This Life In Death

Volume I
'The Struggle'

By Howard Hodgson

This Life In Death

Published by
Chipmunkapublishing
United Kingdom

http://www.chipmunkapublishing.com

Copyright © Howard Hodgson 2024

ISBN 978-1-78382-7152 PB

This Life In Death

This Life In Death

This Life In Death

Dedication

Herein is an entire outpouring of love, despair, a vision of an unimaginably bleak future, a savourer, recovery, a re-affirmation of value, more love, more hard work, some achievement and my whole damn life trying to cope with it all and my own mental frailty written in two volumes:

Volume 1 - 1950 – 1989. 'The Struggle'

Volume II - 1989 – 2024.' The Madness'

All of this is totally dedicated to:

Charles Alexandre Howard Hodgson.

The unique and much-loved son,

of Howard and Marianne.

11th Jan 1979 – 7th April 1982.

My wonderful and unique King of China.

This Life In Death

This Life In Death

Foreword: Dennis Amiss MBE, England International and Warwickshire County Cricketer 1962 – 1987.

When I retired from playing Cricket in 1987, I was approached by Howard Hodgson to join his family funeral business, which had floated on the London Stock Market the previous year. The funeral industry in those days was one of the last to be rationalized, so quickly increasing market share by acquisition was Hodgson's main growth policy. It was an offer I couldn't turn down as it gave me the opportunity to sit on the Board of Directors as the Acquisition's Director, travelling all over England, Wales, Scotland and Ireland.

Howard had convinced me that funeral directors would really want to meet me and that I would be a perfect introducer as nearly all of them were cricket fans. On the other hand, my wife, Jill, was rather surprised that I wanted to join a firm of funeral directors. However, my uncle, Les Amiss, who had his own tyre company and where I had worked when not playing cricket as a youngster, told me he had known Howard's father and he encouraged me to join, telling me it would further my business career.

I started shortly afterwards and was placed into the care of Graham Hodson, who had joined Howard some years before. He and Howard presented me with a new Jaguar XJ 12 and told me how they would pick a town or city which had several funeral directing firms in the area. The rationalization plan was to have one set of staff and funeral vehicles looking after a group of funeral homes and thus maximizing the use of those assets by the economies of scale.

My job was to arrange appointments with family funeral businesses to see if they were prepared to sell to Howard. We had a formula for assessing the businesses' value: so much per funeral per annum before adding the value of the assets on top.

I would meet the area directors of Hodgson Holdings and they would point me in the direction of funeral homes they wanted to buy. Then I would try to arrange appointments with the same to see if they would consider selling. Some, who didn't want to sell, would give me short shrift over the phone. However, many didn't. And so, I built up my contacts and a considerable pipeline of acquisitions was created.

Those who wanted to see me were very proud of their businesses and showed me around with great pleasure. However, they wouldn't have invited me to see them in the first place, if they weren't considering selling. Therefore, the formula proved to be extremely successful.

I recall that during my two-week induction, I went to Thompsons, this was a large company owned by Hodgson Holdings in Liverpool. They conducted somewhere in the region of 3,000 funerals per annum. The first place they showed me was the mortuary. I could not believe what I was seeing with so many bodies belonging to families from all over the city. Then they showed me the embalming room. Well, I must admit I wasn't able to eat for 48 hours after that experience. However, the more I carried on, the more I came to respect the funeral business and their owners who were generally lovely people.

I took the financial details and funeral numbers of those firms who were interested and passed them to Graham Hodson, who would assess the information in order to value the firm. I could make them an offer, which was then sent in writing. I would follow up after a couple of weeks with a phone call. If they wanted to take matters further, they would come down to Sutton Coldfield and be shown around our head office and maybe one of our funeral homes to try to give them confidence that we would carry on running their business well in the future. Some would want to stay on in the business, others would choose to retire.

Once these visits were completed, it was time for a famous Howard Hodgson lunch which would finish around 4.30 to 5pm. Here, they would at last meet Howard, who would then convince them that we would take care of their business and continue to run it well and that money would be made available for new livery, vehicles and a property refurbishment.

This Life In Death

Soon I had acquired over 100 funeral businesses and Howard turned his attention to the North American market as profitable UK acquisitions were becoming harder to find.

He, a company corporate financier called Sandy Fraser, and I flew to Toronto in Canada to meet the second largest US/Canadian funeral group Lowan Brothers. Howard was always on form on such occasions and spoke for an hour about his passion for the funeral business and how he would look after their businesses if they sold to us. It was a remarkable pitch and considering he had had no sleep, he was brilliant.

However, I shall never ever forget their answer:

"Well, that was some talk Howard", said Mr. Lowan. "We thought we were good at selling but we have met our match with you. However, you wanna buy us, but we wanna buy you!'

It was the only time I saw Howard lost for words. None of us expected that retort.

I enjoyed my time in the business. They were very exciting times; we were the vogue UK company of the moment, and we were winning the 'Funeral Ashes Series' consequently. Hardly a week went passed when Hodgson Holdings plc wasn't featured in a TV documentary or a Sunday colour supplement article for one of the national newspapers.

It was also lovely to be part of such a dedicated business where our people genuinely wanted to look after bereaved families and were more concerned about that than the pressures the stock market placed on us.

So, I thank Howard and the people at Hodgson Holdings who took me under their charge all those years ago. They helped me to understand not only the business but to appreciate what dedicated people they were running it and how they were there for all those families who had lost loved ones.

This Life In Death

Those 4 years certainly gave me an understanding of a well-run business and gave me an opportunity to sit on a board of directors for a public company which was an excellent and valuable experience preparing me for when I became CEO of WCCC in 1992.

Dennis Amiss MBE

June 2024

This Life In Death

Introduction

This book seeks to record a life of turbulence and emotion in a fight to recover lost wealth and love from an idyllic childhood, through a hectic journey of much happiness, but also hurt, extreme tragedy, pain, before ultimate success and victory. There are also births, marriages, deaths, love affairs and flirtations galore along the way.

I have been around for many years and, while I'm still working hard and would hope to live for many more, I realise that I might not and should take this opportunity to share my experience of life and the challenges it has held, so that it might help others realise that they can overcome life's slings and arrows – even when sometimes these are self-inflicted.

I hope you really enjoy this roller-coaster ride of will power set against adversity amid a family life, love affairs and the workings of an industry that deals in life's greatest taboo – death.

This is because in the frantic and manic life I have led there is adequate proof that much can be achieved if you believe in yourself and your dreams. You really don't need to be an 'Einstein' to be either successful or just to win when the odds are stacked against you. In fact, most successful entrepreneurs are not academic and are, perhaps, more like you than you think.

I am no psychological expert, I realise that all people are different, that no two lives are the same and that I have no right to preach to anyone about how they should feel or what they should do to cope with their life's problems or deaths affecting them.

However, I also know that we all have our inner demons and secrets and our individual external challenges, hopes, and fears. So, I have decided to share mine in the hope that we both can draw something from you reading them and me writing them.

Therefore, please enjoy my story about my life among the twilight machinations of the funeral directing world and draw from it what you will without using it as a road map to recovery or salvation as I'm not qualified to give to you such direction.

Nevertheless, I really do hope you realise how much is achievable with a positive attitude of mind and that that when I got hit with such a tornado of unexpected grief that such an attitude served me well.

Moreover, I must say that without an inspirational move by one man, my recovery might have not happened at all.

Throughout time each generation thinks it is wiser than the last. However, the truth is that while we all benefit from invention and discovery, we hardly ever learn from previous generations' experiences and apparently almost never from their mistakes.

This is because wisdom is gained by experience and experience is gained with age and then we die, and the next generation must learn from personal experience too just as their fathers did. Such is life and such is our stupidity to put our trust in youth as a guide to the future. It usually disappoints for these reasons.

So, this is also a tale of a young man who steadfastly had to learn from his own mistakes, having believed, like many a man before or since, that he was the first person to tread that particular path through life.

Therefore, this is a story about my life, how I coped with my limited ability, some tall challenges and how song opened the door inside my head to let my grief escape. You may not choose song but there will be another medium for you. You just need to look for it.

I'm pleased to report that writing this book has also been a cathartic experience for me. I have been forced to ask myself some questions which I had never delved into before and have come up with answers which have helped me to understand why all that you are going to read happened – for there is an identifiable recurring theme. I suspect that is probably true with all of us. However, I could not always see it as clearly then as I can now.

This Life In Death

So, I think I know me much better now due to the writing of this tome. My life has been a continual rollercoaster of troughs to peaks and back again and again externally. These have been usually driven by my own internal Piscean swings between pleasure-seeking indiscipline to obsessive drive, determination, and fanatical discipline. I must be a psychiatrist's dream.

Therefore, this book is all about what has been my road from failure to success and my route to happy recovery from bleak despair.

This Life In Death

This Life In Death

Chapter One

Not a Perfect Start (1950 – 1964)

I was born in Edgbaston, Birmingham on the 22nd February 1950. Britain was very different then to the place we know today.

The Second World War had only been won 5 years earlier and a grateful world was now witnessing a bankrupt Britain struggling to maintain what was still the world's largest empire ever abroad, while staving off economic collapse at home.

In 1945, a nation more concerned about creating a socialist 'land fit for heroes' than rewarding its victorious prime minister with another term in office elected a radical Labour government under the leadership of Clement Attlee.

The new government truly meant well but was too ideologically obsessed and so its profound ignorance of both human nature and economics saw it completely fail to halt the nation's downward economic spiral.

Food rationing was every bit as bad in 1950 as it had been during the war and basic commodity imports were cut by the government to minimum levels. For example, timber imports were squeezed to the point where national newspapers were cut back to four pages a day. Even worse the basic petrol ration was abolished, although most people couldn't afford a car in those days anyway. The government even urged the public to smoke cigarettes right down to the butt, adding that it might be good for their health.

Britain had lost one quarter - £7 billion – of its entire wealth winning the war, and in 1947, after the first of a seemingly endless series of sterling crises, the pound had been devalued against the dollar.

The government's response to this economic collapse couldn't have been more damaging. It was ideologically opposed to private enterprise and competition. So, it didn't believe that free market conditions would create a trading environment to steer the economy back to prosperity.

Instead, it preferred to try and run the economy itself – like The Soviet Union had some 30 years earlier. The results were to be catastrophic.

Between 1945 and 1947 six measures of public ownership were carried through Parliament: The Bank of England, cable and wireless, civil aviation, electricity, and road and rail transportation. gas, iron, and steel followed in 1950.

Although, this government's fantastic achievement – the creation of the National Health Service - must never be forgotten and should be universally applauded, its handling of the economy, and in particular its acts of nationalisation, destroyed incentive and creativity and so caused mass hardship amongst the poor and unskilled.

Thirty years later, as Margaret Thatcher's government sold all but The Bank of England back to the people, not even the Labour Party raised much of a protest.

However, in 1950, the cradle-to-the-grave interference by the state had as few critics as it has defenders today.

Birmingham was then, as it is today, Britain's 2nd city. I was brought up in the leafy suburbs of Harborne and Edgbaston and so was cocooned from these hard times.

However, my earliest memories are of travelling with my father to our family funeral business on Hockley Hill, Hockley, a very poor area situated between the Jewellery Quarter and the equally poor areas of Lozells and Aston.

In those days, Birmingham was very like the city we saw in the world acclaimed TV series 'Peaky Blinders' but with bomb damage added.

This Life In Death

The average factory wage was around £9-a-week and a normal Hodgson & Sons Ltd funeral cost circa £14.

Hodgson & Sons Ltd boasted 'since 1850' on its letterheads. It had become a successful funeral business during those years with a series of branch offices in Aston, Lozells, Kingstanding, Erdington and Nechells – as well as its head office and horse stables, which were converted to garages by the time I was born, in Hockley.

My grandfather, who had been born to a gypsy Romany queen, like Pol in 'Peaky Blinders', had grown up to be known as the 'Stallion of Handsworth' before marrying a great niece of Cecil Rhodes – Clarissa Proud - and with her came breeding, education and wealth.

She died tragically at the early age of 42 in 1942 from a heart condition while my father was at Harrow Public School. This loss and the fact that he was not at her bedside consequently weighed heavily on him for the rest of his life.

When I was born, my grandfather lived as a widower in a mansion on Hampstead Hill, in Handsworth Wood, surrounded by an army of domestic staff. He had a live-out mistress whom he never took on his numerous sea cruises on the best liners of the day – the complimentary silver beer tankers he received on each I now possess.

Osmond George Hodgson, as he had been Christened, had been born in 1900. He was the eldest of 2 boys and his younger brother was called Leslie. Both were keen pilots and Leslie, born in 1901, even made it into the Royal Flying Corps during the later stages of the First World War and saw action against the Red Baron. He didn't shoot him down, but neither was he shot down by the famous German ace. Indeed, he survived at a time when a pilot's life expectancy was a mere six weeks.

Both boys were the sons of George Hodgson, who had an amazing way with women. He had married the gypsy Romany queen, who begat his sons, before he expanded his funeral business by opening new branch offices at regular intervals and installing an unpaid mistress in each.

They made funeral arrangements and looked after George's sexual appetite and in return lived rent free. His wife fumed in a rocking chair in her own branch office on the Soho Rd in Handsworth and, as legend has it, put a curse on all Hodgson males as a result.

I have no proof that this was true, but history makes a fair case that she might have done so – and with some success.

The boys also worked for George, who in the late 1920s decided that, as a widower, he wanted to retire. He offered to sell Hodgson & Sons Ltd to them. They were well short of the asking price but Clarissa, of Rhodes fame, came up with the cash and so a deal was done.

Therefore Ossie and Les, as they were known, had bought the business from their father George. And, as he was their father, it was done on a shake of hands and without any restrictive covenants being signed.

George took the cash and promptly opened in competition to his sons close by to their office. The boys had been duped and Clarissa's cash was at risk. Something had to be done.

So, they decided to engage Peaky Blinders, not the Shelby family of course, but real Peaky Blinders – poor, unemployed men with snot coated moustaches and razor blades in their peaked caps – to wait outside his funeral office and follow any family home. Once there they would explain that Ossie and Les would conduct the funeral for 5 shillings (10p in today's money) less than George. The depression was now underway, and times were hard. Therefore, most families were only too happy to accept the offer.

They won the business back but still agreed to buy George out a second time if he left the city – which he did and settled in Brighton before dying in a bombing raid during the Second World War.

This Life In Death

The business prospered in the 1930s. Then came the Second World War. Both men were in their late 30s and funeral directing was a reserved occupation – which meant neither would be called upon to serve in the armed forces.

However, Les was also a talented engineer and saw an opportunity to make a fortune with government war contracts and free himself from serving the funereal needs of the 'Hockley bog rats' as he referred to the folk from there in a letter to Ossie asking his brother to buy him out.

Ossie obliged and so Les left the business, but the war was eventually won and so the government contracts dried up leaving Les without either employment or income.

Ossie refused to have Les back but in 1950, the year I was born, my father Paul, who was 24 and worked for his father, Ossie persuaded him to allow Les, to return. However, it was only on the condition that my father, Christened Osmond Paul Charles, was to take total responsibility for his uncle – which he did until his death in 1970.

Les retired in the mid-sixties but was brought back to re-build a Phantom III Rolls Royce engine in the summer of 1969. He did so and stood a two-shilling coin on the radiator next to the flying lady. The engine started first time and the coin did not fall. All the chauffeur-bearers burst into applause. Les was some engineer!

In 1954 Osmond George was taken ill with cancer. He was told that if he had a colostomy he could be saved. He declined saying that this was no way for a man to live. Consequently, he died the same year. He was only 54.

He was quite tyrannical, and people were frightened of him. My father adored, respected, and feared him in equal proportion. That was usual then, as it had been earlier with Winston and his relationship with his father Randolph Churchill. It is less so today as respect of one's parents gave way to an 'I, me, mine' attitude created during the social revolution of the spoilt 'baby boomers' in the 1960s.

This Life In Death

Osmond George had kept his son on a tight rein with a relatively small salary. Nevertheless, we lived in a very comfortable home in the leafy suburb of Harborne, with a Dr Shirlwell as a neighbour and another funeral director, one Ernie Brain, next to him. Consequently, this part of Croftdown Road became known locally as 'Death Row.'

So, my early memories were of a handsome father, and a beautiful mother, who had been brought up in Harborne, but came from Cheshire stock on her mother's side and whose father came from somewhere around Sedgley in Staffordshire.

He had no parents apparently but had been privately educated at a boarding school. How very strange.

His name was Robert Ward. This was the same surname as that of the Earl of Dudley. As a result, it was always believed, but never talked about, that he was born on the wrong side of the blanket to that noble family and so provided for financially while not being recognised.

In 1952 my sister Adrienne Paula was born. In 1956 my mother, Sheila Mary Kendrick, had her 3rd and final child – Russell Lindsay Robert.

As the 1950s progressed, the Conservative government, which had regained power from a well-intentioned but failed and exhausted Labour Party in 1951, saw the economy recover to such an extent that the then prime minister, Sir Harold Macmillan, told the nation famously, "You've never had it so good' before winning another landslide general election victory in 1959.

And the Hodgson family had prospered too as disposable incomes rose and my father expanded the business without fear of the criticism he may have received if Ossie had still been alive.

He would go off to work armed with sandwiches and a flask of soup each dark winter's morning 6 days-a-week before seven, dressed in his heavy black doubled-breasted overcoat, pinstriped trousers, starched white shirt (with detachable collar) and company tie. His top

This Life In Death

hat was always left brushed and boxed in his office – ready for the first funeral of the day.

During the winter months, he would return each night just before my sister and I were sent to bed, exhausted having conducted 7 or 8 funerals in bitterly cold conditions in usually snow-covered cemeteries, where the coffin's final journey to the graveside could be treacherous as deep snow disguised many traps under foot.

It is worth remembering that in those days the death rate was much higher in the winter than the summer – because bronchitis resulting from a cold or flu killed and folk living in those inner-city damp houses had little chance of survival once bronchitis had them in its grip.

Even in the 1960s I can remember how wake sandwiches would curl up and turn green if not covered with a tea towel in these houses while the funeral was taking place.

Today's big killers, heart disease and cancer were far less then because, if you were poor, there was a good chance bronchitis would get you first.

It should also be noted that around 80% of funerals were burials then – whereas today 80% are cremations.

Burials take longer because the service and the graveside committal are in different places. So how could he have done 8-a-day? This was because funerals were local, journey distances were short, traffic was light, and services were purely religious and often took less than 10 minutes.

Families were given no opportunity to express themselves as they are today with personal music or eulogies. Their expression of love and grief had to be demonstrated by the cost of the coffin they selected, the quality of the floral tributes they bought or the number of limousines they hired.

This Life In Death

The clergy of all religions were very slow to welcome bereaved families' participation in funeral services as a celebration of a loved one's life and were still resisting it more 50 years later in the 2000s.

My father was an excellent funeral director. He was compassionate, kind, beautifully mannered, efficient, artistic, and good looking. As a result, in the decade following Ossie's death the business flourished. He bought out a competitor; he opened one of Britain's first 'funeral homes' – complete with several arrangement rooms, a service chapel, 6 private viewing chapels, a family lounge, and a coffin selection showroom.

He even introduced wash and dress facilities for Birmingham's growing Hindu, Sikh and Afro-Caribbean communities. He had been brought up an Empire boy and would die one, but he was no racist and those communities flocked to him as a result.

Standard stuff today - but utterly revolutionary in the late 1950s.

I enjoyed being taken by him to the office and, even better, the coffin workshops; for we still made our own coffins from either solid oak or elm – indeed as all funeral directors did then.

There were rows of both timbers in drying sheds, waiting to be magically transformed into French polished coffins by the workshop with either a double-raised lid, a single-raised lid, or a flat lid. They also either could have panel sides or plain – and many were likely to be finished with an Aston Villa claret and blue frill and gown set.

The more expensive coffins were always bought by those who could least afford them – because these very competitive working folk wanted to show the street that their 'mam' was the best.

The cheapest were nearly always bought by middle-class families who were already living beyond their means and were buggered if they were going to waste their inheritance on the old man's funeral bill.

This Life In Death

The carpenter in charge of these workshops was a lovely Welshman named, perhaps unsurprisingly, Evans. He had 3 fingers all the same size due to a careless encounter with an electric saw. He was always kind to me when most adults seemed to be an ogre, and I liked him accordingly.

But there was another good reason that I liked him and my visits to his workshops. He had made my 'Fort Apache' from coffin moulding one Christmas and my sister and I had the very best sledges in the snow on the Clent Hills or at Warley Woods when the inevitable winter dump came – all made from coffin off-cuts.

Eventually, Hodgson & Sons Ltd would buy mass produced solid or veneered coffins, like most other funeral directors did in the 1960s.

But, by this time Evans had emigrated to the US with his family. Once there, both his sons were drafted to serve in the Vietnam war. Horribly, both were killed. How terribly tragic and unfair was that? I was in my 20s when I learned of Evan's fate, but I was nevertheless deeply distressed by the news. He wanted a better life for his family, and this was his reward.

However, it was undeniable that my father had made an excellent start to his tenure as head of the family business and with all this success I noticed that life was changing at home too.

Now it was my mother that had her own army of domestic staff – 5 in total; my father upgraded his Ford to a beautiful Jaguar MK VII – in gleaming black as all cars were then; he bought a small cabin cruiser berthed at the Poole Harbour Yacht Club and we became members.

Quickly these boats became bigger and then he switched to sailing a Bermudan sloop in 1959, which infused my life-long passion for sailing.

So, a potential bad decade for me was turning out to be a great one for my parents and as usual I was just there for the ride.

This Life In Death

Yes, so what of me during this first decade? I had grown from a fat baby, who did not walk until 16 months old, into a pleasant looking fair-haired boy. I was shy and reserved like Prince Charles had been as a boy. On the other hand, my sister was outgoing and vivacious – like Princess Anne at the same age. She wasn't academically bright like my younger brother was to be, but she could communicate with adults.

Whereas, I was inclined to be a pleasant observer, a bystander, who really didn't want to be seen or heard and was happiest in the company of my sister, little brother, and beloved parents – especially my father, whom I worshipped.

Worse, it was soon discovered that my problems were more and worse than first appreciated when I was just a lazy fat baby. I was diagnosed with a poorly functioning left lung, I developed asthma, my eyesight wasn't great and that caused me to wear those ghastly circular pink national health specs, made famous by John Lennon 15 years later, but in the 1950s, made me look like the 'Milky Bar Kid' on those famous black and white TV adverts.

Could it get any worse? Oh yes it could! I was left-handed! On no - surely not.

The world had yet to discover that right-handed folk have a left side of brain bias which meant they could learn like a sponge, whereas left-handed people have a right side of brain bias that meant that while they preferred to be self-taught, they were artistic, creative, and individual thinkers.

Today we celebrate the left-handedness of David Cameron, Barak Obama, Prince William – and wow - Sir Paul McCartney and Leonardo di Vinci. However, in the 1950s, my kindergarten 'Fair Days' placed me in a class with other children who were being forced to write with their right hands.

This Life In Death

It was thought that left-handed children were bound to be backward and that the only cure was to force them to write with their right hands.

When my father found out, he visited the kindergarten and informed them I had enough problems without my school adding to them. He insisted that I be allowed to continue to write with my left hand.

He followed my early schooling with interest and much disappointment because I was comfortable in my own little world and was basically bone-idle – clearly not destined to be an achiever, more of an observer from a cosy corner of my life's little room.

Still, he persisted in encouraging me and was never harsh, in the way Prince Phillip was to Prince Charles, despite his obvious embarrassment at his eldest son's lack of anything worthwhile.

One Sunday evening on the long journey back from Poole to Birmingham, he asked me what I was learning at school.

"Julius Caesar". I replied confidently. History was the one subject I liked, was interested in, and paid any attention to.

However, my father had got it wrong and assumed that I was talking about English Literature and the Shakespeare play of the same name. So, he asked me, "Who said 'I come not to praise Caesar but to bury him'"?

"I don't know Daddy – but did we get the funeral?" was my reply. This did nothing for my standing with him.

However, despite this shocking malaise, I was starting to appreciate that, if I was going to get away from being the cause of constant sympathy from everyone towards my parents – for my mother loved and cared for her flawed first born very much too – I would have to do something about it. Moreover, that something would have to come from within the inner me.

xxxxxxx

This Life In Death

I obviously realised that I was not a naturally gifted academic. Therefore, I knew I would have to work hard, believe in myself, and become much tougher if I was going to make anything out of the little talent I possessed. Either this or become a history boffin – which I did consider but rejected as I didn't think they ranked highly as being sexually attractive to girls.

I told myself that I might have to become Captain of England's cricket team, if girls were ever going to like me. As no pretty, or even not so pretty, girl would want to go out with a fair haired, freckled nosed guy in pink national health specs.

Yes – that was it: I had to believe in myself, become tough, do my best and achieve what I could. I determined to give it a go.

I had become obsessed with the opposite sex from the age of six. This took 2 forms. The first was purely sexual and I can remember several of those, "You show me yours and I'll show you mine" conversations from 6 onward before I lost my virginity on top of a Bournemouth bus parked in the bus station in the summer of 1965.

However, the second was harder to explain. When 4, I fell for our 18-year-old French au-pair – much to her amusement. In the summer of 1958, aged 8, I fell madly in love with a 14-year-old heiress to the Bowyer pork pie and sausage roll empire – a delicious looking girl called Cheryl Bowyer. I was truly smitten. I would constantly repeat this desire for older women until I was about 35.

Earlier in 1958 I had been sent to my father's prep school for an entrance interview. This was West House Preparatory School for Boys, 24 St James's Rd, Edgbaston. I was dumped in the bottom class and might not have been even accepted at all if my father had not been an old boy, Captain of Football and ended up as Head Boy.

I had not made a good impression. I really had not expected to, but I knew that I needed now to make some impression when I started, or my life was not going to ever change for the better.

This Life In Death

I had not been there long when I ventured into the gardener's shed in the grounds. On the wall he had pinned a large photograph of the Aston Villa 1957 FA Cup winning side. I looked at it – knowing that both Ossie had been, and my father was an avid supporter. I had not shown any interest in Aston Villa despite some encouragement.

In walked the junior school's big bully with his gang of admirers. His father had a large retail outlet in West Bromwich High Street. He was a West Brom fan. He spat at the photograph before ripping it down and stamping on it.

One second, I looked at him smirking at me, the next he was on the floor put there by my left (yes left) hook to his nose which extracted a squeal, blood, and tears. He leapt to his feet. A minute ago, I hadn't been an Aston Villa supporter but now I was a fanatic. I was ready for him and, if necessary, his friends. However, he ran, and they followed.

God that felt good. Really good. This was the first moment of a different me and I felt great. Pride and self-belief pumped through me to the point of giddiness. I have remained an Aston Villa fanatic ever since and will die one. If you cut me, I bleed claret and blue.

These were early days at West House – and my mother phoned the school to ask Cary Field, the Headmaster, to look out for me as I was a shy and sensitive boy.

"Mrs Hodgson, I can assure you that you have nothing to worry about. Out of the new in-take of boys, Hodgson (Christian names were never used) is the one who thinks it is appropriate to settle everything with his fists".

My mother was convinced he had mixed me up with someone else. He hadn't and I was on my way. The gardener's shed was a watershed moment.

I quickly realised that my new image was built on being a force for good amongst my peers: protecting the less confident who might be bullied, whom I could identify with, while trying to emulate Winston

This Life In Death

Spencer Churchill and Horatio Nelson as my British heroes and believing in the greater good of Jesus Christ and a 100% belief in the Roman Catholic and Church of England religions.

The first I felt was mysterious and compelling, while the second was British. So, it had to be 'high church Anglicanism' for me from the age of 12. And yes – I was asking myself these questions and thinking about the answers at that age.

Nevertheless, while I fought against any authority close to me at school, but accepted my parents' authority at home, the most surprising thing was my 100% backing the establishment's authority over the people. This was nothing like the attitude of the 60s 'Baby Boomer' revolution which was to follow.

As a result, my life had become a complete clash of my Empire values for the greater British establishment and my cocking my thumb against any authority which got in my way at school.

It was a heady mix of 'look at me' here versus support of the British Empire, where I don't matter, there.

Now I was taking a determined control of my own destiny. I could do nothing about my left lung and asthma but learn to live with them, but I decided that I could do something about my glasses.

I decided they had to go. This was the new me. The me who believed in authority but thought that, when it came to me, I was that authority.

My parents splashed out on private frames. They made me look studios. I should have been grateful. I wasn't. I wanted to be a 'hero' and heroes did not wear glasses so I wouldn't, and I didn't anymore unless it was essential.

I was lucky that I was long-sighted rather than short-sighted. I might have had to think again if I hadn't been. But I was long-sighted, so I decided that the new me did not need glasses and that was that. I have tried to find some family photos of me in glasses in the late 1950s and there was but one. The worm had turned.

This Life In Death

My father's good friend was our neighbour our new home in Hamilton Avenue in Harborne. He was a nice man called Denis Evans and he was also our optician. He told my parents that my ridiculous obsession with being too vain to wear glasses was likely to damage my eyesight further.

A couple of years later I read a number plate some distance away to him. He accused me, quite gently, of having memorised it previously. I proceeded to read several others at an even further distance. He declared that this was completely impossible.

I continued without my glasses until my 40s and then turned to contact lenses.

However, back then in the late 50s and early 60s, I steadily progressed through the school. I was never academically gifted apart from my increasing knowledge of history and hugely one-sided patriotic view of the British and its 'sun never sets on' Empire.

Elsewhere, I was an immense nuisance at school and was beaten several times a week as a result. On one occasion our nanny, Gwen,brought my mother's attention to the bleeding stripes on my bottom having been beaten with an aluminium arrow twice within 15 minutes.

It took a lot of persuasion for me to dissuade my caring mother from telephoning the school to complain. I did not want this. I had become the school's 'Robin Hood' and for my mother to have called in might have destroyed my tough guy image.

Moreover, I had absolutely zero resentment about the beatings and just accepted them as par for the course. It was a game. I knew the stakes – get caught and you got a beating. That was life - wasn't it?

Indeed, the headmaster, Cary Field, whom had been headmaster to my father and previously been in the Royal Navy in the First World War and had fought in the Battle of Jutland, was an Empire hero of mine.

This Life In Death

It was he who had beaten me with an aluminium arrow twice within 15 minutes. Did I hate him for this? No, I did not. He had to look to his job of running an orderly school and I had to look to mine of being 'Robin Hood'.

So, the years between 1958 and 1963 became a litany of me behaving badly in an attempt to carve out my own personality and cover up my own short comings in science, maths, and anything else which did not interest me.

I swung out of a window 40 feet up for a dare – beaten. I got dressed at midnight in the dormitory and walked with friends to Five Ways on the way to Birmingham City centre – beaten. Poor science result – beaten. Answering back in class against left wing teachers' views – beaten. Replay this week on week and you have the picture.

However, I was now a good cricketer and had made it into the 1st XI at football a year earlier than anyone else my age. I was also in the swimming team, was the best breast stroker in the school, and was in the 1st XIV at rugby. So, I had my uses to the school too in the highly competitive world of boys' private education as was then.

Nevertheless, it remained war. Me versus the school.

Then, quite suddenly, the school changed tack and my father's old headmaster and his new co-head, a kind man named Mr Douglas, came up with a plan. Robin Hood should know that they were not King John folk but really King Richard people instead.

I listened and bought into this plan. I was made a prefect, then vice-head boy. I also changed tack and became a wonderful enforcer of school discipline.

As a result, in an orgy of mutual admiration, I won the 'Pound Cup' – which my father never had – for the best all-round performance. My father was delighted and although he had always shown me love, that day he showed me total respect for the first time.

This Life In Death

He had his annual drinks party on the night that I brought it home. He placed on his cocktail bar and never tired of telling anyone of his 70 guests what I had achieved. I was blissfully happy. He had always loved me but now, at long last he was proud of me. I'm crying as I write this.

My time at West House was drawing to a close. I had become a much stronger and more wilful boy during these years.

On reflection, I'm very glad I had because my decision to have self-belief and fortitude were to be called on in spades in the years to come.

My parents had been slow to see this change – more just to be happy with the sporting and character-building achievements – having given up on the prospect of any academic achievements years earlier.

However, before we say goodbye to this era, I should mention 2 external things that made a massive impression on me then.

Firstly, in 1962, with my little transistor Radio under my pillow as a boarder at West House, I heard a song on Radio Luxemburg. I thought it was wonderful. I asked the lad in the next bed who the band were. He, Steve Stevil, later to be a very successful singer/composer himself, replied that the band was called the Beatles. I was captivated immediately.

I loved the sound. I immediately started on a roller-coaster ride to the end of the 60s with the band that changed the world. I still have all the original vinyl albums. More importantly, I can tell you where I was whenever Paul McCartney released an album or just a song from then until now.

He has, like Aston Villa, been a massive factor in my life. So much so that in 1992 I turned down an opportunity to meet him. Why asked my publisher?

This Life In Death

"Because I might not like him and that would be my whole life down the toilet", was my immediate response. I needn't have worried, as a few years later, during the Wimbledon tennis fortnight we met by complete accident. We talked. Or perhaps I talked, and he listened to start with at least, as I was so nervous.

Either way, he was as great a guy as I could have wished, and very normal despite being the most famous and talented composer of the 20th century.

I consider that my life has been so much richer thanks to having grown up with the Beatles and in particular him being with me every step of the way since.

Secondly, in 1963 there was the Profumo Scandal involving the Conservative War Minister, John Profumo. This troubled me greatly because, while still being only 13, I could see that the Conservative government had been a good custodian of the economy, and I did not believe that such lies, and corruption could or would survive the test of the electorate.

Indeed, they did not, and Britain was to be subjected to some appallingly bad economic government by Harold Wilson (Labour) and Edward Heath (Conservative) as a result.

Britain's Labour government 1964 – 1970 and 1974 – 1979, along with the Conservative government 1970 – 1974 would destroy the UK's economy almost completely. Indeed, in 1974, under Harold Wilson, we paid ourselves 44% more for doing 4% less.

Trade Union power ran the country and as it increased so did inflation, unemployment, and debt. No wonder the world came to consider the UK national debt as to no better than 3rd world debt.

No one in power seemed to understand that you had to create wealth before you could spend it. This is true for an individual, a family, a small business, a large international company, or a nation.

This Life In Death

It wasn't until Margaret Thatcher was elected in 1979 that the management of the UK economy was reset in the right direction and on sound monetary principles, incentives, and creativity. As she said, "There is no such thing as government money. It is your money, and we spend it".

You will think that I was bound to think like this coming from such a comfortable and well-off environment. You will now be assuming that I was just as bound to be a Tory supporter as I was a Villa fan. This would have been true of my father, but it was not of me.

This was the 1960s, I was a baby boomer and identified with the Beatles, the Stones and Bob Dylan. It was cool to be working class then and it wasn't cool to be a Tory. Mick Jagger knew that and so did I.

However, I was, you will recall, a left-handed self-taught freethinker. I had decided that Britain needed compassionate capitalism to create wealth by incentive and self-determination. A meritocracy with a decent safety net for all and which cared for everyone could only spend cash it had earned – and it needed private enterprise and competition to achieve this.

It was the failure of Karl Marx to understand this that had led all communist and far-left socialist governments to fail. As a thirteen-year-old I could understand how lazy and unintelligent folk thought they deserved a free ride but was amazed that there were intelligent adults who couldn't see how the socialist concept ignored both human nature and the rules of simple economics.

By 1990 most people had seen some sense as the Berlin Wall fell.

I became very ill in the winter of 1963. It was the harshest winter since 1947. Birmingham was still a very polluted industrial city. My asthma was very bad. I collapsed playing football and stopped breathing for over a minute. My parents became very concerned about how I might survive in such an unhealthy environment.

This Life In Death

I had been working hard to pass the common entrance exam to Malvern and hoped to escape going to Bromsgrove instead as a result. Now this!

My parents had become friendly with the Cadbury family, the family who still controlled the Bourneville based world famous chocolate brand. Brandon and Favier Cadbury's son, Rupert, also had asthma and was educated at the extortionately expensive Aiglon College in Villars, Switzerland. They recommended that my parents look to send me there too.

I was horrified. No parents, family, Aston Villa, Beatles, or even communication, other than a weekly letter, for 3 months at a time. I realised that I would climb a mountain only to see another mountain and Switzerland was a landlocked country – so no sailing the seven seas for me.

I became convinced that God or my parents or perhaps both were now paying me back for my wilful years. Clearly, they did not understand that I only adopted such a stance to eject myself from the pitiful malaise of my first pathetic eight years.

Couldn't they see that I was trying to make the best of a bad job, that I was just a little mischievous rather than bad. I believed in Jesus, the Queen and always stood for the National Anthem – even when I was alone when one of the then only two TV stations closed at around midnight by playing it.

But no matter how I tried I could not convince my father, who believed that it was essential for my health or my mother who also believed this but, in addition, loved the social possibilities of mixing with the great and the good at this, one of the world's most expensive, schools.

To pay for this was an amazing sacrifice by my father as, although he was a successful businessman and much appreciated funeral director, that now had graduated from Jags to Aston Martins, his income did not run to these levels of expenditure and so inherited stocks and shares had to be sold to fund my exile.

It was decided that I would stay on at West House an extra term and start at Aiglon in the summer term of 1964 and that I should go from weekly boarding to termly, even though I lived only 2.5 miles away, for my last two terms at west house.

I had enjoyed being a weekly boarder in 1962 and the first 2 terms of 1963. However, being a termly boarder in preparation for being dumped in a foreign land-locked country for an eternity was a different matter and I started to feel permanently homesick.

Asthma immediately struck me down in the autumn and my friend, Steve Stevil, replaced me as left-wing in the 1st XI. He scored, was awarded his colours and deservedly kept his place. I was dropped.

Now nothing was going right. I was a termly boarder, in preparation for going to some bloody school for either ill or badly behaved rich British or American kids and to cap it all, I had lost my place in the West House football team after being a star in it for over a year.

I felt like weeping and took myself away to an empty classroom in case I did. Once there, I weighed matters up. This was all new to me. It was an external crisis not an internal inadequacy. I was either going to weep and feel sorry for myself or I was going to do something about it.

I remembered that little boys of seven were sent away from their civil servant English parents in India, all the way back to a strange and friendless England to be educated at harsh Victorian schools. This was the Empire. This was British stiff upper lip, and they were expected get on with it.

How dare I think of myself as a fit young man to be associated with them if I was going to bemoan my lot now aged 13? I decided there and then that I would double my effort, I would not complain about going to Aiglon again but would pretend to be looking forward to the challenge and lastly, but not least, I would win back a place in the school 1st XI.

I looked at the team sheet and decided that the weakest player was a pleasant boy called Neal (his surname). He was centre half. I had never played in defence even in the playground. The next morning, I told Mr Thomas,our sports master, that I wished to play for 2nd XI at centre half. He was surprised but reluctantly agreed. Within a fortnight I was back in the 1st XI at centre half, also having stopped moaning about being sent to Aiglon, and immediately won the colours that had previously eluded me despite having scored lots of goals as a naturally left footed winger.

It was at the end of this term that I won the Pound Cup. That little chat that I had had with myself was about different problems to those of the gardeners shed some 5 years earlier, but nevertheless an important watershed moment too.

My changed attitude for the better also saw me rewarded by my father insisting that I be allowed to spend my extra and last term at West House as a weekly boarder.

In addition, my parents also took my sister and me to London for the half term break as a treat. We stayed at the Westbury, rather than the Ritz, where they usually stayed, as a cost cutting measure because of my impending school fees.

I was still behaving like an officer and a gentleman on the outside but each day that passed I knew the dreaded flight to Geneva was drawing ever closer. I was feeling more home sick than ever – but you would have never guessed it.

This Life In Death

Chapter II

Exile (1964 – 1966)

Eventually, on the Friday before the 1964 FA Cup win of West Ham United over Preston North End, my parents and I boarded a plane for Geneva. The next day, we caught a train to Aigle and then took a taxi to Villars. I was still smiling at them but shivering inside.

They stayed for 5 days while I settled in. Then it was the last day, the last lunch, and the last walk back towards the school. I couldn't eat at lunch but put a brave face on, nevertheless.

We started on the last walk. It was agreed that we would part at the halfway point – a bend in the road where the telecabin was.

We arrived there. I kissed them both goodbye. We went our separate ways. I walked about 30 yards and stopped and looked back to get just one last glance of them. My mother was striding away. My father had stopped and was looking back at me. Something snapped and I ran to him, threw my arms around his neck, and wept emotionally while sobbing apologies for such an act of weakness.

He was kind and, without being asked by me, announced that he and my mother would return to see me in 6 weeks' time. I grabbed this thought and dried my eyes. I walked back to school cheered and determined to give it a go – however much I hated the place.

I had taken an entrance exam some months earlier and passed it. So, I was surprised to be asked to take another on my first day at the school. I considered not giving of my best in hope of being rejected – but that wouldn't have been 'cricket' so I dismissed the idea.

The Aiglon entrance exam had seemed very strange to me when I first took it. There were no subjects to write about, just lots of silly questions. This second exam was very similar.

This Life In Death

The next day, the headmaster, John Collette sent for me. Oh God, here we go again, I've only been here five minutes and I'm already in trouble. I trudged off to his office in the house called Claremont fearing that I had already let my father down by failing this silly test.

I entered and was invited to sit. I had been invited to take a 2nd IQ test to ensure that the 1st was correct. It had been. Then he asked me if anyone had ever explained to me about IQ. I shook my head.

"You have the 2nd highest IQ in the school and as a result we are going to put you straight into the 4th year", he explained.

Now it was my turn to think that there must have been a mistake. But no. I was sent off to the 4th year A stream to try and cope with a six-term syllabus and be ready for end of term exams in 10 weeks' time.

My wonderful newly discovered IQ immediately told me that it hadn't ever helped me with academic lessons before and that to attempt to cram in 2 years of such into 2 and a half months was several bridges too far. Nevertheless, I determined to give it a go with the stoic attitude of a good Christian Empire boy.

Now I had to also meet my fellow pupils at this extraordinary place. Aiglon had about 150 pupils in those days based in 3 houses and a chalet for misfits. I was in Alpina where the housemaster was Sir Toby Coghill. There were about 50 of us billeted there.

The school then was around 90% either British or American and about equally split. Nearly all fell into one of four categories – poor health, too thick to get into a decent British public school, sons of famous American divorcees where neither parent wanted their child, or the sons of US Army generals stationed in Berlin (remember the war in Europe had only ended 19 years before and British, American, and Russian troops still controlled Berlin). These boys were paid for by the US government.

After dinner, I sat with some, cautiously hoping to be accepted and perhaps even make some friends. They introduced themselves to me:

This Life In Death

"Hi, I'm a Burton, you may have heard of us – the high street tailors". Of course, I had as there was a shop in every UK high street.

"Hi, I'm Charles England, my stepfather (ironically a man named London) owns Singer Sewing Machines". There was one of these in just about every home across the world.

"Hi, I'm Rupert Cadbury". I already knew about him and thought that it was his, and his bloody chocolate making family's fault, that I had been stationed half-way up a Swiss mountain.

However, he was to become a very close and dear friend throughout my time at Aiglon. He was a gentle and decent chap and on free afternoons we would slip out to a little known or frequented bar in Villars, run by a very old man called Paul Robert, and drink several pints of strong local beer together while reminiscing about Birmingham and the fact that we both fancied each other's sister. It was a wonder we were never caught.

And so, the introductions went on: a son of Lord so and so, a son of a four-star US general, a son of a famous Hollywood film director, whose Christian name was Sam, and sons of a couple of ambassadors and TV stars etc.

Then it came to being my turn to introduce myself. I was the son of a Birmingham funeral director. No, I wasn't they all declared – almost in unison. Yes, I was I insisted. Impossible they replied. Then an American called Toft declared that he knew the answer.

"Who is it in that photograph next to your bed? The good-looking guy with an Aston Martin" he demanded.

"That's my father" I replied.

"I got it. Hodgson's old man is a spy, like James Bond. His fees are paid for by the God damn Limey government".

This Life In Death

Mass amusement? Not at all. They all believed Toft was right and even Rupert never came to my defence – having never been told about me previously by his mother.

I remember thinking that my mother would have hated that we had not been worthy of a mention!!

Charles England, stepson to the Singer sewing machine empire, was also a new boy like me. His parents had arrived at the same time as mine and with the same purpose. They had even stayed in the same hotel.

Charles was the same age as me. Happily, for him he had been placed in the bottom stream of the 3rd year, where he proceeded to bully his fellow students from the moment he made their acquaintance.

He was not bright, but he was massive – about twice my weight and at least 4 inches taller. A sort of 1960s version of Billy Bunter. He was spoilt rottenly by his mother, who doted on him, and I suspect that his stepfather had little say in what Charles said or did.

As new boys we both had awful jobs to do being each the bottom rank in the senior school. This is how Aiglon worked. Your rank dictated your status and your pocket money. If you worked hard, you were promoted, and your weekly allowance went up. If you didn't or were a rebel you were demoted, and your status and pocket money went down.

The headmaster, John Collette had been a housemaster at Gordonstoun, the school that had educated a happy Prince Phillip and an extremely unhappy Prince Charles there in Scotland. Aiglon had been based on the same Kurt Hann principles of character building rather than academic achievement as a result.

I had already worked out that this was just as well as most British chaps at the school were either too asthmatic, and so their education had been constantly interrupted, or thick to be academic and the Americans were even years behind them.

This Life In Death

Charles England and I were both in Alpina. His job was to clean the boot room – where we kept our athletic gear in the summer, football boots in the autumn and our skis and boots in the winter. Mine was to clean out the showers. Both places would be inspected by 'Standard Bearers' (one rank below prefect) and marked nightly.

Two or three weeks into this term of my discontent, I was returning from church in my Aiglon blazer, shirt, and tie to clean the showers before dinner. I entered Alpina on this sunny evening via the boot room where Master Charles was doing his job - brush in hand.

"Your mother should have taught you to go to church in a 100% white shirt - that one has a check".

I ignored him but he barred my way with his brush.

"Get out of my way England".

"You make me", he taunted and cracked me on the shins with his cleaning utensil.

Pushing, became shoving and that became punching and then gouging in his case. However, as asthmatics will tell you, when you must fight for every breath, other physical pain doesn't seem so bad.

So, I was glad that I had refused to be bullied and not avoided this fight that I was now clearly losing. Nevertheless, I hoped someone would arrive to stop it before I got killed.

Soon boys, indeed lots of boys, arrived – but they did not stop the fight, rather they cheered me on as Charles had succeeded in making himself universally unpopular in less than a month at the school.

Eventually, we rolled across a row of lockers before falling some 2 feet to the stone floor where we continued to roll. When we stopped, I was on top. I pinned down both his arms and offered to accept his surrender in my typically British Empire act of fair play.

This Life In Death

However, Charles did not surrender. Instead, he broke an arm free and smashed me in the face. I pinned it down again and without mercy repeatedly smashed his face with both my fists.

The roar of the crowd and his squeals seemed to dim into the distance as I let all my rage about everything go.

Then a decent American Standard Bearer called Carl Fisher arrived to stop proceedings. I jumped up and left for my room. Once there I sat on my bed and felt thoroughly ashamed of myself. I told myself that I had behaved no better than Charles England – no, far worse.

Before too long Sir Toby entered my room. He never visited boys' rooms and therefore, I knew why he had now.

I stood up and, in a voice close to breaking into sobs, expressed my sorrow and shame. To my surprise he was kind and understanding. He told me to change my torn and blood splattered shirt and come with him.

We went up one floor to England's room. Lady Coghill was already there alone with him, sitting on another roommate's bed. England was sitting on his bed and writing a letter to his parents. His face was a shocking mess. Both eyes were black, blue, purple, very swollen, and almost closed.

Sir Toby gave us a fairly kind lecture and told us to shake hands before going down to dinner, which was by now well under way.

I put out my hand, but Charles refused to accept it. Instead, he told Sir Toby that he was writing to his parents to ensure that he was removed as housemaster and that I should be expelled.

I couldn't believe my ears. He was digging his own grave, and I was actually starting to look as if I was actually a decent chap by comparison.

Sir Toby and Lady Coghill tried to convince him again but again he spurned their advice and this time even more rudely.

This Life In Death

So, he stayed in his room, and I went down to dinner with the housemaster and his wife. I couldn't believe my luck. However, it was short lived. As we entered the dining room a huge cheer went up with everyone banging on the tables too. A furious Sir Toby put the whole house on silence for the entire dinner as a result.

Nevertheless, I did not receive further punishment and had announced my arrival in much the same way as I had at West House. It only really occurred to me when recounting my story to you that this was no accident as I now understand that from eight years of age onward, I had become determined to be a quasi-James Bond and was completely terrified of lapsing back into being that bone-idle, pleasant idiot which appeared to be my lot in the first eight years of my life. There were two Howards and the first version had to be kept in remission at all costs.

No wonder I was mixed up. Half of me just wanted to be at home in the bosom of my family while the other half wanted to be brave, courageous, and bold. Half of me wanted to win the applause of an authority I respected, while the other wanted to be appreciated by the rebel quarter of the boys at Aiglon – loving the Beatles, the Stones and Dylan while hating haircuts.

So not only did I want to run with the hare but hunt with hounds, but it was a schizophrenic Piscean me who had unexplained internal conflicts about God and the Empire versus wanting to be Paul McCartney and have as many girls as possible. The real problem was that I genuinely wanted to have both aspects in my life.

Three or four weeks later both England's parents and mine came out to see us for the Whit bank holiday – although there was no half term break for us. They arrived on a Friday and so England and I were granted exeats to have dinner with them. We rode up to the hotel on bikes together – now on speaking terms again - and as we entered the drive my heart took flight as I saw my adored parents sitting on the terrace by the entrance. But wait: they were having drinks with Mr and Mrs Singer Sewing Machines. Shit. This might be difficult.

This Life In Death

Charles beamed to see his parents too. After our brawl he had shown me respect and was a lot nicer to me than to his poor classmates. There was no animosity between us now – but what about our parents?

We jumped off our bikes and I kissed my mother and shook hands with my father – as this was expected in those days. Charles approached his parents and his mother immediately boomed out, "Who did that"? pointing to his two still black eyes a month on from the event.

"He did", he replied in a matter-of-fact kind of way without any meant accusation. He evidently had not posted or been allowed to post his letter.

"We had better go into dinner as Howard has to go to Lausanne tonight. See you later" said my mother and I was whisked away before a confrontation with Singer Sewing Machines could develop.

Indeed, I did have to go to Lausanne. This was because I had been selected to represent Aiglon for the 400-metre race in the ADISR Swiss national championship of schools for 1964 at the Olympic Stadium in Lausanne. There were three age groups – junior, moyen, and senior. I was 14 and so was a moyen.

Obviously, my parents were flabbergasted by this but no more than me. My asthma had not prevented me from becoming a good cricketer, a very good footballer, and an excellent hockey goalkeeper. But running races had always been a bridge too far.

However, since arriving in Switzerland I had not had one day's asthma, and my body was not only tanned but gaining strength – despite operating on only one and a half lungs. I should now express wonderful gratitude to my father's financial sacrifice – which I do in any event.

However, I suspect that I had grown out of an illness which is reputed to come and go in seven years cycles. I was 14. It left me and, to date, has never returned despite me smoking very stupidly, from the age of 16 until I was 42.

My parents had always been very liberal with giving me alcohol from a very young age. My mother used to pour whiskey down my throat to revive me during serious asthma attacks as a three-year-old. She also would make me drink a small brandy before any swimming race from 10 onwards and my father would allow me a Watney's Pale Ale while sailing with him from the age of 9.

Therefore, now 14, they had no problem with me having a couple of glasses of wine at dinner before I sped back to school to catch the yellow post bus from outside Claremont to take us to Lausanne, which was down the mountain and then along the Swiss side of Lake Geneva.

From birth I had suffered from being awfully car sick. I was renowned for it everywhere I went. They already knew about it here at Aiglon – and I had only been at the school 6 weeks. I was duly placed in a front seat just behind the driver with Toft - my American friend who thought my father was James Bond.

We set off, soon JC's, (as John Collette was known) Bentley Continental overtook us as he was coming, like my parents were, to support the school on the following day – and I thought to myself, "My Daddy helped pay for that car" with a little smile.

However, that thought was soon forgotten, as the bus rolled heavily round each of the scores of double bends down the mountain. I started to feel terribly travel sick. I tried to put mind over matter but by the time we were accelerating passed Chateau de Chillon next to the lake I was desperate and even worse as the falling summer sun was dancing on the lake and making me dizzy too.

I told Toft I would have to ask 'Mac', our athletics coach, if we could stop. He told me that Mac would be 'really mad' and that I should stand and put my head by the small quarter-light window to get some air. Stupidly I did.

This Life In Death

Now I thought that I was about to faint but instead vomited horrendously out of the window a huge dinner that had been washed down with both Coca Cola and wine. The effects of this were catastrophic. My projectile effort managed to enter each and every open quarter-light on the left side of the bus and spattered all the senior boys towards the back in puke which pebble-dashed their faces and smart Aiglon blazers and ties.

In addition, several following cars also got coated, the first of which was a white E-Type Jaguar with the roof down which started to swerve all over the road while using the windscreen washers and wipers. I was later told that the woman passenger was having a fit – her evening outfit for perhaps a dinner in Montreux ruined and her bouffant hair annointed with my dinner.

Chaos reigned. I don't think that before or since I have ever caused as much chaos in such a short moment. The yellow post bus limped into the Olympic village, where we were all staying for the night, as a sorry sight. I watched, as we were led away, the poor driver looking at his task with a bucket in one hand and a sponge in the other.

I crawled into a top bunk in the huge dormitory, nobody was horrid to me, but my shame was complete. This was like being seven all over again. I had let everyone down. My last memory as I lay there was some American saying, "My God, I've even got Hodgson's puke in my underpants".

I determined something had to be done.

The next day all teams paraded round the Olympic Stadium before the races began. I kept thinking that I must do something special to atone for the previous evening. I determined that the only thing was to win the race. However, I also knew that this was extremely unlikely. Nevertheless, I would give it my very best effort.

Then it was our race. I lined up. I decided that I would not pace myself but would run it as a sprint and die, if necessary, in the effort.

This Life In Death

Everyone knows that only a fool would attempt to run the 400 metres like a 100-metre-dash. But then, when in this mood, I was a fool.

The starting pistol banged and the Aiglon racer dashed off into a lead. I was several metres ahead at 100 metres; at two hundred metres I was still in the lead; at 300 I was still there, but my lungs were bursting, and my legs felt like jelly and everyone else was catching me up fast.

I knew this meant I needed to ignore any physical pain. I had to be like those mothers, who have been known to lift a car up to free their child from underneath it.

The pack was getting ever closer, but the finish line didn't seem to be. Just a few more paces I kept promising my collapsing legs. Then the line was crossed and I, by only a whisker, was deemed to have won the ADISR Moyen gold medal for the 400 metres. I collapsed and puked up what little was left of the previous evening's dinner.

JC was ecstatic – especially as we did not win much that day compared to other Swiss schools or, more importantly, our great international rival La Rosey.

My parents were speechless, and my mother felt totally vindicated for putting my father to such expense. The wonderful Swiss air had done its job. My father had seen the effort and felt the pain of those last 100 metres. He hugged me as well as shaking my hand and whispered that he was very proud of me. For the first time, since arriving in Switzerland, I felt almost happy.

Yet again, drive and determination had been my friend and helped me turn a disaster into a triumph. This only served to harden my attitude to everything and was to become my solution to every problem. Of course, this was far too simplistic an answer to all of life's problems.

The second half of the term didn't see me become any happier and naturally, although I worked very hard, and this was, in fairness, acknowledged in my end of term report, my exams results were the disaster everyone anticipated they would be given the impossible catch-up task that I had been set.

I didn't mind that as I had tried my hardest without anticipating any reward; I didn't mind the 6:45 am alarm bell, or the following 10-minute PT drill and two minute cold showers; I didn't mind the schoolwork. Masters, and boys had both treated me kindly. Indeed, I was popular with everyone. But I hated the weekends, as I had yet to learn how to abuse the planned camping expeditions; and the long separation from my family.

I had remained dreadfully homesick throughout the 12 weeks and could not wait to board the overnight train, which stopped especially at Aigle station to collect homeward bound British Aiglon students, bound for Calais and the ferry to my beloved England.

My reunion with my mother at Victoria station in London was joyous and my happiness complete as I was reunited with my father, sister, and brother that evening in Birmingham. The next day we left for our modest holiday home in Poole. There was no happier young man on the planet.

The summer of 1964 was glorious; England was playing Australia for the Ashes – that's cricket for those who might not know; The Beatles film 'A Hard Day's Night' was released to huge critical acclaim as Beatlemania was engulfing the world and I was well, sailing and most important of all at home.

Of course, there was always the nagging thought of returning to Switzerland in the back of my mind – but I knew I would be flogging a dead horse if I tried to persuade my parents that I should be allowed to leave.

Towards the end of the holiday, I was reading about Villa in the Sports Argus while sitting with my maternal grandfather Robert – perhaps of unadmitted noble birth. We were very close due to our love of cricket. I put the paper down and told myself to take advantage of this moment with him as I might not see him again. He had only one lung having lost the other because of a gas attack by the Germans in the First World War. He smoked 40 untipped cigarettes a-day despite this. He was now dying of lung cancer. I was right, he died in the November, and this was followed by my great hero Sir Winston Spencer Churchill in the January. They both represented great loss and subsequent sadness to me.

Eventually, the 14th of September arrived and following being taken to see 'The Sound of Music' starring the wonderful Julie Andrews, as my brother's 8th birthday treat the night before, I was braced for another awful term.

People who told me that they would give their right arm to go to Aiglon were swiftly answered by me that I would give mine to go to Villa Park instead.

However, although still very resentful about being there, I had to admit that my second term was a much more palatable experience than my first. I was no longer a new boy; I had been kept in the 4th year 'A' stream and made form captain; I came top of the class; I was made Captain of the Aiglon successful moyen football team and was top scorer; I played every game for the 18-year-old 1st XI, despite only being 14, and was that team's top scorer too – notching up over 2 goals per game; and Rupert Cadbury and I shared a room together – so now I had a true friend to talk to.

So, this was a much happier term, and I was still able to balance just about being a model Empire boy with my desire to be a 'dedicated follower of rebellious fashion' and an increasing obsession with the opposite sex.

When I returned to the UK at Christmas, my father met me at Heathrow Airport. He took me into London and to the Ritz Hotel. Before lunch we went down to 'Laurie's Bar' in the basement. 'Laurie' was the barman. I was only 14 and not supposed to be in a bar. But he allowed me to sit on a stool in a corner at one end of the bar and sip a ginger beer shandy while my father socialised at the centre of the bar with other drinkers.

This Life In Death

A large rotund and bald American entered and noisily exclaimed to Laurie,

"This country is finished. You are all living on past glories. Your Empire has gone. London is the arsehole of the world".

To which my father replied, "And I suppose you are just passing through".

The bar erupted into laughter mixed with applause.

I was very proud of him.

I was by now more relaxed and resigned to accepting my life of exile. I was also terrified of getting spots and couldn't wait to attend the dancing classes that I and my old friends from West House and its rival, Hallfield, had been booked into. I would be re-united with my childhood best friend 'Bogey' Jones from the former and my life-long friend to be, Simon Draycott, later to become a successful QC, from the latter.

These classes were held in a dance studio in Monument Lane by the Ivy Bush on the Hagley Rd in Edgbaston. They were organised by 2 old spinsters as a sort of coming out operation for young local public-school boys who boarded and equally well-off middle-class girls who didn't.

I suddenly realised that I was at a huge advantage. Aiglon had done me a favour. I had met lots of English and American girls at Swiss 'finishing schools', as they were then described, and was not shy of engaging in conversation with them. Indeed, I had a girlfriend in one, her name was Emma-Anne, and she came from Birmingham too – but the one in Alabama rather than England.

I was tanned, had blond hair - which was quite a bit longer than the other guys, was spot free and not tongue tied. Moreover, I did not speak like Bertie Wooster. Therefore, I was far closer to being a Beatle or Rolling Stone than any contemporary. I quickly became keen to take full advantage of this.

This Life In Death

I can't say that I really became a good dancer because of these classes, although I do remember how to do the military-2-step nearly 60 years later. It probably wasn't too important as by then formal dancing was already losing ground to the less disciplined jigging about that is called dancing today.

I can say the whole concept was great, because as a result of these lessons, most parents then held little drinks parties for their children's friends around Xmas which was attended by all dancing class attendees. Boys would wear suits and ties and girls party frocks. Sausages on sticks, crisps, weak shandy in large jugs and soft drinks were provided.

The start time was usually 19:30 and parents arrived to take their young teenagers home 3 hours later. Initially, everyone chatted as the album 'Beatles for Sale' was on continuous repeat before some dancing and then the lights went down with about an hour left.

This is what I was there for. I needed to make sure that I was dancing with the girl I wanted to be with just before then – so you had the one you wanted as the last hour of 'snogging' began. Kissing, then French kissing, before my left hand slipped inside her bra – very exciting for a 14-year-old boy but nothing further was contemplated then – as the swinging 60s were still in their youth and so were we!

Yes, as Macca, was later to write 3 years later in 1967, on the glorious Sgt Pepper album, 'I have to admit it's getting better'. I was growing up and was to identify with that lyric. It was getting better but was I going to be able to keep it going that way?

The winter term of 1965 began with my introduction to skiing. It was to join sailing and horse riding as a favourite pastime forever. I still have a great time with all three over 50 years later – sailing in the summer, riding in the autumn and skiing in the winter.

Skiing was a much more dangerous sport then than it is today and, as the winter term progressed, it was quite usual to see an increasing number of boys with legs in plaster while trying to get from A to B on crutches.

I still didn't like Aiglon but it seemed to like me. I was promoted up the ranks to Standard Bearer Candidate when only just 15. I finished top of the 4th year A stream and so started in the 5th year A stream that autumn. I came top of that too having been able to jettison the science subjects that I detested.

To ensure I got into the 'upper 5th' I knew that I needed to pass all subjects – even those that were to be dropped – during the year and in the end of year exams. This presented me with a serious problem because, while I was by now very proficient in English, maths, history, geography, art, and French, I was totally disinterested in physics and chemistry and useless at both as a result.

Something had to be done – as I had managed to persuade my father that I could leave Aiglon at the end of the summer term 1966, provided my 'O' level results were good. My asthma seemed to have been cured and I could see that the huge school fees, along with prime minister Harold Wilson's 19 shillings in the pound tax bills, were becoming an impossible burden for him and so took the opportunity to talk to him about being allowed to return to England.

A new English boy had arrived at the school called King. He was academically very clever and did not appear to have asthma. So, I'm not too sure why he was there in the first place. He was also quite neurotic and a little odd and therefore a prime candidate to be bullied – which he was.

I hatched a plan which would be beneficial to both of us. I would ensure he didn't get bullied if he sat by me, let me copy his science and did my science homework for me. Therefore, he got physical protection, and I had good science marks. We both kept to our side of the bargain, and we were both happy.

Then it occurred to me that there was a huge problem looming. What about the end of term exams? Without King's help I was bound to fail hopelessly both papers. How were we going to overcome this considerable hurdle?

It was decided that I would school him in forging my handwriting: he would get himself sat in front of me: he would do his paper and then change pen and hand writing and do mine: at the end of exam, when we were asked to pass our papers forward, I would pass some jottings: he would add my exam to those and pass them forward along with his own exam too.

Physics was first and the plan worked like a dream. I got 65%. He got 83%. I pointed this out to him. He rightly counted that if I had got 83% it might have caused an investigation. Now it was chemistry's turn. King was late. Someone else took his place. They refused to move. The teacher told King to sit somewhere else. He glanced at me as he went. He could see that I was not pleased and looked suitably terrified as a result.

The exam was going to be a disaster now. I had to think quickly. I completed it as best I could and then, with an Oscar winning performance, made myself vomit towards the end of the exam.

Later on the results revealed that I had only got 2 % but it was decided that, as I had done very well in all the other subjects and had been ill during the exam for this one, it would not count against my passage to the upper 5th.

At the end of the exam, a worried King was waiting for me outside. He was extremely apologetic, but I told him to forget it. I hated bullies and liked him anyway, so the deal was still on. He was still the scientific genius, and I was still trying to be James bloody Bond.

I did very well in 5A and was either 1st or 2nd on every fortnightly review. I often changed places with a boy called McLaughlin for one of those two positions. He gave the impression of not having to work as he was so clever – whereas I knew that I did and started revising for my June 1966 'O' Level exams in September 1965 with a very meticulously designed programme.

This Life In Death

I had returned from the summer 1965 holiday very focused on good results and increasingly determined to have it all my way. The school wanted me to sit French. I refused. They said that without it I was not taking enough subjects. I said I would take Religious Knowledge. They said I couldn't because the resident vicar had said that he couldn't teach it. I replied that they should send for the Oxford Board course and that I would teach myself. I was insistent and won.

This did not impress JC when he found out. It did impress the rebellious British Baby Boomer camp that I had always been half in and half out of. Indeed, at the end of the autumn 1965 term, they had done an end of term sketch of being me helping a sick boy out of church when I could see him slumped in his pew.

JC had singled me out for praise for this in the following day's morning assembly. This had really painted me as a goodie, goodie two shoes. However, as the term progressed, I had more and more come into conflict with authority over my education, which I arrogantly thought I knew much better what was needed than the school did.

Therefore, I was drawing closer and closer to the rebels and further and further away from the established authority. Then they asked me to appear in the end of term sketch. It was anti-church and anti-Aiglon. The stage set was the Villars Anglican church. A guy called Rhodes, no relation, was the vicar. He started with a version of the Lord's Prayer that referred to mouldy school daily bread. A pupil becomes unwell, and everyone runs to haul him out and thus escape the rest of the service – everyone that is except me.

They were taking the 'Michael' out of JC's commendation of me, and I was joining in. Understandably, he was not amused. The dice were being thrown by me. I was going to get home my way and the enemy had become the school establishment as a result. If I had relied on reason more than I had on gut feel, the result might have been different.

The rebels loved having me walk 100% over to their side and JC did not. An admiration of him by me and a liking of me by him disappeared almost overnight and the autumn term of 1965 finished badly. However, this turned into all-out war when I returned to school in the new year of 1966 to find that I had been billeted in the misfits' chalet.

My mother had scheduled a trip to see me in February. I discovered that she was coming during the skiing expedition long weekend of trudging up mountains with skins on the bottom of our skis. My request to be excused this form of hell so I could see my mother was denied. However, I had other ideas.

On the Thursday afternoon before the weekend in question, I got separated on purpose from my ski group and arrived back at school just before they were sending a search party out. I collapsed next to the school. Mrs Phillips, my house matron, and Miss Trott the school nurse, were sent for. I explained that I had fallen and couldn't move my left leg.

They carried me up four flights of stairs and the school doctor was called. He examined me and pronounced that I had strained ligaments and would not be able to ski. My two nurses wanted to know who was going to look after me as the whole school was going on the expedition. I was happy to inform them that my mother would be in Villars.

It was arranged that I could be sent in a taxi to her on the next evening and would stay for the duration of the expedition. I hobbled up to her room on crutches. She had brought me a feast of Beatle and Villa articles and magazines. What a result!

We started down for dinner. My mother suddenly stopped and asked, "Where are your crutches"?

"You didn't believe any of that shit did you"? I replied with a wink and a shy smile.

I'm sure my actions were suspected but nothing was proved and so I got away with it. However, it was perhaps yet another nail in the coffin of my relationship with the school establishment.

This Life In Death

I became increasingly pompous and arrogant in my refusal to accept any school authority that I did not agree with. Worse, I took to simply doing what I felt like when not working. I was demoted back to Senior Badge rank with every justification as a result. I took up smoking and drank beer whenever I could as long as I had fulfilled my revision quota – for I remained still an obsessive worker towards obtaining my 'O' Level results.

This was in complete contrast to my new friends who were all at least two streams below me and couldn't care less about their 'O' levels in the least. But they were now my buddies and I had turned my back on being an Empire boy now that I was, in my opinion, a man. Complete rubbish of course – but not vaguely uncommon with 16-year-old boys – especially today when parental respect and control are so much less than they were then.

My final term at Aiglon began with me picking another fight with the school. I had decided that I wanted to leave as soon as I had taken my last exam, which was some four weeks before the end of term. My parents, who were now distracted by other matters as we shall see, had agreed. I informed the school and awaited a response.

Due to my rigorous revision timetable, I had just about dropped out of sight from any sports activity but did find time to organise a masters vs. boys cricket match. This was certainly the first and probably the last such event of its kind ever held at Aiglon. I captained the boys and we won.

During the game, as I was fielding, JC appeared behind me on the boundary. He told me that I would not be leaving after my last exam but would remain until the end of term. Shamefully, I disrespectfully told him that this was not his decision but mine. He said no more but wandered off.

The next weekly letter I received from my mother informed me that Mr. Collette had written to my father informing him that I could leave now or stay until the end of term. To leave now would mean not taking my 'O' levels. Checkmate to JC, I had lost and had to accept it. I stayed, took the exams, which were all passed – including the self-taught religious knowledge – and I actually behaved better.

All of this is well documented in my final headmaster's report dated 17th July 1966:

'Howard is pompous, arrogant, self-opinionated, and inclined to think he is always right. He has small streaks of brilliance, but his ultimate success will be limited by narrow-minded drive and determination. Arrogance is no virtue and he must learn this...' This was but the opening and it got worse as it went on.

For years I saw this as a statement of war. Now I read it and realise that it is a true reflection of me then, written by a truly gifted, intelligent, and caring man who knew his pupil much better than the pupil knew himself.

Moreover, although I can still feel the pain of not wanting to be there, I can honestly say that Aiglon did me a lot of good and I took from it much more than I realised at the time. This was because despite initially hating it and then fighting it, I agreed with its belief in fairness and good character. I had come to the school with these principles, and I left with them strengthened.

People like JC, Christopher Reynolds, (another housemaster) Sir Toby, my history teacher Mr. Parsons, and others, not least my German matron Mrs Phillips, whom I fantasised about, had dedicated their lives to making these rich and often cash spoilt but love starved boys' lives better and more secure.

Twenty-six years later, in the summer of 1992, I was invited back to give the end of year graduation speech to the now co-ed school. This was usually reserved for famous parents like Roger Moore, Jackie Stewart, or Sophia Lauren and certainly not an old boy who had left just one rank up from where he had started.

Therefore, it was hardly surprising that the new headmaster, Mr. Parsons, who had taught me history and English language, JC having retired and sadly died by then, referred to me in his welcome, as 'the most unlikely old boy I can recall to ever be invited back for this purpose'.

In 2000, I visited the school again while on a skiing holiday in Villars. While standing in the reception of Belvedere, another Aiglon house, Mrs Phillips, walked in and without prompting said, "Hello Howard, how are you"? We hadn't seen each other for thirty-four years. She still looked great despite now being in her sixties.

So Aiglon was left behind in the summer of 1966. I returned home to see England win the World Cup and follow that with a fortnight on a cheap package holiday to Palma in Majorca with my best pal 'Bogey' Jones. The cost was only £14 each including flights and full board. My father gave us an additional £5 each to spend. We felt like millionaires, despite Harold Wilson's currency restrictions, and embarked on what was to be an orgy of sex and booze that lasted the entire time with only the briefest of respite for sleep.

I had lost my virginity to a girl much older than me on top of a Bournemouth bus the summer before in an instant of excitement and was now determined to practice as much as possible in order to become a proficient performer in what had become my favourite sport.

Now the summer was ending the hard facts of life had to be faced. For the last 3 years, I had believed that life in Birmingham, England would be bliss and yes, I was delighted to be home. However, there were serious issues for my family and me to face.

This Life In Death

Chapter III

Out of the Frying Pan & into the Fire

(1966 – 1972)

My parents' marriage, which had never been quite as wonderful as I had always wanted to believe as a child, was becoming increasingly strained. My mother thought my father drank too much and was having many 'flings' with the attractive barmaids he came across in the private members clubs he frequented. He was guilty as charged.

In truth, my father had been changing by degree for several years. The young man that was my wonderful daddy; so kind and artistic and who had worked so hard in the decade following his father's death had suddenly looked over his shoulder to realise that his tyrannical father was no longer there and that he was now the boss and free to do as he pleased.

As a result, he had taken his foot off the accelerator and had engaged his best friend, a genial man called Stan Edwards, who had spent four years in a prisoner of war camp during the Second World War, as the business's manager and chief funeral director. He had taught Stan to be an excellent funeral director, but Stan was no businessman, and the times were changing in Birmingham.

The old inner-city areas, where Hodgson & Sons Ltd funerals largely came from, were being demolished and the indigenous population moved away. No houses = no people. No people = no deaths. No deaths = no funerals – QED. A simple equation that Stan missed, and his absentee boss was not focusing on. Moreover, other areas which hadn't been demolished, like Handsworth for example, were increasingly being populated by the huge influx of immigrants from across the Commonwealth. These people were mostly young and so had a relatively low death rate.

This Life In Death

Therefore, although the business was still being very well run professionally and remained the City's top funeral directors, with the Oaklands Funeral Home a shining beacon of excellence, there was no business plan to deal with shrinking numbers of funerals.

This would prove to be an increasingly serious problem in the future. This is because about 80% of a funeral directors' overheads are fixed and must be paid irrespective of the number of funerals arranged.

If you exceed the budgeted number of funerals, your business becomes extremely profitable because you have already covered 80% of your costs and only have to cover the 20% of variable overhead cost thereafter. However, if you fall short of that budgeted figure you are not covering the fixed costs and this spells disaster.

Therefore, the seeds for business disaster were being sown a decade before they would explode into the last chance saloon. Moreover, the storm clouds of family disharmony had been gathering even before I went to Aiglon. However, initially they were only occasional, and we had continued to enjoy the largely blissful happy family life of my early childhood.

Nevertheless, when my parents did argue even then, it was usually late at night and could end up in physical confrontation usually caused by my father having consumed a considerable amount of alcohol.

I had been woken up on occasion from the age of thirteen onwards to break up these parental battles. However, once resolved, I had preferred to put them to the back of my mind in the hope and childish belief that they would never happen again.

As a little boy of eight, I had dreamt that my father had changed from the man I adored and worshipped. I awoke and was relieved that it been but a nightmare. I was to pretend that these episodes were just a bad dream and would not be repeated for many years. Naturally, I was to be proved wrong.

This Life In Death

Also. it should be remembered that there are always two sides to every story. My mother had been brought up an only child and was the daughter of an extremely selfish and strong-willed woman that her husband, Robert Ward, of perhaps noble birth, had put up with only with the solace of a mistress to turn to for most of their married life.

My mother had inherited a lot of her mother's genes and, as an only child, was not used to sharing or thinking of others. For example, when ill as a child, it was my father who had sat up with me night after night as my mother found illness or imperfection in others hard to deal with.

So, I always felt that if she had shared more with him, encouraged him more and criticised him less, there was a chance that he might have avoided that slippery slope of ill-discipline and lack of self-esteem that he was destined to descend.

Of course, perhaps they were never well suited even when they married in 1949. However, divorce was still a complete social enigma in the 1950s and so they did their best to make the most of it and, to be fair, kept their love affairs, for my mother was not the innocent she made out in that regard, and personal disputes out of earshot for most of my sister and my childhoods. My brother, who was six years younger than me, was to be subjected to the full force of their increasing acrimony from a much earlier age than us and became deeply affected by it to such an extent that he has used it to excuse his largely wasted talents.

Now the reality of their mutual incompatibility had to be faced as I was living at home permanently. This was something that I had kidded myself would be a perfect life while at Aiglon but was now to be forced to see that it was not and was strewn with emotional and sometimes violent scenes.

As usual there was the relentless conflict going on inside my head which had to be dealt with. I had achieved good 'O' level passes because of my determination to get away from Aiglon. However, now

61

that I was home, I seemed to have lost that drive and determination. I was far more interested in wearing fashionable clothes, going to parties, and taking as much advantage of the swinging 60s with the opposite sex as possible and often with more than one at a time. The officer and gentleman part of my personality had almost disappeared altogether.

As my hair grew longer my interest in my 'A' levels became less by almost equal proportion. Moreover, my parents' own problems seemed to increasingly occupy them and therefore, they hardly seemed to notice that I was only really going through the motions of college work.

I suppose I could try to excuse my behaviour by claiming to have been going through that awkward age of '16 going on 17' or even blaming my parents, as my brother has been apt to do for the most of his life. But the truth was that I was throwing all that I had gained from many years of hard work away in the pursuit of fun - and that meant wine, women, and song and I seemed to have little interest in anything else, other than going to Villa Park.

One Saturday in October 1966, I hoped to combine the pleasures of the flesh with a trip to Villa Park. My parents had been invited to a wedding, and getting on well for once, went off to attend happily, leaving me with the instruction that a taxi would arrive with my little brother and a friend of his, when school finished at lunchtime, and that I should then take them on in the taxi to Villa Park to watch Villa play the great Manchester United, who boasted amongst other great players George Best, Bobby Charlton, and Denis Law.

No sooner was my father's car out of sight, than my new girlfriend, was whisked into our home and my bed. We did not have access to the pill and feared her becoming pregnant, so I dutifully wore a condom. We made love.

It was good. I was sixteen and so loaded up a second time to do it all again. However, the taxi arrived and so instead we hurriedly dressed, said goodbye and I jumped into the taxi.

This Life In Death

At halftime Villa were winning 1-0 against the run of play, I bought the boys a hot dog each and told them not to move while I went to the 'gents' – which was a polite, if somewhat inaccurate description of the men's urinal.

Here one queued until it was your turn to join 30 or so other men peeing against a steel wall which then fell into an open trough and all drained away like a small river amid a horrid stench.

I started to pee, but nothing hit the steel. Why? I looked down; to my horror the second but unused condom was filling up like a balloon; then it dropped off the end of 'William' with a loud splash and floated passed my fellow pee-ers, who to a man looked at it and then turned to me. I would have wanted the floor to swallow me up if it had not been so grubby. Football stadia were still very Victorian in 1966.

United equalised with five minutes to go and so a day that had started so well was now going from bad to worse.

However, a little known player, called Tony Scott, won the game for Villa in the last minute. As a result, I quickly forgot about the maiden voyage of my good ship 'Condom'.

Six months later I was seventeen and had passed my driving test. My father gave me an old Ford Anglia immediately, which I proceeded to smash up three times in as many months. He was naturally furious with me for bumping up the company's motor insurance premium as well as being an embarrassment to him when forced to ask Stan Edwards to make yet another claim.

However, my father was still fond enough of me to buy me a brand-new Triumph Herald in the summer of 1967, as he thought I would be safer racing around in that than an old banger. I was indeed very spoilt and had done nothing to justify this new car. Worse, I was to drive it just as fast and at weekends, when they were sailing in Dorset without me, would drive all over the place to visit various girlfriends who were holidaying in the Cotswolds or even North Wales.

This Life In Death

On one occasion, I took my little brother with me as he had been left in my charge. He was nearly 11, but nowhere near old enough to go on such expeditions. Nevertheless, I put him in the back of my car with a pillow, and a blanket, while he was still in his pyjamas. As it didn't occur to me to take any clothes for him, he was forced to visit the gentlemen's toilet in the Liggon Arms, Broadway, in the Cotswolds on a mid-Sunday morning dressed that way.

Lennon & McCartney were still writing together but by now it was more common to start a song separately and then the other would help polish it up. Who wrote what was given to the Rolling Stone magazine by John and, with the except of two songs, this list was later agreed by Paul. However, you can tell who the originator of which composition is as long as you can identify the singer's voice – as they always sang their own songs.

In 1966, Paul McCartney had become the senior contributor on the Revolver album with not only the most but also easily the best songs. Then in the summer of 1967 the Beatles released the pinnacle of the 60s musical extravaganza, the album that changed modern music like no other – Sgt Pepper's Lonely Hearts Club Band. McCartney dominates this album too while the Beatles continued to change the world.

I was completely caught up in this whirlpool. I wore Cuban heeled boots, a military jacket, flower power shirts, flared jeans, on which I wrote girls' phone numbers, and chiffon scarves. I even grew a Mexican moustache. I was indeed a 'dedicated follower of fashion' and by now completely out of control.

My only saving grace was that I didn't do drugs like all my male pals. They would pass round a big joint while sitting in a circle surrounded by joss sticks. Most of the girls didn't smoke pot like me – so we did other things.

The parties or 'raves' as they were called were nothing like those of that smart middle class set back in 1965. There were huge affairs, with no class distinction and often took over houses in any district of the city or countryside.

As some of my older friends were at university by now, I could end up at a 'rave' even in another town all together. I went to one such event in Leicester. I came with a girl and left with her the next day but not before I had got to know three others intimately overnight.

That sounds alarmingly atrocious in our politically correct society of today. However, it was the 'done' thing then and girls, who had just been liberated by the pill, were suddenly extremely keen to be very sexually promiscuous. This was driven by peer pressure and fashion as well as sexual curiosity. If you were a girl who had remained a virgin by the time you were 18, you were either frigid or ugly or both. Unfair but true – and when has fashion or peer pressure ever been kind or sensible?

On the way to one such 'rave' in a barn in the beautiful Warwickshire countryside near to Stratford-Upon-Avon, a crazy cortege of 'ravers' cars were speeding to the venue at idiotic speed when a Morris Minor couldn't take a bend and flipped onto its roof. The other 'rave-mobiles' stopped. I noticed flames were coming out of the up-turned engine as the occupants scrambled out. However, there was still a girl in the back of the car. She was upside down and banging on the window.

I wasn't courageous because I didn't stop to think. One second, I saw her and the next I was dragging her out and we both scrambled away just before the Morris became a crematorium.

There was something cynical about the baby-boomers of the 60s. I believe it was a reaction to Victorian attitudes and the heroics of our fathers in World War II.

So, none of my friends thought my action was heroic, rather that I was a silly fool for risking my life. But there was still enough of that Empire boy wanting to be James Bond in me that made me act instinctively.

This Life In Death

In the autumn of 1966, following my return from Aiglon, I had started at Birmingham Tutorial College. It was known locally as 'Bantocks'. This was the surname of the founder and his two sons who worked with him. It was really a crammer where people of all ages and abilities came to pass exams that they had failed or were likely to fail.

I had chosen it because it was situated only a five-minute walk away from where we lived in Edgbaston; it didn't start until 10:00 in the morning; there was no weekend attendance and very little, if any, homework. My father, had agreed because it was a lot cheaper than me joining a sixth form at some British Public School and he still had my sister at boarding school and my brother due to go to the expensive Malvern College – which meant a substantial amount on school fees still had to be found.

I had decided that my three 'A' level subjects were to be history, economics, and British Constitution, because I somewhere in the back of my distracted brain thought I might become prime minister one day. What a ridiculous self-delusional idea.

The place was a terrible choice for me because one needed self-discipline and I seemed to have lost mine altogether. Therefore, it was bad for me, and I was bad for it – being totally disruptive and leading anyone who would follow away from their studies.

Matters were bound to come to a head sooner or later and in the spring of 1968 they did. God only knows how it had taken 20 months to do so. I had convinced some pals to go for a lunchtime drink. Some girl students wanted to come as well. The numbers grew and about 15 students decided to join the cortege trip to the pub.

We had an hour and a half break – which was generous. However, I suggested going to a pub on the other side of Birmingham, where we all had a great time and rolled up back at the college as the few remaining pupils were about to go home.

Old man Bantock was rightly furious. We were sent for and lined up in his office to explain ourselves. I elected myself to be the

This Life In Death

spokesman. To my chums' relief, I explained that it had all been my fault and that I would take full responsibility.

The old chap listened but then pulled out his battery-operated hearing-aid from his ear with a scream and we all heard it blare out the "Radio One is Wonderful – Bee Bee Cee" - the BBC sung jingle of that time.

I burst into fits of Errol Flynn type hilarity while the others tried, more politely, to disguise their mirth. That was enough for Mr. Bantock senior. He dismissed the others while telling me he would be phoning my father. So, there we have it. This was my third and final school Principal and I had managed to drive all three mad.

Naturally, he did call my father, who had left my mother by this time, and gone to stay at his country club in Worcestershire. Old man Bantock explained that, while I was a gifted student of history, economics, and British Constitution, and likely without much effort to get good 'A' level grades, he could no longer put up with the anarchy and disruption which accompanied me to his establishment.

However, my father used his considerable powers of charm and persuasion and it was agreed that I would be given one more chance. I was to be summoned to my father's solicitors, Cartwright & Lewis on the Bristol Rd going towards the city centre. There, old man Cartwright would give me a 'good talking to'.

I was staying at that time with my best friend Simon Draycott at his house. There his mother presided over and ruled, as a quasi-modern-day Miss Faversham. She often stayed in her nightdress for days, while entertaining a local villain called Sid to chunks of Cheddar cheese and glasses of white wine in the 19th century style kitchen.

Simon's parents' marriage was running the same course as mine. His father was an eminent and famous Q.C. and he was rarely at home due to his cases or perhaps his lack of desire to be there. Consequently, I couldn't work out if Betty Draycott lived in such a dangerous and decadent way to draw attention to herself or just because she liked it.

She was, and would go on being, very kind to me over my ongoing trials and tribulations during this period. She flirted with me, and she mothered me – and I welcomed both.

On the day of my appointment with my father and Mr. Cartwright, I received a call from my girlfriend, who informed me she was "late". This was not good news. She might be pregnant. I was barely 18 and she was 17. Moreover, this was not the first time that this had happened. The previous year had seen me use a lot of my inheritance from my grandmother on a Harley St termination when she was only 16. Her parents were impressed enough by my action to allow us to go on seeing each other. I can't recall if my parents ever knew. I think not as I'm sure I would have remembered if they had.

I duly arrived for my stern lecture at Cartwright & Lewis. I was ushered into a typical lawyer's office of the day to see a genial elderly gentleman sitting at his desk with my father next to him and therefore opposite me. So, it was to be war I immediately decided.

I dressed as if I was the fifth and only fair-haired Beatle in full Sgt. Pepper regalia. Old man Cartwright cleverly ignored this provocation and spoke to me sensibly and calmly. I tried to listen politely even though I disagreed with a lot of what he said.

He informed me that Nottingham University was prepared to accept me to read history and Leicester (I think) to read economics according to Mr Bantock. He went on that I had enjoyed a privileged life but that the world was changing, and university degrees were the thing of the future. I could see all of that – but a thought was screaming out to me at the back of my head. This was that by the time I had finished university the family business would have gone under as my father took zero interest in it, 'Uncle' Stan, although a brilliant funeral director couldn't, and dear old great uncle Les had by now neither the wit nor the energy to save us.

This Life In Death

When Mr. Cartwright was finished I presumed it was my turn. I was wrong. My father thought it was his and started to express, with a lot of reason it must be said, his disappointment in me. This was quite fair and appropriate but the hot-headed me listened for about 30 seconds before exploding.

"You talk to me about me? What about you? Thanks to you if I go to university there will be no bloody business left to support this family".

I leapt out of my seat and sprang out of the room, the building and on to the forecourt in what seemed like one step.

I had decided in one moment to reclaim my life, my drive and determination and set a goal which was to shape my life forever. Jesus Christ! This must be completely insane. I had not entered the Cartwright & Lewis office with any such thought in my head. But now, in the twinkling of an eye, this was my life's goal and I was going to become the saviour of Hodgson & Sons Ltd and then make it the country's biggest and best funeral director – come hell or high water.

I jumped into my car, headed towards the city before turning left into Wellington Rd and ran out of petrol. Suddenly, reality kicked in. My girlfriend might be pregnant, I had no money, old man Bantock hated me, my father had just, understandably, disowned me, my car had no petrol, and I would have to walk back to Draycott's home.

Once there, he played 'Like a Rolling Stone' by Bob Dylan on the stereo, which was appropriate but perhaps a little unkind, while I looked into the embers of a dying fire in the drawing room grate. This was a new low and perhaps the lowest low I had ever experienced to date. Earlier ones had been forced upon me. This one was completely of my own making, and I knew it. My family was in ruins, and I had done nothing positive to save it. My efforts at West House and Aiglon had resulted in a sex-mad teenager who lived for the next 'rave' and, quite deservedly, my future was rock bottom.

Betty Draycott flashed her cleavage at me and told me to cheer up. A faint smile passed over my face. The maybe pregnant girlfriend, an extremely beautiful girl called Susan, then telephoned the Draycott's to let me know that she had got her period – well that was something but not enough to lift my spirits.

I knew everything was absolutely awful and that most of it was down to me. I asked Simon to play the Beatles instead of Dylan, like a child wanting some comfort, and I fell asleep in front of the fire in the drawing room.

I was awoken very early by the old Bakelite black telephone ringing early in the butler's pantry. The Draycott house was a very large rambling place where we had enjoyed and endured many 3 day long 'raves' while his parents and younger siblings had been away in Leatherhead during the previous two summers.

I knew no one else would hear it upstairs in this Victorian house, so I got up and answered it – just in case it was important. It was not important to the Draycott folk, but it was important to me. It was my father.

He was pleasant and to the point. He would like me to come over to the Cray Combe Country Club for lunch so we could discuss my future calmly. I jumped at the opportunity and genuinely apologised for my rude and hot-headed behaviour of yesterday. He didn't accept the same but neither did he reject it. He did ask me to dress appropriately.

Betty lent me a pound which nearly bought 10 litres of petrol in those days so I could rescue my car. I bathed, shaved off my moustache, and dressed as he had asked, with the help of some borrowed clothes from Simon's father – without his knowledge but with Betty's blessing. I can't recall dressing like Sgt Pepper again.

I arrived for lunch, which was preceded by a couple of George VI scotches drunk in the cocktail bar by my father while I drank a ginger beer shandy. Then we went into the beautifully appointed and white table clothed restaurant.

This Life In Death

He ordered a splendid two course meal, but I was too nervous to really enjoy it as we were discussing my future. Eventually, he declared that if I would buckle down, and drop back into society rather than out of it, he would organise for me to become an apprentice at James Summers & Sons of Cardiff. He did not think it was fair on his own staff for them to teach me all they knew and then one Monday morning me become their boss. I readily agreed.

He also demanded that I start to look like a funeral director rather than a rock star and that I go to work in an Evesham pork pie factory owned by a fellow club member for a fortnight in order to learn some discipline. Again, I readily agreed.

So, we were reunited and pals again and I was deliriously happy. He asked me to stay the night in a local pub as the club was full. I happily consented and drifted off into a contented sleep almost straight away. What a difference a day makes!

After the eventful fortnight in the pork pie factory, which might become the subject of another book one day – which included a sacked employee shitting in the meat pie vat, and five haircuts in 5 days, I was ready to be taken to meet Morlais Summers – the senior of three active Summers in the Roath Court Funeral Home, Cardiff.

My father drove me there in his second hand and old Bentley – as my school fees, his increasing drinking, and falling funeral numbers were starting to cramp his lifestyle somewhat.

My God, I thought, Roath Court was even more resplendent than the Oaklands. Morlais showed us round personally – a rare honour - and introduced me to his brother Cuthbert, a more readily likeable man than Morlais and his extremely nice, but sensitive and dominated son Paul, in whose care I was placed.

We then went for an expensive lunch, which was the last I was to have for some time, before my father dropped me and my case off at the Penylan Hotel which is where I would be billeted for now. Then he was gone and with him the nicer things in life. However, I did not care too much.

I might be living in a very cheap hotel. I might have to be up at the crack of dawn every day to fit out coffins. I might have to stay in the funeral home some nights without extra pay to be on 24-hour call. I might have to stay out driving Morlais from night club to night club until the early hours but still clock in at 7:30 while he slept until 11:00. I might only be paid £8-a-week for all of this. I might not look now so cool with my locks cropped. I might not be able to 'pull' as many women as a result.

Indeed, all of this was true or potentially true. However, I was on the first rung of a very important ladder. I believed I was going to become a very successful and important funeral director. I was going to help my father rebuild Hodgson & Sons Ltd and we were going to offer the best possible standards of service and facility imaginable to bereaved folk of whatever colour, religion, or class.

This was my goal, and I knew then it would become my life's work — even if it wasn't quite as cool as being either George Best, the famous footballer, a Beatle, or prime minister. This suddenly did not matter any more. I had rediscovered my drive, determination, and discipline. I was very happy and even more so to learn that my father and mother were reunited.

I hoped this all signalled a new beginning for the business, the family and me. Naturally, I was hoping for a miracle but thought that it was better to be positive and believe that it was possible than let my nagging suspicion that their relationship was doomed come to the fore.

I was put to work in the coffin fitting department, which was by the garage. Neither were in Roath Court but established about a mile away. It was run by small old man called Billy Pring. He was, at first, suspicious of me. I was after all English, and my father was a friend of his boss. However, I was very polite, respectful, and showed a keen desire to learn. He warmed to me as a result and even more so when he realised that I embodied the sixties sexual revolution and would advise to go after the young married girls at Routh Court. Why? He explained that when a loaf had been cut into no one missed a slice. This speaks rems of the power of the old Victorian values which were still hypocritically followed by the older generation still alive in the sixties decade of promiscuity. I really liked Billy. He was a character, and I can see him clearly in my head now some 55 years later.

A lovely lad called John was the coffin fitter. He was 24 and therefore 6 years older than me. He was married with a young son. He taught me how to fit 'ready-made' coffins and I taught him to have fun – when Billy was not around.

This was the summer of 1968. The Australians were over again for the Ashes. We would fit out all the coffins as early as we could and then disappear into the adjoining coffin store, where there were some 500 coffins of all sorts of price and size. Here, we used the last lane, which was about 25 yards, as a cricket wicket. We had a bat, a scoring system worked on which coffins we hit, and we had our own test series – England vs. Australia. I was English so I was England.

On other occasions we would use the power staple guns as sub-machine guns and engage in rapid fire fights. We did our work very diligently but, as this was the summer and the death rate quiet as a result, we made the most of the rest of the day – when really, we should have been putting linings into coffins for the coming winter upsurge.

Before too long, I was moved into the garage to become a 'grease monkey' in the pit under the DS 400 Daimler hearses and limousines. I didn't like this as much as I was terrified that my perfect complexion would be ruined by the oil which constantly dripping from them as I greased their axle nipples. However, I was quickly moved on after I had filled a senior funeral director – for Summers had seven FDs – one Mr. Miller's company car with oil but used a quart jug instead of a pint one. The result was that when I turned on the engine all four hearse and eight limousines were lost in a cloud of heavy carbon monoxide smoke which had about 20 staff members sputtering and dashing to the exit.

Next, I was deployed on hospital removals with a decent older and bald man called Percy. He took me home to meet his wife and was kind to me. As we tripped around the five or six local hospitals on our route to bring in six plus bodies placed on racked shelves in the ambulance we might stop for a coffee. Percy drove as he said he did not wish me to crash the Ford Transit ambulance as he might be sacked. He had been warned that I thought that I was either Jim Clark, Graham Hill or Sterling Moss.

After a couple of days, when we stopped, I bought a packet of cigarettes, a Coca Cola, and a Daily Express, which I proceeded to read as he drove. He looked at me and told me that he should be the one reading the paper.

"Not a good idea when you are driving", I answered.

"OK wise guy", he replied as he pulled over. From then on, I did the driving.

From there, I worked in the mortuary, which was brand new and the state-of-the-art, learning about body preparation and embalming. The chief embalmer and his assistant were odd folk – but then I have found since that most embalmers are a little different to ordinary folk, unlike funeral arrangers or conductors, who are usually perfectly normal.

I usually was allowed to go to meet my parents in Dorset each Friday evening. However, occasionally I had to stay and do my turn on the Saturday morning rota. On one such occasion, I was about to depart for Dorset when a home removal request came in. Apparently, it was on the top floor of a block of flats. The police said that it might be best to send three chaps as it would be both difficult and unpleasant. I was commandeered to be the third bloke just as I was getting into my car to go to Dorset.

This Life In Death

All three of us, Percy, a fat man called Tom and I sat in the front dressed in our spotless white ambulance coats. All the way there I steeled myself. I must not let my father down. This was my first home removal and however bad it was, I must not let my father down under any circumstances.

The summer of 1968 was a glorious one. It had been hot for weeks. The elderly man who had died had been apparently dead for some time. He was an Indian Sikh that had entered the country illegally. The police explained that, as a result upon his death, his family had panicked and shut the door and left him there for several weeks before neighbours had noticed very unsavoury smells emanating from the apartment. The police had put their heads round the bedroom door but not ventured in.

Now we had to. We did. The smell was appalling but that was nothing. We strode into the room armed with the body bag. They were wearing surgical gloves; I didn't have any. As we moved across what we thought was black lino, we quickly realised that we were mistaken. Instead, it was a crust of dried blood, which we broke through and all three of us started slipping and sliding on the red liquid blood beneath.

I slipped over and was horrified to see red blood oozing up between my fingers and on to my chin as I was propelled across the room on my front. I looked as if I had taken part in the 'Chainsaw Massacre'.

Nevertheless, we had to get on with it. As Percy went to lift a leg, it came off in his hand. Maggots were pouring out of every part of a body well on the way to final decomposition.

We eventual got the gentleman, or what was left of him, into the 'cricket bag', as the body bags were known, past the frightened family and sheepish policemen, into the lift, down and on to the American stretcher in the block's hallway. From there it was wheeled to the waiting ambulance.

This Life In Death

All the way back in the ambulance my two older companions were heaving and having to stop to vomit. I was fine.

"What the hell are you made of", demanded the embarrassed fat Tom in his 'Valleys' lilt. "Are you upper class English made of stone"?

"Leave the boy alone. He put you to shame", responded Percy before I could answer for myself. And it was true. For once, I had not let my father down.

Of course, life in Cardiff was not all work. So how did I entertain myself in the evenings? I occasionally went to the local cinema to watch my favourite Clint Eastwood films like 'The Good the Bad and the Ugly' which was a huge hit in 1968 and which caused his other 'spaghetti westerns' to be all shown again and again. But I mainly stayed in reading up on Davies' 'Law of Burial and Cremation' or having a beer with the travelling salesmen in the shabby little hotel bar pontificating about politics. This caused some raised eyebrows as I was only 18 and looked 16. However, I was polite with it and so was tolerated by them.

Although I was only paid £8-a-week, I was managing to save £1-a-week. I soon had a little war chest of £10 in my back pocket – well I did until I took a local girl that I had met to the cinema. On the back row I let her get into my trousers and in all the following excitement failed to notice all £10 go missing. When I discovered this the next morning I arrived at work with a face as long as Livery Street. I don't think she nicked it rather that it fell out but either way there was a lesson to be learned.

As the summer progressed into July my great friend from Bantocks, Pete 'pyjama top', a name I gave him due to his liking of striped shirts, came down to stay in the little flat I had found next to the hotel. Pete was a bit like the young John Lennon in so far that he was very short-sighted but hated wearing glasses, which meant that I got to choose the better looking of the local girls we attracted in St Mary's Street in the city centre, wandering up and down dressed in our Wrangler jackets and flared trousers. We would pretend to be French, know little English and be lost. It worked nearly every time.

Pete's dad was called Cadwallader and was a rich road haulier. Pete had arrived in a very large Rover saloon belonging to him. We used this car for not only to attract and then entertain girls but also to engage in our other favourite sport of pedestrian squirting. We would use a pin to alter direction of the windscreen washers, so they pointed towards the pavement. Then we would drive around until we saw someone and would stop to ask them the way. As they bent down to give us directions, we would squirt them in the face and drive off. Childish yes – but we were still kids, and such pranks were about as naughty as we got. We never thought to carry knives and then use them on folk as you read about daily today.

However, we very nearly got a good and deserved thrashing because of one of our more outrageous 'likely lads' pranks.

We were in a downtown disco. Pete, as we know, didn't like wearing his glasses when picking up girls. Thus, he had to rely on me. I spotted a gorgeous Afro-Caribbean girl. She was so pretty and wore knee length white socks and the shortest mini skirt in the joint.

She beckoned to me and drew me in like a magnet. Pete followed and started to dance with her friend. I hadn't considered Pete for a second. He was now dancing with a white girl from the 'Valleys'. She was perhaps most accurately described as a spotty strawberry.

I suggested we go for a drink. We left the disco and got into Pete's car. My beautiful girl and me were in the back and the spotty strawberry next to Pete in the front. Pete put on his glasses so he could see we he was going. He looked at his dancing partner and immediately flashed a furious look in my direction.

We drove some distance to a country pub. I was having a fantastic time in the back, while Pete's knuckles were white with rage as he gripped the wheel and drove like a lunatic.

This Life In Death

Once at our destination, the girls went to the ladies and Pete exploded.

"So, you don't like yours"? I cheekily enquired. "Then let's go mate".

We did. How completely ungentlemanly.

A few days later, we are trawling along St Mary's Rd in Cardiff, being two lost French boys as usual, when I spotted the gorgeous white socked girl with a group of Afro-Caribbean boys coming towards us.

I told Pete to put his head down. We both did and they passed. Phew!

But then came a tap on my shoulder. It was her.

"You didn't expect to get away with that stunt did you".

Her friends were some yards away. They had stopped and were waiting for her.

"Where did you go the other night? We looked everywhere for you" was my ridiculous reply.

"Why you..."

In an instance, she signalled to her friends and I grabbed Pete by his Wrangler jacket and we darted into a crowded pub, barged our way through the bar and out of another exit. Then we ran as fast as we could.

Pete suffered from asthma, reached for his inhaler and said he must stop. I grabbed his jacket again and pulled him along.

"They will kill you". I gasped.

"And whose fault would that be"? he wheezed.

xxxxxxx

This Life In Death

We shared the flat with a lad called Roger Brookes. who was a little older than me and had started as an apprentice at Summers, where he now worked in the garage. I called him Billy Bollock because he was fat and round.

One day Morlais Summers, in a rage about something, arrived in the garage, a place I had never seen him come to before. He fired Billy on the spot, for no other reason than he was angry, and Billy Bollock was the first person he came across. This was outrageously unfair and utterly despicable but in 1968 quite legal. Moreover, Morlais didn't know and never even asked Billy's name, saying, "You're sacked whatever your name is. Now get out of my sight".

Billy couldn't bring himself to tell his father, who was the main pilot for Newport docks, that he had been fired so he continued to stay on in the flat until his money ran out later in the year. I really believe that Morlais would have even forgotten about the incident 20 minutes after it had happened. However, Roger would never forget it for the rest of his life.

Morlais was a tyrant that the whole staff of perhaps 60 at Summers were extremely frightened of. He hardly ever spoke to any of them, and they never dared address him unless he spoke to them first. He often reduced his pleasant but timid son to tears and on occasion to the knowledge of other staff members who could hear the rantings across the whole of Roath Court. His brother Cuthbert, an altogether nicer man, seemed to steer clear of him and my father was always very respectful to him. He was, indeed, a Dickensian character that made Ossie Hodgson look like a social worker.

Nevertheless, it had been a very happy summer, and, as one of the greatest all-time modern compositions, Hey Jude, was released and catapulted to Number 1 on advanced sales, I went on a late summer holiday to Majorca with my family, content that I was making good progress in my chosen career and had an amazing sexual encounter with an older woman in my parents hired Seat while they were having dinner.

This Life In Death

However, as summer turned to autumn and then winter, my progress slowed. I was working as hard as ever but being taught nothing in return. At Christmas, while lying on my bed and listening to the new Beatles 'White Album', I decided something must be done. Oh no please don't, I can almost hear you say.

For the past two months, my working day consisted of going to Thornhill Crematorium and acting as the fourth bearer perhaps six or seven times a week. This was cheap labour and not a proper apprenticeship. But perhaps things would change after Xmas. They didn't and I wrote to Morlais to inform him that I was not cheap labour but an apprentice.

He sent for me. I was not frightened of being screamed at and approached his office confidently. I entered. He handed me a third class rail ticket back to Birmingham with the words, "Go and do some slave labour for your father".

Jesus Christ – I had done it again. I could now add my failed apprenticeship to my other dubious accolades of fights with school and college authorities. I was now nearly 19 and the last 11 years seemed to have been one long fight with all of them.

On that wet January afternoon, I got on the train more conscious that I had yet again let my father down than having a feeling of anger about how unfair it was. I think that was because I accepted that life simply wasn't fair and that it was a lot more unfair on other people less well-off than me.

On my arrival home, I was surprised that my father already knew the news I was dreading to give him yet again. Even more surprising, was his pragmatic reaction to it. He thought that I had probably learnt everything that I was going to learn and tomorrow he would come with me to sort out my top hat, morning tails and pinstripe trousers. I was going to work for him at Hodgson & sons Ltd.

This Life In Death

I was appointed both assistant conductor and manager to Stan Edwards, the position occupied by the recently retired Uncle Les. I couldn't believe my good fortune. I went to bed happy.

Upon starting work, I was to realise my charge of slave labour against Morlais was not 100% fair. I was able to introduce improvements to the viewing system, the chapels, the composition of the garage orders for the next day's funeral fleets schedules, and many small but labour-saving devises in the mortuary and coffin fitting shop. These were gratefully accepted by my father, if not quite by Stan.

On the other hand, Hodgson & Sons conducting of funerals with military precision and timing was vastly superior to that of Summers. My father had taught Stan, and he was now teaching me in this bitterly cold winter of 1969 when the Beatles performed 'Get Back' on the roof top of their Saville Row Apple offices, which closed Saville Row as people rushed from everywhere to hear Macca, belt out this wonderful song – which remains my mobile's ring tone 54 years later. This made the front pages of all UK papers as the nation had hardly seen or heard of the reclusive fab four for two years other than on the occasional vinyl album or single.

I was keen to learn, and I took to the Hodgson precision style – as if every funeral was a state affair however expensive or not it was – like a duck to water. It fitted in so well with my 'narrow minded drive and determination'. It was disciplined and precise and I loved it.

Nevertheless, despite being dressed like a funeral director, I still had to be the fourth bearer. I was paired with what seemed like an extremely nice 60-year-old midget called Harry White. He was about 4' 9" and I was 6'. This meant that, when the coffin was resting on my shoulder, it was above his head and that on occasion when we turned right, he would walk straight on, unless I caught hold of his coat.

Twenty years later I was to lose two discs in my back. While my surgeon was contemplating if this had been caused by either my bowling action at cricket or lunatic jumping of fences on horses, I was able to suggest that lifting 1,000s of dead bodies and shouldering 100s of coffins opposite Harry White was the probable cause.

My work and dedication to my chosen profession in general and Hodgson & Sons Ltd in particular, impressed my relieved father. Stan was able to also draw some benefit as he soon persuaded my father that I should be allowed to conduct Saturday morning funerals instead of him. This allowed him to have a two-day weekend. I was delighted.

The first funeral I was to direct for the firm was a Sikh funeral leaving from a house behind St Michael's church at the top of Soho Hill. As usual the deceased had gone home in his coffin an hour before we were due to depart from the house for Perry Barr crematorium, so that the circa 500 mourners could file passed his open coffin in two groups – men and women.

As we rounded the church the house came into view. The women were already on the second of the two hired corporation double-decker buses. The men were crowded outside the open front door of the house. This was all quite usual. Then to my horror the open coffin with an elderly Gentlemen in his smart grey suit, white shirt and blue turban appeared through the door and was being passed overhead towards the hearse. Oh God.

I reacted calmly and quickly. I managed to find his eldest son and persuade him that his father should return inside so the coffin's lid could be put on. This was done and quickly the coffin was back on the trestles in the sparsely furnished front room. I put my top hat down on the linoleum floor to assist the hearse driver secure the lid. I turned round to retrieve it to see a little boy peeing in it.

I reported this to the old man and Stan, who now shared my father's grand office having given up his own small office to me. My father was reading something. He didn't look up but replied that I should get another and the cost of which would be deducted from my wages at £1-a-week.

This Life In Death

"But I didn't ruin it", I complained.

"But you will never put it down on the floor again will you", was his reply.

I didn't. This was indeed a good reminder. My wages were only £9-a-week. Out of that I was obliged to give my mother £5-a-week. This left me only £4 which was just about me to support my official girlfriend and still be able to explore, as any skier would, beyond.

Thus, I wanted my cake and halfpenny - have a favourite run but still a wish to ski down any ski slope I had never skied down before. This sounds very bad today by Woke Society thinking, but then was thought to be normal.

Indeed, I had seen the British movie, Tom Jones, which had preceded the Beatles invasion of the US a year earlier in 1963 by winning four Oscars. This 18th century British costume drama romp was a world-wide success. I sort of thought that I was Tom Jones – a young man with a heart of gold, a sense of British fair play but quite unable to keep 'William' in his trousers. I had a very good moral compass as long as sex was not involved.

My appreciation of film and music was more extensive than I have written about so far. You are entitled to think that I only listened to the Beatles, Dylan, and the Stones when it came to music from the story to date. However, I loved all the Mersey Beat artists of the early 60s, the resulting artists from the Sgt. Pepper explosion like Pink Floyd, Barry Ryan, The Kinks, The Small Faces and many more. I had also progressed to love 12 bar blues and jazz artists like Robert Johnson, Billie Halliday, BB King, and Lou Reed. And, amazingly, I, by now, had also started to adore Beethoven, Mozart, and Tchaikovsky. This love of music will become a very important factor later in this life's saga.

On the film front I watched the avalanche of new 60s avant-garde films avidly. British and French films led the way. However, it was an old-style western which was to become a huge aid to ensuring my libido was satisfied. This was the film 'Butch Cassidy and the Sundance Kid' starring the already huge star Paul Newman and a newcomer to stardom, Robert Redford. I thought Newman was very cool, not as cool as Clint Eastwood, but very cool. I thought Redford was very good, but I didn't know anything about him.

However, my mother thought she must have had a love child with him, and I was it. I couldn't see this and had only ever just wanted to be like Beatle Paul or Eastwood. However, a lot of folks seemed to agree with her, and with women, this became a serious attraction which I was to benefit from but had not earned in my own right.

Over the next 50 years I was often to wish that I had received £10 for every time I had been approached with the comment, "Did anyone tell you that you look a bit like Robert Redford." However, this is not true of those who believed that I was Robert Redford. For these folk would either think it was my fault that I wasn't rather than their mistaken identity or they simply would not believe me.

Once having lunch in Canford Cliffs in Dorset with my third son Jamieson, a woman approached our table and asked politely for my autograph. I informed her that I was flattered but that I was not Robert Redford. She refused to believe me and only left after some persuasion. However, when she had finished her meal, she returned and told me that she would never watch a film of mine again; she would tell all her friends what an 'arsehole' I was and left the restaurant fuming.

"Why don't you just sign next time. You'd be doing Redford a favour", was Jamieson's advice.

So, I could just about get by as I lived at home, had a three gallons-a-week petrol allowance and £4-a-week spending money. Then, one day, something tipped scales even further against my ability to entertain myself when off duty.

We had finished the funerals for the day. I was composing the next day's A fleet (Stan) and B fleet (me) garage orders as we were conducting 10 funerals a day in this very busy March when a knock came upon my door. It was our receptionist, who was also the telephonist, as was the case in those days. Her name was Jean Startin, and she was a very nice girl.

"Mr Howard", for then in Victorian tradition, my father was Mr Paul, I was Mr Howard and Stan, not being a Hodgson, was Mr Edwards. "Mr Howard, there is a young lady in the arrangement room who needs to see the boss".

My father was at his club as usual, Stan was not around so she had turned to me. I duly obliged and went to see this young lady.

I entered to see a truly beautiful young woman about my age. She had dark red hair, a milky white complexion and a few small freckles across her nose. She was tall, with beautiful long legs and delicate ankles.

"Mr Hodgin, I need your help", she began in a broad Birmingham accent, which was to be expected from a girl from Aston.

I didn't correct her mispronunciation of my name and let her tell her story. She had had a baby boy out of wedlock. He had died at two months of age. She had come to Hodgson & Sons Ltd as we did children's funerals free of charge, which is normal today but was uncommon then. However, she wanted some extras which were not included in the free package. These, she had been told would come to £10. She didn't have £10. But she would pay us back at 10 shillings-a-week. She looked pleadingly at me.

"Of course," I replied and granted her wish. She smiled sweetly and left.

The next morning, on one of my father's fleeting visits to his office, I went to see him and explained what I had done. He listened and when I had finished simply said, "she won't but you will".

She didn't and I did. Moreover, at £1-a-week. So now my disposable income was down to £3-a-week for the next 10 weeks.

This Life In Death

My father had only done what Ossie would have done to him. It was a family business way of life that was still alive then at the end of the 60s despite the social revolution of that decade.

My life seemed to be following a pattern of hope in the spring, a joyous summer, and a disastrous autumn. Now my parents determined to make yet another attempt to make their marriage work. They bought a new family home called 'The Woodlands' in the countryside south of Birmingham. It was less resplendent than previous homes in Edgbaston as the business wasn't as prosperous as it had been for all the reasons already given. However, it was a charming house and all of us hoped that a corner had been turned.

This was, of course, a hope against hope. My father's increased reliance on alcohol and my mother's criticism of the same when he was sober was a recipe for disaster. On occasion he could be the wonderful man of my childhood but increasingly he was not.

There was a very tense atmosphere at home as a result and inevitably a violent battle was bound to break out again at any time. When it did, I got caught up in the crossfire by defending my mother and was dismissed from the business for my trouble.

So, I went to work for Ashton Ebbutt, a large funeral director in South London, having approached and been interviewed by the boss Laurie Ashton, given a beer and offered a job as he liked me, and thought that I would make an excellent addition to his firm as I had Hodgson and Summers pedigree. Meanwhile, my father had left the new family home again.

I slept on the living room floor of my old friend Simon Draycott's flat, who fancied himself as an actor at that time, and was at RADA as a result. The flat was shared by four would-be actors and was a complete shambles. Nevertheless, I was extremely grateful for somewhere to rest my head.

However, suddenly the turmoil that was associated with these parental disputes came to a swift end as the family had found a common enemy to unite against.

Over the years of whizzing up and down from Birmingham to Poole Harbour and back my father had become acquainted with the landlord of the Lamb Inn in the village of Filkins in North Wiltshire – a convenient watering hole about halfway between the two locations.

In 1964, my father had borrowed around £10,000 from his father-in-law, Robert Ward of perhaps noble birth, just before the latter had died. He had used the cash to buy a new funeral business, JH Hartland in Coseley, situated between Birmingham and Wolverhampton. This to be his last positive action to try and solve his falling funeral number problems.

He had decided that this landlord chum, one Cyril Clements, would make a good funeral director. After all, he had served in the Second World War, like Stan Edwards, he had a resemblance to the actor Leslie Phillips, like Stan Edwards; he was charming, like Stan Edwards; but he wasn't honest unlike Stan Edwards.

Now five years later, at the end of 1969, it was discovered that he had been embezzling JH Hartland's cash. He was dismissed immediately; my parents were reunited once more and I was summoned home and made manager of JH Hartland. I was still only 19 and only a veteran of some 18 months service. However, I had been well taught at two academy companies, which I was only too aware of, having worked through that autumn at Ashton's who were not of that standard of service or facility.

Throughout my life I had let my father down. However, I knew that I would not this time and I didn't. JH Hartland had arranged circa 200 funerals a year, therefore around 4 funerals a week, when it had been purchased. Cyril had increased this to five a week over his five-year stint. However, very quickly I pushed the figure up to seven a week. Numbers were up, money was flowing in, and my father was delighted. He and I were getting on as well as we could after all that had happened.

Sadly, my mother did not help matters in this regard by using my success there as a weapon with which to taunt my father by suggesting that I would do a better job than him at Hodgson & Sons. This resulted in him giving me the nickname 'Mary's Boy Child' and drove a wedge between us when there was no need for one.

Nevertheless, perhaps we still could make something of this last chance saloon effort. The Beatles' Album 'Abbey Road', which was McCartney's most powerful contribution to date, ensured the world's favourite band remained just that. It was also decided now, by my mother, that it would be better for her and my father if only my younger brother remained at home with them. My sister was already boarding and so it may be better if I paid my £5 a week housekeeping to someone else.

A posh old lady, who owned a large house by St Peter's Church in Harborne, Birmingham and took in paying guests to pay for its upkeep, was approached and a room for me was found to stay in Monday night to Friday morning each week.

The peace was just about holding at home, it was a pleasant summer, work was going as well as my father would allow for on a shoestring budget, and the Beatles released their last album 'Let it Be' amid rumours of them being about to break-up, with John Winston Lennon announcing that he was fed up with being a member of Paul's backing band. Ted Heath became prime minister much to the joy of the posh old lady who invited me into her sitting room and offer me a sherry as we watched the results come in.

Then, as the summer was drawing to a close, I was hit by a landslide of setbacks which were to blow away life as I had known it forever.

My mother left our Dorset apartment while all of us children were on our boat in Yarmouth, Isle of Wight, because she suspected my

This Life In Death

father of having an affair with a younger woman. She caught him red-handed. This was now the end and we had to face that.

Then McCartney announced with the release of his solo album that he was leaving the Beatles and my Beatle comfort blanket was withdrawn and lastly, and hardly surprisingly, my long-time girlfriend Susan decided that she had had enough of my habitual womanising and finished our relationship.

The first disaster of family destruction was bound to happen sooner or later and there was nothing I could have done more to prevent it. However, when the end came, it felt very bad. My wonderful childhood was to become a blurred memory. My family, which I had been fighting to preserve, was now blown asunder, and would never be re-established. The father, that I loved and admired so much was turning into a monster before my eyes, and my mother had de-camped to our Dorset home, which had been bought with her inheritance and so she felt safe there. But that also meant that now I was separated from her and my siblings, all of whom I was very close to.

It felt like Aiglon had moved to Warwickshire and I was a lad again. Worse, I knew deep down that this was not as bad as it would get.

The Beatlesbust up certainly was not my fault, but it just seemed to shout that the world as I knew it had gone with the coming of the 70s. The Susan departure was 100% my fault, no more than I deserved and the only surprise was that she had hung in there for so long. However, that didn't stop me missing her now that the roof was falling in everywhere else, and I could no longer turn to her for solace.

I tried to stay close to both parents initially and spent the August bank holiday in the Midlands with my father. I realised that if I was to save him and the business that I would have to stop his drinking and his millionaire life-style – both of which seemed to be increasing now he was liberated from the critical scorn of my mother and faced with the encouragement of his new girlfriend.

This Life In Death

Her name was Michelle, she was, at 26, only six years older than me. She loved partying and she clearly believed that my father owned a forest where money grew on trees.

My father was still only 44. However, that age was considered to be lot older than it is today, and he was now adding a mid-life crisis to his self-destructive nature. I could see immediately that she would blow every penny he had left before moving on.

She was staying in the 'The Woodlands' in my sister's room with my father because it boasted the only double bed in the house. I was staying in the bedroom that I shared with my brother. There was a guest staying in my parents' bedroom.

She had come with Michelle as a kind of chaperone, although God only knew why as my father and Michelle were publicly affectionate in every pub they frequented in the area.

Her name was June Gumley. She was also 26, exceptionally beautiful with platinum blonde hair, a superb figure and had been a bunny girl at the London Playboy Club, near Park Lane, before returning to her native Birmingham. There she had taken a job behind the cocktail bar at the Highfield Club, where my father was a member and increasingly spent his days. Indeed, it was here that he had met Michelle.

We all retired for the night in the early hours of the morning. I lay in bed, and failing to sleep, was trying to find a little light in the corner of my mind. I couldn't find any: Aston Villa had been relegated to the old third division for the first time in their illustrious history; the Beatles were no more; my father was killing himself, hell bent on an orgy of self-destruction; our family business would be ruined as a result; the rest of my family were a hundred and fifty miles away; and I had deservedly lost my girlfriend.

Personally, I have always preferred McCartney's rock songs such as 'Helter Skelter', 'Get Back' or 'I Saw her Standing there'. Of course, he is perhaps more famous across the globe for his Beatle ballads

This Life In Death

such as 'Let It Be', 'Yesterday', 'Here There and Everywhere', 'I will', 'And I Love Her' etc.

However, the ballad 'For No One' off the 1966 'Revolver' album is easily the most meaningful song ever written to anyone who has lost a love.

Lines like 'The day breaks, your mind aches you find that all her words of kindness linger on when she no longer needs you', and 'in her eyes you see nothing; no sign of love behind the tears cried for no one – a love that should have lasted years. You want her you need her and yet you don't believe her when she says her love is dead; she no longer needs you' – all hit a chord that makes you cry out "Exactly".

McCartney wrote this, I believe, over the loss of Jane Asher, whom he had taken for granted. Of course, it is a wonderful melody, but the genius is in the lyrics that describes the pain perfectly.

I could not get this bloody song out of my head as I lay there. It went round and round and with each revolution I was going down, down to a place where I didn't want to go but couldn't stop.

I have always been useless, as you have seen and we shall see further, at expressing any pain or unhappiness. Stupidly frightened of showing any weakness, stiff upper lip has always been my 1950s Empire moto. But I needed a cuddle. Yes, a cuddle, not sex, but human bodily affection.

My mind turned to June a little way down the landing. However, it also quickly told me that she was six years older than me and that she would only be interested in rich men in their 30s and 40s and not a penniless boy like me.

I remembered that I had met her before, on a trip to the Highfield Club with my father, when I was perhaps only sixteen, and had thought then that she was both beautiful and a lovely person who had taken an interest in a 16-year-old boy. But, of course, she was too beautiful and too old and so the bar was set too high for me.

This Life In Death

But my 'mind ached' still so badly, I felt so alone, and I was so desperate. I screwed up courage and got out of bed. I was trembling with nerves as I walked towards where she slept. I touched her shoulder, and she awoke.

Her sparkling pale blue eyes opened, met mine and without a word she pulled me into her bed. She cuddled me, she mothered me, and she loved me.

We started with a very gentle love which ended up with a very passionate and boisterous sex before falling asleep in each other's arms. My dark night had turned into happy dawn.

She was a much better and more experienced lover than me – but I was a very willing pupil and she had saved me from dark despair. As I write this over 50 years and many highs and lows later, I can still feel, and even taste, every little bit of that night's emotional roller-coaster. I'm so pleased that I took courage into my hands and went and I'm even more grateful that she accepted me so wonderfully.

In the morning, we lay there chatting. I with my head on her bosom, stroking her flat tummy. I noticed some very tiny stretch marks on both of her hips. She noticed that I had and volunteered, without being asked, that she had become pregnant a few years before but had had an abortion. I was not shocked. Who was I to be shocked about such matters. She went on to explain that my father had paid for the abortion.

How nice of him I thought. It never occurred to me to consider why he had.

I am glad that it didn't, for it might have spoiled a perfect moment of relief. Of course, in reality nothing had changed: my father, aided and abetted by his new love, was still hell bent on ruining all of us; the rest of my family were in exile; Susan had gone and neither she nor the Beatles were coming back.

However, June had stopped the song 'For No One' in my head and I wanted to hold her in bed or even just her hand out of it.

This Life In Death

Michelle rose before my father, realised where I was and quickly reported it to him. He seemed delighted by the news. He didn't say why, but, looking back, I suspect he took it as an endorsement of his new relationship.

The next two days were spent with June, holding hands, and chatting. She told me that she had fancied me when I had met her at 16 at the Highfield Club. I told her that I didn't believe her. She told me that I had seemed as pure as driven snow.

"More like driven slush on the M1", I replied.

"Howard, you have no idea what life is like in clubs serving married men who drink too much, slap your bum when you pass and think you are only fit for one thing. You treated me as a lady – and were a nice-looking clean boy".

The next weekend she invited me to stay Saturday night at her home. This was a semi-detached council house in Accocks Green, not far from the Robin Hood roundabout.

When I woke, exhausted from another night of passion, it was time to shower and join the Cumley clan in their garden for a huge breakfast fry up. There were a lot of Cumleys and, all these years later, I can't remember who they all were.

However, I remember her father. He was a self-employed race-course bookie. He was probably a bit of a rogue too, but he had a kind face.

He greeted me with, "So, you're Paul's lad. A real gent is Paul". Another clue about the abortion flew over my head undetected.

"Where did you grow up"? He asked.

"Birmingham", I replied.

"You don't sound like it", he counted in his broad Brummie accent, which his daughter had lost somewhere in London.

This Life In Death

"Cut me and I bleed Villa's claret", I responded determined to hold my ground.

"I wouldn't say that, or we might find out. We are all Blues here", he chuckled.

Her mother, a very homely woman, arrived with a huge plate of fried eggs. I stood up as she approached the table – just as I had been taught to do.

"Ooow! What a toff", he taunted.

I just smiled and seemed to have passed his test as he became very pleasant after that.

September meant school time for my siblings. My sister to start her last year and my brother to start life as a boarder at Malvern College where he had won a scholarship.

My parents realised that this posed some problems as things stood. Therefore, it was decided that my mother would move back into the Woodlands and my father and Michelle would move out. I can't recall where they went – but it would have cost a lot of money for sure.

At Hodgson & Sons things were being very well run. Stan was perhaps the finest funeral conductor I had ever come across, and I had got to grips with the finances and the administration and was applying a mixture of my own ideas with those things I had learned at Summers.

However, there was a problem. My father and Michelle were now spending money at the Highfield and Ambassador's Clubs or on shopping sprees in London much faster than Stan and I could earn it.

Our financial controller, a very large and decent lady, named Pat Lane, informed me that she had seriously big bills from my father's clubs going back months that she had not got the bank facility to meet.

This Life In Death

I spoke to Stan. We agreed that something had to be done. He was by now not treating me as a novice schoolboy, but he was understandably nervous about approaching my father – who had turned from an enlightened, caring funeral director to something that made even Morlais look reasonable.

Stan was over 50 and if sacked might find it hard to get another job.

My father was now obviously in a tyrannical mood and did not want to be opposed. Stan was my father's best friend, but, as he pointed out, this would count for nothing as he was not, after all, a Hodgson – unlike me.

So here we go again, another moment when this foolish and stubborn young man was once more to place his head into the mouth of the lion.

I met my father with the ever-present Michelle, for dinner at the Ambassador's Club in Edgbaston. I told him that the business needed investment capital, that it was being bled dry and that we could not settle the bills he was charging to the firm on top of a salary which he wasn't earning.

He was furious and told me to get on and do my job and leave the finances to him, while Michelle added that making 'tax losses' was something that every successful businessman did as I would realise when I was older.

I pointed out, as politely as I could muster with so much anger in my head, that in order to take advantage of tax losses one had to make profits on which tax might be due first. These words of wisdom fell on deaf ears.

Nothing was resolved and I left the dinner more worried than ever. I had failed to get through to my father the seriousness of the situation. He seemed so besotted with Michelle or perhaps just wanted to go on as he was and continue to live the crazy dream of 18-hour drinking seven days a week.

This Life In Death

During the weekends of this autumn of 1970, 'Pete Pyjama Top' and I would go one Saturday to see his team, the famous Manchester United with George Best, Denis Law, Bobby Charlton et al, and the next mine, the currently less successful Aston Villa.

June and I still saw each other, but I was starting to wander a bit with other girls, as had been and was to continue to be my constant failing.

There was a school chum of my sister called Linda, who looked as if she had had a brilliant 'boob job' but hadn't; a friend's ex Maltese girlfriend called Jeanette, who was extremely pretty and, even now and again, Susan who loved the sex but no longer me.

I was to stop these romps with her, as I realised, that now it was me who wanted more than that and that she never would. So, self-preservation kicked in before I ended back in the place of 'For No One' where I was on that night when June had saved me.

There was also a very trim German girl, whose name was Ingrid, My mother had gone to Dorset with my brother, my sister was staying in Edgbaston with her boyfriend, who was to become her husband of over 51 years to date, and I was alone in the Woodlands. I can't remember where we met but she came home with me and like my father, before me, I took advantage of my sister's bed. She was slender and had both Germanic stamina and appetite.

As a result, we only fell asleep at about six in the morning and did not wake until after midday. We showered and dressed, and I took her to Stratford-Upon-Avon for lunch.

However, by the time we arrived there was only a Chinese restaurant still open. With no other choice open to us, we decided to have lunch there. She had never been to a Chinese Restaurant before as she had been brought up in post-war Germany where there were none.

She didn't know what to order as a result. I said I would order for both of us. I did. Soon a finger bowl arrived and was placed in front of her.

This Life In Death

"Vat is this"? She enquired.

"Your first course. You drink it from the bowl. It is a very popular Chinese soup", I replied with a dead pan face.

She did and the restaurant erupted into laughter. She was not amused and informed me that after she had told her father, who owned a toy factory in Mainz, about this prank, he would probably have me killed.

Thank the Lord that we won the war was my immediate thought.

June still often stayed the weekends and on one Saturday spent the evening with my mother as I had to go to receive an award at my football team's annual dinner.

My mother said she wasn't too keen about this. I thought that this was unusual for her, as she was lonely without my father, even if he had become a nightmare to be with.

As I was driving home that night my dim-witted brain suddenly put June's comment, her dad's comment, and my mother's comment together and realised that I was probably sleeping with my father's ex-mistress.

However, I shrugged the thought off and told myself that this was 1970 and therefore, not really important. I mean if John Lennon could have a dirty weekend in Spain with Brian Epstein to get McCartney & Lennon changed to Lennon & McCartney, then this was small beer by comparison.

When I arrived back at the Woodlands, I found them enjoying sherry and watching the late-night movie on BBC 2 together. Perhaps, I had got it all wrong? I decided to let sleeping dogs lie.

My mother, who went on to live until 94, was a very strong personality. I was later to state that she made Margaret Hilda Thatcher look like a supporter of gay liberation rights for lesbians in Lambeth.

This Life In Death

I might have derived my artist flair, imagination, and sporting prowess from my father but the drive and determination to have it my way at all costs, came from my mother.

She was now 44 and had been dumped for a younger woman. She decided to take matters into her own hands. She remembered an old sweetheart of her youth, a chap called Peter Hafner. He was older than her; had a distinguished Second World War; was an usher at my parents' wedding; worked for the steel company Stuart & Lloyd's; was married with two sons at Bromsgrove and lived near there.

She contacted him. He invited her on a business trip he was about to make to Scotland. They started an affair immediately. Therefore, just as Michelle had ended my parents' marriage so my mother ended the Hafner's marriage.

Now any last hope of a reconciliation had gone. Even though my father seemed quite annoyed by this latest turn of events. I can only put that down to a 'what I do is OK but not if you do the same' theory he might have harboured.

All concerned parties, except for Michelle, engaged solicitors and serious war broke out everywhere. Mrs Hafner was suing Peter for divorce and my father, with the hypocrisy of a Champagne socialist, started proceedings against my mother.

I attempted to stay out of this and work with Stan to keep Hodgson & Sons going. However, it became inevitable that I would get dragged into proceedings.

My father cut down or off, I can't recall, my mother's allowance. She countered by demanding the £10,000 her father had lent my father back. He refused.

I went to see him and Michelle and stated that while I didn't wish to take sides and would prefer not to comment about any financial settlement, he should remember that the £10,000 was not ours but belonged to Robert Ward, of perhaps noble birth, and therefore should be returned to his only surviving relative – my mother.

This Life In Death

I could see that immediately that this was going to be a crucial moment. My father didn't have £10,000 knocking about in a drawer somewhere and Michelle was determined that he was not going to even attempt to raise it.

I was becoming too much of a pain in the rear end for Michelle. I wanted to restrict my father's drinking, his spending and now this.

She joined the argument and told me to stay out of my father's affairs. I countered that this £10,000 was owed by my father to my mother, was not her business and that it should be repaid.

Michelle answered that by bursting into tears.

I was fired on the spot.

Moreover, my company car was confiscated and put in the corner of the Oaklands garage with the wheels removed while it rested on bricks - in case I attempted to steal it back.

Now I had no job, no home, and very poor future prospects. Moreover, I had been propelled into my mother's camp permanently as my father and I were no longer on speaking terms. This meant any last chance of his salvation had also gone as Michelle had him all to herself.

I applied for any job going – and there weren't many - but without success. I even failed to get a porter's job in the Birmingham fruit market for £8-a-week. There were only two applicants. Me and a very thick and illiterate lad and I was not chosen.

I just could not accept this and asked the interviewer why I hadn't been selected. He smiled and told me to look at my hands. He said they were not the hands of a labourer and that I wouldn't have stayed in the fruit market for long, whereas the other lad would probably work there for years. Of course, he was right but then this didn't help right now as my mother, and I, were penniless.

This Life In Death

I had a flat in near the Licky Hills on the way to Bromsgrove. Without a car it was very hard to get to. Moreover, how was I going to pay the rent in any case?

This apartment was much better than the last in Bearwood. I shared again with Paul Bullas and we were living almost a civilised existence except for one thing. We managed to fall out with the two middle aged ladies who lived below.

For once, this not my fault. Indeed, it was entirely Paul's fault.

Firstly, he decided to wash some socks in the kitchen sink. It was a pleasant day, I was on the balcony at the front. It looked for miles over Longbridge and Selly Oak to the centre of Birmingham. Suddenly I caught sight of a stream of water running down the road. I followed it, out of curiosity, back to its source. It appeared that this river was coming out of our building. I shouted to Paul to come and look. He did, went white and ran back inside.

He had left the sink tap on. The socks had blocked the plug hole. The water had overflowed onto the kitchen floor. It had then brought the ceilings down in the two apartments below us on the second and first floors, before escaping out of an open door.

The two ladies below us were at work. They were not amused by the mess they discovered on their return. They made this abundantly clear to Paul. Luckily, for me, I was out.

Secondly, when we first arrived there, we only had one set of apartment keys. So, I would give these to Paul, and if he was still out when I got home, I would climb up the balconies from the ground floor to our third floor flat and enter by the unlocked balcony door.

However, one evening, I had the keys because I knew he would be home later than me. But it didn't work out that way and he arrived first.

He decided to scale the building a la me. This was not a good idea as he was at least four inches shorter than me. Nevertheless, he made a valiant effort and got to the second floor but failed to get to the third and shat himself while trying.

I arrived home at about 1:00 am, saw his predicament, let myself into our apartment and then pulled him up to the third floor. He explained what had happened and fetched a washing bowl of hot soapy water to throw onto the balcony below so that the 'two lesbians', as he referred to them, would never know that he had been there.

He lent over the balcony and chucked the water. He missed the balcony floor completely with the result that the hot soapy water went through an open window, as it was a hot summer's night and into their living room.

xxxxxxx

My mother had left the Woodlands and she and Peter had been lent a sizeable house in Handsworth Wood by our family dentist and friend of my father, who had retired to live in the same apartment block as my mother in Poole.

He had always liked my father but could see that his drinking and now the influence of Michelle had driven him off the rails. So, he, like many of my father's friends, was sad but firmly set against him.

Then my mother was summoned to her solicitors to hear of an offer my father had made. I went with her. The Old Man was prepared to hand over JH Hartland instead of re-paying the £10,000 and in full and final settlement of all other matters.

This was music to my ears. I advised her to take it. I told her that I would run it, build it and eventually, as it got stronger and Hodgson & Sons got weaker, we could buy that and so save the lot. There was a God after all.

This Life In Death

The solicitor asked if he could see my mother on her own. I left the room. Once I had gone, he told her that it was his duty to advise her that I was far too young to take on such an endeavour and that as a mother of three; in a marriage of over 20 years' standing; and protected by the 'Married Woman's Property Act' that she would receive a lot more.

Sadly, for me then, and my mother forever as we shall see, she listened to the solicitor and not me. The offer was rejected accordingly.

The divorce case proceeded to court. The night before my father called me and told me that if I would appear to give evidence against my mother, I could have my job and car back. I declined.

So, I was not there the next day. Cartwright & Lewis represented my father. The actual solicitor was a man called Alan Greesebar. My father had sued over my mother's adultery. The case was proved by my sister's evidence, which he had insisted she give.

Accordingly, he had won, and as there were still guilty parties in divorce cases in those days, and so he took all the spoils of this war.

He got custody of my younger brother, which left Russell to the mercy of a wicked, drunken stepmother. My sister was going to continue to live at the Woodlands with my father and therefore no award was made to my mother in the case of either child. My father got to keep the Woodlands and she the Poole apartment, which she had bought with her own money anyway. Thereafter, she was to receive only a mere £5-a-week from him in support.

Game set and match to my father and a disaster for my mother. She was shocked but not broken. She seemed very happy with Peter, and I resisted the desire to remind her that she could have had a really decent funeral business going some 370 funerals-a-year instead of £5-a-week if she had listened to me.

During the build-up to the case, I had been busy finding some meaningful employment. I had seen an advert in the Birmingham

This Life In Death

Evening Mail. It said I could easily earn £100-a-week. That was ten times anything I ever had been paid.

I duly went along to the offices of Tri-Star Investments Ltd to an introduction meeting which was attended by some 40 people. We were given questionnaires to fill in, which seemed suspiciously like the Aiglon IQ test to me.

Then a charming chap called Digby Jarman went through a visual presentation about how savings were being destroyed by inflation and how only by saving in an investment trust could you protect the value of your money.

Next, he demonstrated on a blackboard how once you had sold a few plans, you could start to build a team to sell more and earn 'override' commission.

It looked to me like something my 'narrow minded drive and determination' might be well suited to. I was keen to be accepted and approached Mr. Jarman to ask how I had done in the test. He replied that he couldn't tell me as it would be marked by a computer.

At the time I didn't appreciate that this was complete rubbish, and everyone was accepted. It was but a clever way of making applicants worry about acceptance rather than whether they wanted to do this 'part time' job, worked after a normal day's work.

I duly phoned back, was accepted, and couldn't wait to get started. I went off like a rocket, sold a few plans and then started building an Empire of people working for me. Within two months I was Tr-Star's most successful senior consultant not only in Birmingham but the UK. I had overtaken Digby Jarman on the way and now reported to the branch manager, a very decent 41-year-old local football referee called John Taylor. We will hear a lot more about him later.

One of my early recruits was a young, very tall, Kashmiri called Rasiq. He spoke hardly any English and under today's FCA regulations would never be accepted to sell financial service products. But this was 1971 and there was no FCA back then.

This Life In Death

After a few weeks he told me that he wanted to become a consultant.

"You haven't taken the steps to become a consultant", I replied.

"Hodgson, I have but I fell down the stairs", was his logical reply.

He started to advertise to build a team by placing an advert in the Evening Mail and using the local phone box as his office to take the replies. He moved in an armchair and blocked the door.

This phone box was near his family home in Ladywood right in the middle of the red-light area. A gang of local prostitutes wanted to kill him as they couldn't receive any calls due to his occupation of the box.

One Saturday afternoon, he asked me to visit a house in a very poor area with him. It had no glass but boarded up windows. Inside, there was but one sofa, a gas fire on, despite it being a hot summer's day, a cat breast feeding her litter, a woman breast feeding her baby and two fearsome looking and agitated Irishmen.

"This Paki", began one.

"I'm Kashmiri", interrupted Rasiq.

"Whatever. You", continued the Irishman, "said that if we both took out a £4-a-month plan we could cash it in two years and make £10,000 each. Is that true"? he said as he turned to me.

"No, it is not", I replied very quickly and added that I would see that their cheques were returned before they were sent to Wolverhampton for cashing.

"Why you bloody Paki swindler", the other Irishman exploded as he looked even more likely to be a member of the IRA than ever.

"Leave him to me", I said as I grabbed Rasiq by the collar and beat a hasty retreat to the door.

This Life In Death

Once outside I asked why on earth had he told them such an appalling lie and added that he could have got both of us killed.

"Because they would not have bought the plans if I had not", was his reply.

I got into my little second hand Triumph Spitfire, affectionally known as 'the bone shaker', bought with the £500 my maternal grandmother had left me.

"What about me"? demanded Rasiq as I started the engine.

"You walk" I replied in my best Clint Eastwood impersonation.

As I drove away, I thought, how different my life was now on this hot summer's afternoon, in the middle of Birmingham poverty, than it had been the summer before sunning myself on my father's yacht.

My advert campaign, which was run from Betty Draycott's butler's pantry old black telephone, there were to be no mobiles for another 15 years, plus my recruitment of friends, who needed work, was successful and soon I had a growing army of mainly young men who worked for me.

I organised them well by insisting people in my team, built teams too, and that those teams also built teams and so on. Every recruit must make a minimum of six appointments-a-week and achieve a one in two marketing ratio.

All activity, was recorded on a spreadsheet I devised which recorded people's names in each team vertically down and the dates horizontally across the sheet. This gave me perfect control of who was supposed to be doing what, when and how successful they were.

People who did badly were verbally beaten up and threatened with the sack and thus the loss of this marvellous opportunity to change their lives.

This Life In Death

Every associate reported in each evening to his team manager and so on until I was finally phoned by my direct team at times which started at 22:00 but didn't finish until after midnight. Of course, the drawback to this fanatical control was the bigger my operation got the later the finish.

All Birmingham Tri-Star salesmen went to Dr Johnson House in the city centre on a Monday evening for the weekly motivational meeting which also gave them a chance to bring personal introductions who could be recruited into their teams.

I placed all my people on the front three rows. Then during my fist banging oratory, I would have individuals stand up, relate their achievements for the week and demand a round of applause from the 250 plus folk in the room.

Then I would ask all my people at the front to stand, run around and look at other people. I would ask them if they wanted to be part of our success or join a less successful team.

Naturally, this drove the other consultants mad and soon my operation was known as 'The Hodgson Youth'. However, our superior motivation, organisation and individual success meant that our success bred even more success.

Our people turnover was high, but the retained growth was higher, and this SS style operation was much better marshalled than other teams and soon over half the seats on a Monday evening were taken by people who worked for me.

My right-hand man was my flat partner, Paul Bullas of 'washing his socks fame'. He had been a long-standing friend and ex-boyfriend of my sister. He had narrowly escaped being tracked down and shot by my father for taking her virginity some three years previously.

My father, who had never met Paul, was to meet him later in 1967 and like him very much when my sister and I introduced him as her new boyfriend called Henry Schnider.

This Life In Death

Another close senior ally was a guy called Philip Dunn, who was training to be a solicitor and needed the money. It turned out that our mothers had been friends for years, having been to school together.

Philip was a light-hearted and likeable lad. Almost immediately after training, he reported a £25-month sale. This was on a young Japanese woman and was worth a fortune to him, me and helped keep me to stay at the top of the leader board. However, come the end of the week, he failed to hand it in, and I had reported it to John Taylor.

He explained that she kept asking him to go back. I told him to go back and 'give her one'. He replied that he couldn't as he was engaged. He was but the real reason was that he was gay – but he wasn't to come out for many years.

Something had to be done. He gave me her address in Edgbaston. It turned out to be in the same very pleasant apartment block where I had said goodbye to my grandfather seven years before.

Paul needed to borrow my car to go on a couple of appointments with a new recruit, so he dropped me off there and arranged to come back for me later.

I rang her bell and was invited up.

Her name was Kako Smith. She was 28, Japanese, petite, and kept promising to sign in a minute. However, instead she told me that she was Yoko and that I was her John Lennon as a prelude to seducing me, which I had rightly suspected was what this was all about.

However, she was insatiable, and hours passed as we went from the settee, to the floor and on to the windowsill. At that point, one of her children entered to demand a drink and she told the little lad that there was milk in the fridge over my shoulder and in between her heavy panting.

This Life In Death

Eventually it was all over and an exhausted me got out the application form and my pen. Seeing this she told me to come back tomorrow.

"What"? I said.

"Me no sign now or I will call the police to say you raped me", was her reply.

I finished dressing in the lift and rushed to my car to find poor Paul fast asleep. I had missed all my nightly reports for the first time ever and had totally failed to secure the sale. However, I determined to go back and complete the sale as invited the next lunchtime.

On arrival, I was warmly greeted by Kako as if our last conversation had never taken place. In the drawing room sat a Swedish woman, who had dark hair and was as tall as me. Her name was Anna, she lived in the above apartment and was probably around 40.

Kako explained that they would both like to take out £25-a-month plans but preferred their salesman to be naked. I explained that I would need to have signed application forms and two cheques for the first month's premiums. They duly obliged and as a result so did I.

I allowed Philip to keep the KaKo sale but took the full commission on Anna's. Amazingly neither plan lapsed. I declined Kako's invitation to present to a group of her friends as I feared I might die on the job at the tender age of 21. However, from time to time she came to my apartment when work allowed, which was good for both of us – me because my schedule did not allow for normal relations and her because her husband was in the merchant navy and away a lot as a result.

Although by now, in theory at least, I was earning a fortune, compared to any previous wage, I still had a huge cash flow problem. I didn't earn a salary. I was paid commission only and that took about two months to arrive and was subject to the deduction of lapses. So, the pot of gold always seemed to be at the other end of the rainbow.

This Life In Death

Moreover, I was young, needed the money and didn't mind working day and night to get it. Therefore, I decided that a daytime job, with a salary, needed to be added to this night-time job. It would mean getting up at 7:00am and finishing work at 2:00am the next day six or even seven days a week before having dinner in an Indian restaurant and going to bed around 4:00am. I would only get two to three hours sleep a night. Completely mad. But I was hungry, angry with my father and determined to succeed even if it killed me in the process. My motto had become, 'The only way is up'.

But jobs were very few and far between at the time. So, I decided to approach a friend of my father's called Doug Ellis – yes, the famous 'Deadly Doug' of Aston Villa. He asked me to come and see him after work one Wednesday at 6:00pm.

I set off in 'the bone shaker' in good time but ran out of petrol on the Hockley Flyover. I abandoned my only valuable possession, except for my ADISR gold medal, and ran the mile and a half to his office in Cannon St in the city centre.

I arrived on time and was grateful to be kept waiting so that I might appear more composed and less sweaty. Eventually, I was invited into his office.

Doug Ellis was a self-made millionaire who owned a chain of travel agents and had started a pioneer package holiday company just as the working man was looking to go to Majorca instead of Blackpool or Bournemouth for his holiday. His company in this field was called Midland Air Tour Operators – or MATO for short. He was also Chairman of Aston Villa.

Doug and my father had been good friends for over twenty years, and both were members of the Highfield Club. However, Doug frequented the place a lot less than the Old Man and had overtaken my father as one was going up and the other coming down in the world.

This Life In Death

I couldn't remember meeting him before. However, he was charming, offered me a seat and asked what I would like to drink.

I thought a scotch on the rocks sounded worldly and so blurted that out. What a fool, I hated scotch due to my mother tipping it down my throat as a child to revive me from asthma attacks. He obliged and I faked drinking it until he went to his private bathroom, when I tipped it into a plant pot next to where I was sitting. Upon his return he poured me another.

We got on very well. He didn't mention it, but he was going through a difficult period with his son Peter, who was to become a good friend in later years. Unlike him, I did mention that I was going through a difficult period with my father.

We chatted about my father, Michelle, whom he didn't like, my mother, whom he did, and Aston Villa and then, at last, we came as to why I had come to visit him. I told him that I was well suited to business economics. He replied that he didn't believe in accountants let alone economists. However, he added that I was a good salesman because I had sold myself well. I was appointed manager of the MATO shop in Cherry Street in the city centre with immediate effect. My salary was to be £20-a-week, which was over twice as much as that which Hodgson & Sons had paid the boss's son.

I walked back to the Hockley Flyover really pleased and was even happier when I discovered that the police had only moved 'the bone shaker' into a side street rather than the city pound. With two incomes coming in I could not only eat but also afford to fill the car with petrol.

Life at MATO was much more pleasant than at Tri-Star due to both the normal hours and the security of having a weekly pay packet. Moreover, I got to become friendly with Villa players like Bruce Rioch and Willie Anderson because I booked their holidays for them.

There was another bonus too. My work schedule never allowed for any time off and so that meant no girls. As a result, all previous female friends had drifted away – even June had gone back to

This Life In Death

London. Of course, there was Kako but I remained a little nervous of her with good reason. So, I might as well be either a male prostitute or a priest as matters stood.

However, there was a very sweet girl who worked in the Cherry Street shop as my only assistant. I can't remember her name because I started out by calling her George – and that is who she became to me, and this was 52 years ago after all.

George and I became good friends. She must have been only 18 and came from somewhere like Yardley or Sheldon and, to her, I was an old man of 21 who spoke like an aristocrat or a BBC Radio 4 announcer.

However, the 60s social revolution popularised by the Beatles, where it was cool to be classless, plus my own fall from a high place and a genuine liking for people whatever their colour race or religion, meant I really did judge the book rather than the cover. Perhaps one of the few saving graces of this psychiatrist's dream patient.

One evening after the shop closed at 5:30pm, neither of us wanted to leave. I think we both knew where this might lead. We started teasing each other, had a water fight which ended up in the basement with us both ripping off the other's clothes and making passionate love on the piles of MATO summer and winter sun brochures stored there from the previous year.

This became a regular feature when the office closed each evening except Friday – when I would go for a drink with Doug at 5:30pm sharp to his command. I had gone to at least three of these weekly chats before I had summoned enough courage to decline a scotch and ask for a beer instead.

During these Friday evening sessions, I realised that Doug really did not believe in accountants or any form of ordered administration. He was a brilliant blue-sky thinker, a charismatic man with drive who could expand sales almost at will but had little time for the mess that was left in his wake because of his actions.

This Life In Death

This became crystal clear when one lovely summer's evening Doug announced that he wanted to promote an accountant called Geoff in answer to my very politely put point that while sales were going very well, I thought that MATO's administration was not quite up to keeping abreast of the expansion.

I said he couldn't do that. He looked at me and said he was talking about Geoff.

"You know Howard. Geoff, he has a drink with you sometimes at lunchtime. Geoff, who has an office two down from me and has been here for nearly 15 years. What's wrong with him"?

"Nothing but he came here from the Alfred Marks employment agency in New Street 15 years ago and he is still paid by them, and you still pay them for his services", I replied in a very respectful tone to try and soften such bad news.

Doug genuinely wasn't worried by this. He smiled and joked, "You are more than just a pretty face then". I smiled and never let on that it was a female senior member of staff who had let this slip in a moment of work related 'pillow talk'.

Doug was pleased with me. He asked me to write a review of the group's departments to find out where savings could be made, and operational efficiency improved.

His senior staff were horrified by this news, and my popularity fell like a stone. However, I wasn't deterred, and my mother typed up my findings to present to him. But glorious summer turned into autumn and there were to be more upheavals as seemed usual at that time of the year.

Stuart & Lloyd's was now a part of the nationalised British Steel Corporation. Peter Hafner was offered, and rightly accepted, the MD role in a subsidiary company in South Africa.

My mother determined to go with him and changed her surname to Hafner to avoid any controversy. She wanted to put the dog Scamp down as a result. I said no. Scamp had always lived at home with her but was, as you may recall, my dog, given as a Christmas present in 1959. I said no way and my dog came to live with me at last and everywhere I went so she came too.

Before she departed, my mother came to say goodbye to me at my new flat, which I shared with Paul Bullas, in Bearwood. It was a dump. She looked round and cried. I told her that I was 21, a big boy now and that Scamp and I would be fine. I didn't tell her that I needed to look up because looking down was just too awful.

Nevertheless, she called her friend of over 20 years, Doug Ellis, and asked him to look after for me while she was away. He replied that I was a 'grafter' and might oversee a very large business by the time she returned.

Then Tri-Star offered me to be the branch manager over Stoke-on-Trent. I would be paid commission on every plan written in the Potteries. I didn't like Tri-Star's directors and I loved Doug. However, I suspected that his enthusiasm for my rationalisation plan was less than I had hoped, and I would never get rich working for him as my earnings were not in my own hands.

Therefore, I went off to Stoke and only with Scamp as a friend. I was very lonely and homesick. So, I decided not to move there but travel each day from my flat in Bearwood. At least without MATO I didn't have to get up at 7:00 each morning.

The Stoke operation was small and I set about building it. I must admit that I really missed my Birmingham team and when I looked at their business volumes, as published in the weekly company magazine, they appeared to be missing me too.

Then one evening after my introductory meeting of only a handful of people had finished and as I was preparing to put Scamp in my new Marcos to return to Birmingham, two men walked in.

They were called David Meakin and Joe Worthington. They had worked for a front-runner of Tri-Star called G&S, but now worked for a company called North West Mercantile. They were here to convince me to switch to that company.

I went for a drink with them. I drank Coke and they tea. They wanted me to head up a start-up for them in Birmingham.

It was a Thursday night that became a Friday morning as we planned how to do it and my terms for accepting. I was exhausted and stopped the Marcos to sleep before I got on the M6.

It was now November and cold. Scamp and I snuggled into my great leather coat with a fur collar, a parting gift from my mother, and slept happily. I was going home to be King of Birmingham and I was certain that I would make a fortune.

I busied myself on that Friday planning to see my previous team leaders and then even went further and decided to go for all the other Tri-Star Birmingham consultants and their teams. I had to act fast as anyone who turned me down would alert Tri-Star to this proposed coup.

All consultants bar one but including Digby Jarman, agreed to join me and a meeting was held at the Watford Gap Services on the M1 late on that night for them to meet David Meakin. This meeting went well and so everyone was to come across to NWM under my leadership.

On the Saturday evening my old Tri-Star direct team met at my new flat in Sheldon, which was close to Elmdon Airport, now known as Birmingham Airport, and again shared with the ever-faithful Paul Bullas.

I rehearsed them in what they must all say to their team members. Then they were dispatched to do the same. Philip Dunn asked if his fiancée could stay with me, and he would pick her up later. I readily agreed as I thought she was a raven-haired beauty.

Left alone together, she quickly challenged me to a wrestling match. I immediately agreed and we had a lot of fun rolling around on the floor together. It could have easily gone further as I really fancied her. Perhaps she fancied me too? Who knows – or perhaps her sexual needs were not being met, as nearly a decade later, Philip was to announce that he was, and always had been, gay.

However, for once in a life where self-inflicted damage has often been caused by sexual urge, I controlled myself as I knew I needed total focus to succeed, and that Philip deserved better than that from me.

I also recruited the Wolverhampton Tri-Star manager, one Andy Johnson and his whole branch, and eventually the Birmingham manager, John Taylor himself, who would be with me for the next 20 years.

NWM Birmingham went off like a train and quickly the meetings at Dr Johnson House, where I had taken over the booking for Tr-Star, were packed with over 500 attendees.

We raided their stage props and constructed an extra four tiers on the stage with me on top of the lot and so high up that I could feel the heat of the stage lighting above my head.

All the way from the audience, up past 3 other tiers on either side, were wide steps carpeted in royal blue. This meant that award winners felt like they were going up to collect an Oscar. The motivational effect was brilliant.

Indeed, it was all a bit like a Third Reich rally – except I only dealt in motivational dreams and there was no hatred of anyone. It helped get normal folk to think that they were special and, along with my other reporting and recording systems, meant that we were soon writing around 80% of the NWM business – with only 20% being written by the Wolverhampton, Stoke, Manchester, Leeds, and Preston branches.

This Life In Death

Chapter IV

The Need of a Family

(1972 – 1975)

I was determined that this was only to be the beginning. Within 3 months we were opening a London branch and I was appointed 'Southern Director'. I now believed that I was unstoppable – a Messiah who could give ordinary folk a chance of a better life by self-determination rather than social service hand-outs.

Of course, this was not vaguely true. However, the mixture of my fanatical conviction, drive, determination and oratorial skills to make normal folk think that if they stuck with me, they would end up very rich, meant that they believed it and so did I too.

Indeed, one Irish guy called Eccles, believed it so much that he started popping into estate agents and collecting brochures for the very best properties in Streetly, Edgbaston or Solihull.

Winter was turning into a blossoming spring and as usual my fortunes rose as the days got longer. It was decided to open a London office and one was selected not far from Wembley Stadium on the North Circular.

I chose David Murphy, of Irish decent but brought up in London to be the branch manager there. David had made consultant in Tri-Star without being in my team. He was raw, poorly educated and, like a lot of white East End Londoners, more than a little racist.

However, he had drive and determination in spades and when he got over the fact that I insisted that he did not call his predominately black team 'coons' and realised that they wrote the business upon which he was paid, David Meakin and I thought that he would do as our 'man in London.'

So off he went but things did not go well and after a month David Meakin, who was as pleasant as I was not, and I went to London to confront him about his failure and the outrageous statement that London would never work because the only people who wanted a part-time job were 'coons.'

We were still operating out of a hotel in Westbourne Terrace by Lancaster Gate, as at this point the Wembley lease had not been signed yet. David Meakin, who went weekly to do an introductory meeting in the hotel, was sharing a room with David Murphy, and I had my own room booked for the one night stop-over.

After the introductory meeting the two Davids went for dinner, and I joined them after I had taken my nightly reports on reception – as there were no mobiles in those days.

Murphy was blaming the 'coons' for his poor showing and Meakin, coming from a very devout Christian non-conformist family, was blaming him instead. This discussion went round in circles for several hours, during which time we had all gone back to their room.

It was about six in the morning when Meakin ordered a pot of coffee. It arrived just before peace broke out when Murphy, a young version of Alf Garnet, had conceded that perhaps he was wrong about his assertion that the only people in London who wanted a part-time job were 'thick coons' and agreed that he would not be referring to people from Nigeria or the Caribbean as 'coons' in future.

Meakin, at this point, and in an act of most unusual irresponsibility for him, threw the metal coffee pot against the wall. It made a huge crash and rolled down the room towards the door.

As it did a knock came on the door. Murphy and Meakin disappeared down their beds like rabbits bolting into their holes. I was left alone, to face this awkward scene. I called out "Wait."

The knocker didn't. It was a Spanish chambermaid. As she opened the door it hit the coffee pot and it rolled back down the room.

"I said wait. Now look what you have done," I protested as I pointed to the coffee-soaked wall.

This Life In Death

Scamp started to bark at her, and she fled screaming something in Spanish. Within seconds the door was flung open by a very attractive young woman with deep red hair and a heavy French accent.

She very aggressively told me, while the other two cowered down their beds, that all night drunken partying, which other guests were complaining about, and falsely accusing the poor chambermaid of damaging the room, was completely unacceptable.

This was only partially correct because we had not been drinking. However, before I could make that or any other point, she turned to go.

I was furious. We were spending a fortune in this less salubrious of the Barclay Twins hotels, and I was not being spoken to like that by the housekeeper. Without thinking, I did something I had never done before nor since, I clicked my fingers as I said, "Hey, hey, hey."

She swept round came up to me and clicked her fingers in my face with the words, "My name is not Hey, Hey, Hey." She tossed her long hair as she swivelled round and was gone. Only then did Meakin and Murphy emerge from beneath their bed covers.

Before, leaving in my Jaguar XJ6, complete with 2-way radio and an Air Call sign of Jet 183, I decided to have lunch in the hotel restaurant. Sitting a few feet away was the French housekeeper with her fiery eyes looking the other way. So, I threw a packet of sugar cubes at her to attract her attention. It hit her on the back of her head.

Once more she spun round but this time to face me and said in a voice that rang around the whole dining room so that every cheap-skating American tourist could hear, "Why don't you just fuck off?"

So now it is French housekeeper 2 and me 0. My parting shot to Murphy was, "No more calling anyone 'coons' and I will be back next Thursday, and you line up Froggy to have dinner with me." He assured me it would be done without pointing out that it might be a trifle hypocritical of me to go mad at him for calling folk 'coons' while I called this young lady 'Froggy.'

This Life In Death

Next Thursday I duly arrived looking very smart having been assured by Murphy that 'Froggy' was on for dinner. However, as I parked my Jag, I noticed her going out with the other housekeeper, a very Germanic girl called Spaue.

Murphy assured me she would be back soon, but she didn't appear. Then it was time for my nightly calls. I took these on reception and in between chatted to the Egyptian night porter whom I had nicknamed Nassar. I liked him and he liked me back because I treated him as a friend and much more politely than the red-neck American tourists who treated him like dirt.

These nightly reports came from Birmingham. They were made by my senior consultants. Melvin Edges, a wonderfully gentle guy – who was always so positive in his deed, while proclaiming "You don't expect to get paid, do you?" He had a very colourful Irish wife called Bernie and I became their second son's godfather. Philip Dunn, who will play a big part later in this saga, and, amongst others, a guy called Rog, who worked for a transport company in Sheldon, slept in a caravan in their enormous garage with his girlfriend and their cat, cleverly named 'Cooking Fat.' He was older than us and in his thirties.

I seem to recall that he was on the phone when two very drunk Icelanders walked in. One was very large, the other quite small. They were making a noise. Scamp barked at them. The small one kicked my dog. I put the phone down and punched him on the jaw. The big one punched me. Now we are wrestling, going round in a circle, and crossing the reception from end to end with me hitting the little one and the big one hitting me.

I could hear Rog's voice saying, "Hello, hello, what's going on?" every time the fight passed by the phone on the reception counter.

Then, as this square dance passed for the second or third time that counter, Nassar was standing on it and launched himself on to the big Icelander and sat on his shoulders beating him about the head. So now Nassar is hitting the big guy, who is hitting me and I'm hitting the little guy, who is also having his ankles nipped by Scamp.

This Life In Death

This punch-up went on until the police, who did a proper job in those days, arrived, called by I don't know whom, to break it all up.

Apparently, the big one was married, and his wife was asleep upstairs. She was awoken and came down in her nightie. The big guy took one look at her and threw her down with such force that she slid across the marble floor and out of the door with her nightie up round her neck and exposing her everything to Westbourne Terrace.

"Right, you're nicked" said the sergeant in charge and both Icelanders were hauled away. Nassar and I were left just as 'Froggy' was coming in.

My God, I looked a mess. My new suit was wrecked, never to be worn again. My shirt was torn and covered in blood, mainly mine. My bottom lip was now very fat, and with blood dribbling out of the corner of my mouth and nose. My right eye was nearly shut. My hair looked as if I hadn't bothered with it for a month. Oh shit!

Murphy had arrived during the fight. He was apparently a judo black belt. However, his contribution on this occasion was to dance around making noises with his arms in combat position. He had been a lot less effective than either Scamp or Nassar in defending me.

He was explaining why he couldn't have got involved as he was a black belt when 'Froggy', much to my amazement, asked me to follow her. I did.

She led me to her room. She bathed my face and cleaned it up. She ran a bubble bath and told me to get in. She put her hair up and joined me. The enemies of the previous week were now in a warm and wonderfully soapy bath together.

We chatted. I became aware that she had been brought to England by Frederick Barclay, half of the Barclay twins fame, who owned the hotel and saw him for dinner about once a week. However, she was engaged to a Frenchman called Jean-Pierre, who at 34, seemed very old to me but I said nothing, wishing not to be offensive.

This Life In Death

"When will you get married?" I asked.

"Oh, I'm not" she replied.

"What?"

"I decided to marry you instead."

"Oh no I'm not getting married – I'm only 22."

We were married 3 months later.

Moreover, without which, much of what comes next would never have happened.

She took me to her bed, and you know what happened next. I told her I would be back in a week, and I was.

Then she took me to a local pub by Hyde Park. She said that she knew everyone there and I knew no one and that she could leave me now if she wanted.

She didn't know about my past as you do now. She had no idea of how self-protective the person that she was talking to had become. I smiled and said, "Good night then." She said she didn't want to go. I knew at that moment I had come from 2-0 down to recover to win the match.

However, not only was she beautiful, but I also saw in her a quality of ambition that was always missing in other girls in my life. She could be the woman to help me re-build the Hodgson dynasty. As I drove back to Birmingham, I kept considering this.

I knew that I was likely to want to be unfaithful in the future, but this was in my genes and wholly my fault and not hers. I realised that I would have to try to keep this less savoury part of my character under control. I also knew that I would be very unlikely to meet anyone as beautiful, fiercely loyal, decent, and wanting to build a family and an empire with me.

This Life In Death

I ached to have a family of my own now that my childhood family had been ripped away from me. I thought it enormously unlikely that I would find a woman better to share this task than 'Froggy.'

So, when I arrived back at my Sheldon apartment, I called her and asked Marianne Denise Yvonne Kiatibian to marry me. She said yes and booked a flight to tell the poor unsuspecting Jean-Pierre that it was over.

I was happy – I sensed that 'that family belonging' was coming home. Melvin, who was to die of cancer some 40 years later, noticed my 'up' mood and said, "You are not going to do something as silly as that are you?" But when he met her, he was as star-struck as everyone else at NWM. This was clearly one of my better decisions and so it was to prove to be.

I bought Marianne a portable TV and took her everywhere with me as the business grew by the week and new branches were opened every month. She improved her English by watching 'Emmerdale Farm', 'Harriet Back in Town' and 'Coronation Street' and became addicted to all three.

The wedding was set to take place at Studley Parish Church on 12th August 1972. My mother flew in from South Africa to be there, met Marianne and took her to see 'Last Tango in Paris.' They became firm friends. I also introduced her to my father and Michelle. My father was enchanted with her and remained so until his death. Michelle , who was by now married to him, a wedding I did not attend, was now hell bent on organising mine with Marianne.

I didn't mind as it made my father happy and that pleased me. We were by now reunited, and I was more worried about him than ever. He was unbelievably frail for a man of 46 and still drinking and spending far too much money – which increasingly he did not have.

However, this wedding expenditure was being charged solely to me, and so Michelle went for gold and was to blame Marianne, when I eventually got the bills, wholly unfairly, as my fiancé was a young French girl and had placed herself in Michelle's hands.

In the meantime, there was another hiccup before we got to go down the aisle. An affair? No. You might have already guessed that if it wasn't that it was bound to be that I had fallen out once more with authority, and you would be right.

David Meakin's partner was a Yorkshireman called Peter Warburton and he lived in Saddleworth. He was a good father but, as a short Yorkshireman, he was bound to have the small man syndrome in spades. Half of him was delighted with the money that I was making him, but the other half was dying with jealousy of the 'Beatles' status that everyone held me in within NWM.

Every Tuesday my men and I, Bullas, Edges, and Dunn etc, now all full time, would journey up the M6 to the Manchester office in Albert Square – to the right of the town hall. We hand delivered the plans written the previous week and collected at the Monday night meeting. They all had hand-written dockets attached which contained essential details.

Digby had been installed as manager of the Manchester branch and was happy to get away from his recruit (me) as a result.

There, Peter would chair the meeting of the ever-growing meeting of full-time guys. David did all the work, but Peter liked to appear to be the boss. This suited both. Peter could appear to be important while watching cricket on TV and eating Maltesers, whereas the kind-hearted David, could blame any unpleasant decision on Peter.

These meetings had always been in awe of the Birmingham performance. However, on one Monday the plans were lined up in front of Peter branch by branch. This was usual and, as was also usual, the Birmingham pile was higher than the others put together by a factor of eight.

But, on this day Peter was complaining about the quality of administration. He picked on the huge Birmingham pile. He read out

This Life In Death

the first docket, it was wrong, as was the second, third, fourth and so on.

I was nearly bursting a blood vessel in my temple, so I needed to explode, as I knew Melvin and Paul had been up all-night writing these dockets. I grabbed the pile and took off the top slice. Further down nothing was wrong. Peter had had the whole pile gone through and had any with a mistake put at the top.

I demonstrated in a flurry of fury what he had done. Not then, but soon afterwards, I was suspended for insubordination. I was, initially, devastated. Here we go again I thought. Then I reminded myself that it was me who had created the NWM success.

This was the first time that I can remember me using smart cunning to get what I wanted rather than just drive and determination.

I invited Philip Dunn and his fiancé to join Marianne in London. From there we de-camped to my mother's apartment in Poole. We had a great time and while I was having a great time the NWM volume went down the toilet.

Within a week Peter arrived at my apartment in Sheldon and invited me back to join the board and take control of the marketing operation of the whole country. Marianne could not believe how cold I was with him until he was virtually begging. He did deserve it, nonetheless.

Fences were mended and I was re-instated and promoted and David was appointed my best man at the forthcoming wedding.

Michelle had ensured that no expense was spared. The church in Studley and the reception at the Arrow Mill in Alcester were covered in flowers, champagne flowed as if I owned Moet & Chandon, the food provided for over a hundred guests was fit for royalty.

My mother looked elegant and fragrant. She was still only 46. On the other hand, my father, who was six months younger, looked very ill. He was released from hospital to come to the service but was not permitted to stay for the reception. His smart grey tails hung off his gaunt frame. He was yellow and his eyes bloodshot with jaundice. And yet despite all of this somehow, he still looked very handsome and even debonair with his now greying temples.

Marianne was given away by her great uncle George, who lived on the Avenue de la Grande Armée by the Arc de Triomphe in Paris. He was very well off.

Doug, as Chairman of Aston Villa, was at an away game with them, but sent a lovely telegram. Sandra, Philip's fiancée had too much to drink, and I held her as she vomited over the old stone bridge and into the mill stream. My father, mother, sister, and brother had been all in the same place for the first time in two years – but I could feel the tension created by this more than the love. I knew my happy childhood memories were now just that – memories. Scamp, the one lasting connection with those memories featured in a special photograph with just me.

Marianne's two sisters and her brother were there too. My younger brother, Russell, fell in love with all three Kiatibian girls – especially his new sister-in-law whom he had an almighty crush on. And I met her brother Alex. He was to become a lifelong friend and is every bit as much today some 52 years later.

After a 36-hour honeymoon in Paris, chez Ton-Ton Georges, we returned to the small apartment in Sheldon and to a regular pattern. I would leave for the NWM HO in Altrincham, near Manchester at about eleven every morning and leave Scamp with Marianne. She would go to the laundrette and do the shopping and bring everything home in her 'walking bag' as she called it. It was a shopping bag on wheels. She would then do a bit of housework before settling down with Scamp to watch all her favourite soaps on the TV. This was doing wonders for her English – which was just as well because I wasn't.

I took great delight in teaching her expressions which might be useful to her such as 'Bugger off' meant 'See you later' etc.

This Life In Death

Once in the HO, I would take the reports for the whole country with the help of a pleasant Peter Warburton protégé called John Firth while Joe Worthington worked on the next edition of 'The Broker' – the NWM weekly in-house propaganda sheet known as a newsletter. Us three plus Peter, David, and the finance director, one Gordan Sellars, made up the NWM board.

Today, going all the way from Birmingham to Manchester and back daily just to receive calls that I could have received at home seems mad in a post covid and environmentally conscious world, but then to stay at home would have seemed very strange and was never even contemplated.

I would leave work usually around one in the morning, call Marianne via Air Call to let her know that I would pick her up at three and we would go to a local Indian restaurant for dinner. We would flop into bed at four thirtyish, make love and then repeat the whole thing again 5 times a week.

I was becoming exhausted, so we decided to move to Manchester and duly bought a house in Wythenshawe, which was owned by the Manchester United striker Ted McDougall and our next-door neighbour became the Manchester City manager, Malcolm Allison, as a result.

We moved in April 1973. I did most of the heavy lifting because Marianne had become, much to our indescribable joy, pregnant. This was the second rung up the high ladder back to happiness and success that I craved so much.

Marriage + children = a family and then you build a dynasty was the clockwork process going on inside my head without any doubt, debate or considered alternatives.

Ironically, we had no sooner moved into this spacious four bedroomed house with a sizeable garden and illustrious neighbours, than I was sent back to Birmingham to resurrect the fortunes of my original branch.

This Life In Death

You may have noticed that financial service businesses can expand quickly, unlike funeral businesses which take a long time to build. The same is true in reverse. As you have seen Hodgson & Sons had been going wrong financially for a decade but was still surviving whereas, an equity linked life office built on part-time labour and financed by indemnity terms can go down the toilet in a fortnight.

So, I was despatched to Birmingham as a matter of urgency and billeted, with Marianne and her brother Alex, in the Grand Hotel, opposite Birmingham Cathedral and not from the MATO Cherry Street office where George and I used to frolic just two years before when, in my mind, I had been but a boy.

This was the summer of 1973. It was hot and the IRA were either blowing up or threatening to blow up parts of Birmingham daily. This led to numerous bomb scares every week at either the Midland or Grand Hotels in the city centre.

With the hours and the effort that I was putting in, the additional distraction of bomb scares with the hotel being emptied on to the cathedral's lawn across the road at any time was just too much.

On one occasion, having been aroused at 4:00am in the morning I was soaking in the bath at about 11:00am when a second alarm sounded, and another evacuation was announced.

I had had enough. I stayed in the bath and thought to hell with them. Luckily for me it was a false alarm. However, such reckless action was not just me displaying my usual narrow-minded determination to have it my way. I was starting to suffer from the effects of three years of living without sleep and never relaxing.

Within a few days I collapsed. I was rushed to hospital with a suspected heart attack. It wasn't a heart attack, but complete exhaustion was diagnosed as the cause. I was ordered to rest.

NWM recalled me to Altrincham, and I was appointed MD of their printing company called Powerhouse Press and told to go home not later than 6:30pm to be with my increasingly pregnant wife.

This Life In Death

I had lost my licence for three speeding offences and NWM engaged an old friend of mine from the Bantocks days, Leg Davis as my driver. I liked Leg a lot. He had followed me to Tri-Star and then NWM Birmingham. Now he was my driver. This was good as I had someone to chat to. However, he was one of only three folk that I have known who defy the laws of common sense by having passed a driving test. A guy called Freddy and a girl called Christine were the other two and we will come to them later on.

Leg only seemed to accelerate when he saw brake lights light up on the cars in front of us. Very strange.

He was a kind-hearted decent lad from a successful Jewish family who lived in a very pleasant house in Edgbaston, Birmingham. He was also very naïve, gullible and didn't always think things through properly. So, he came across a bit like David in the 2000s TV series 'Heartbeat'.

One day, he knocked on my door at Powerhouse and asked for some time off. I asked why.

"I have to see a doctor" was his reply.

"Why?" was my response.

Initially, he didn't want to tell me but after a little coaxing he volunteered that he had yellow mucus coming out of his willie.

"You don't need a doctor. You need to go to the VD clinic" I advised and told him to go immediately. He thanked me and asked me not to tell a soul. I assured him that I wouldn't.

Moments later the Powerhouse Press sales manager came in and asked if I knew that Leg had a dose of the clap.

"How do you know?" I replied, genuinely shocked.

"I just met him on the stairs on the way up here and he told me."

This Life In Death

Within minutes my phone went. It was Marianne asking me if I knew that Leg had VD.

"And how the hell do you know?" I asked almost doubting what I had just heard.

"He just called in to let me know on his way to the clinic" was her astonishing reply.

On the following Saturday night, David Meakin, Leg, who was driving us and was my guest for dinner, Marianne and I were having a great dinner at 'Blinkers.' This club was made famous and hugely successful because it was frequented almost nightly by the fifth Beatle, George Best – perhaps the best footballer I have ever seen play the game. I was also to become friendly with him when he opened his own club 'Slack Alice's' in early 1974. He would sit there nightly, immaculately attired in black tie and drinking champagne. The club was not always full initially as he had helped create a huge success at Blinkers and it became clear that it was a haunt that people were reluctant to drop.

During that dinner Marianne asked Leg how he had got on at the clinic. Leg replied that he was on a course of penicillin. David asked if he had told the girl that she had VD, as unlike with men, it could go undetected. Leg said that he had kind of told her.

"Kind of told her! Either you told her, or you didn't" I exclaimed with some surprise.

"Well, I didn't actually tell her. I went to Cloisters, the club where I met her. She wasn't there, so I told the waiter to tell her next time she came in."

Leg looked amazed as the three of us fell about in hysteria. I worried that Marianne might give birth a month early. She worried that she might pee at the table.

Leg had paid the young lady back in spades without a clue as to what he had done.

This Life In Death

As the days went by and the birthday approached, Marianne took to reclining on the very comfortable settee we had bought when we moved into Saxfield Drive. We listened nonstop to 'Band on the Run.' Earlier in the year Macca, album 'Red Rose Speedway' had been well received but 'Band on the Run' put him back at the top of both the single and album charts for months. To this day, I still associate it with this period of my life.

As twenty-three-year-olds with their own home, an XJ6 Jaguar as well as a Triumph TR6, we looked to be doing very well. However, earlier that summer with the collapse of the Birmingham branch, the NWM lapse rate had caught up with it and had meant that urgent measures needed taking to avoid financial disaster.

We have seen how long it takes to build a funeral business and how quickly you can build a financial service business. The same is true in reverse. So, while Hodgson & Sons had been soldiering on despite my father's profligacy, NWM could come tumbling down quickly by comparison.

All directors had their salaries capped at £7,500-a-year. That was still very good in 1973 when most people had to survive on £1,000 per annum or less. However, it meant we had to make choices. We had decided that a private gynaecologist took priority over anything else.

As a result, Marianne survived on just two pregnancy outfits, one red and one in navy blue for nearly four months. This was hard for a young fashion-conscious French woman but borne by her without complaint.

The gynaecologist's name was Mr. Jones. In those days there was no way of telling what the sex of the baby was before the birth. Mr. Jones asked me what I would like the baby to be.

"A boy born on Christmas day please" I replied.

"Well, I can't guarantee that" exclaimed Mr. Jones.

This Life In Death

"In that case, I may not pay your fee. I mean if I ordered a sack of coal on a Wednesday and you delivered a sack of coke on a Thursday, you wouldn't expect to get paid would you?" I joked but with a straight face.

This was lost on Mr. Jones, who turned to Marianne and told her that she had married a crank. Many of you might agree with that.

On the 19th of December, I had neglected to take the doctor's advice and was working late with the ever-faithful Leg. The phone rang at about 9pm. It was Marianne. Her waters had broken. Action stations. But wait, my Jag was in the dealers' garage being serviced and Leg, Marianne and I would never fit in the TR 6. We would have to use Leg's Japanese car. It was also a two-seater sports car but a little bigger.

Leg and I raced round to the house, and with a great deal of difficulty got Marianne in on my knee and departed for Withington Hospital. Once Marianne was installed in a delivery room, I returned to Leg who was waiting in reception. I told him to find a comfortable chair as it might be a long night. He did and I returned to sit with Marianne.

She was a petite woman and from the back you could not see that see was pregnant. Her weight gain was all baby. So, we had been warned this might take some time. It did. Minutes became hours as I held her hand as she gripped mine in obvious pain. There were no epidurals in those days and the only thing they administered was oxygen when the pain was too much.

Then I was ushered out, again quite different from today. By now it was getting light on the morning of the 20th. I fell asleep waiting in the reception only to be woken up by Leg.

"She is having the baby" he announced with some confidence.

"How do you know?"

"I heard her screaming."

This Life In Death

Then a very tired looking Mr. Jones was coming towards me. I stood up. I was a bit dishevelled, hair tussled and my leather coat over my shoulders. As he walked down the corridor I waited expectantly. I would know with a minute the news I had longed for.

He arrived. "Well, Mr. Hodgson, you are the father of an 8lb 8-ounce fine baby. We had to use the forceps to assist with delivery I'm afraid."

"Yes, yes" I interrupted impatiently.

"Boy!!!"

I turned to the other expectant fathers and punched the air as if I had scored the winning goal for Aston Villa to win the League.

He added, but I hardly took in, that he would expect his fee settling as a result even if my son was five days early.

Howard James Paul was presented to me. He looked wonderful. I went on to have six children. They all grew up to be beautiful looking. However, not all were to be that beautiful at that moment of birth – other than to their parents.

Howard, however, was perfect. He had a full head of hair, which was Beatle length, big round McCartney eyes and the look and colouring of my father. He didn't look a bit like me – and I couldn't have cared less. Rung two back up the ladder had been achieved in the most delightful way.

Howard James Paul was a cross between James Paul McCartney and Osmond Paul Charles Hodgson and I considered myself to be the luckiest man alive.

This was truly the most perfect moment of joy since my childhood and finally banished that feeling in the pit of one's stomach of insecure homesickness. The Hodgsons were a family again.

This Life In Death

Marianne, stayed in hospital, as everyone did in those days, for over a week. When I arrived to take her and 'Little H', as we had come to call him, home, she was ready, but he wasn't.

"I can't dress him" she explained.

"Why?"

"Because I might break him."

I dressed him and we left for home, the start of the three day week, caused by the 1974 miners' strike, and national paralysis which led to a general election and the end of the Heath Government.

We were to have our own series of crises too.

Howard had only been home a couple of days when I noticed yellow mucus coming from his left eye. We took him straight to the doctor. He sent us immediately to the Manchester Eye Hospital. They diagnosed an infection caused using the forceps when he was born. He would have to stay with them.

We were shocked and distraught about being separated from our son. We asked if we could wait and see him settled into his cot. They weren't too keen, but I insisted, and they relented.

Some twenty minutes later we were ushered into a private single bed ward to see 'Little H' tucked up in the bed.

"What the hell are you doing? He's a fortnight old and you've put him into a bed! Are you mad? He could easily suffocate. Why isn't he in a cot?" I exclaimed in disbelief.

"We don't have one" was the young doctor's answer.

I couldn't believe it. My son had been given a serious eye infection by one hospital and was now having his very life put in danger by another.

"He will be fine. We know what we are doing" he said to reassure us.

This Life In Death

"He had better be fine or you won't be" was my reply.

He accepted that, unlike today, when I would be arrested on charges of threatening assault against a health worker.

We wandered outside into the cold January night air. Marianne, burst into tears and I held her, while holding back my own as I had been taught since childhood.

It was a very worrying moment. However, three days later, Howard was deemed well enough to come home, and we were both relieved and happy.

However, within a week Marianne was taken ill. My father and Michelle had been to stay for the weekend to meet Howard.

My father had been thrilled and I can still see the joy on his face as he held his first grandchild in his arms. He and I were now on good terms, despite all that had happened.

He had even asked me to return to Hodgson & Sons Ltd, as Stan Edwards had become ill, and he wanted me to replace him. I had declined as I knew that I would be powerless to stop the firm's and his decline without the power to do so. However, this conversation had all been handled without rancour or bitterness.

As soon as Michelle arrived, she dragged Marianne off on a marathon shopping trip and then expected her to wait on her hand and foot when they arrived back at home.

Marianne had been doing this, while starving herself to get her petite figure back and still having to look after a child that she believed she might break. It was all too much, and no sooner were my father and Michelle a mile away on their way back to Warwickshire, than she collapsed.

The doctor was called, and he discovered she had blood poisoning and that had caused a very nasty abscess under her two front teeth. She was put to bed and ordered to stay there.

This Life In Death

This wasn't a problem for me because I could bath, feed, change and dress Howard. Moreover, thanks to the three-day-week I was working from home anyway and he could sleep next to me while I worked on the dining room table.

I hadn't reckoned on Pele. Pele was Malcolm Allison's golden labrador. Mr Allison was away from home having his well-publicised fling with a young woman called Serena Williams, while leaving the dog with his wife Beth.

Beth was an extremely likeable woman whom Marianne and I had got to know quite well in her husband's absence. Indeed, Marianne even confided in her that she liked seeing me walk around the house naked. Beth replied that so did she as I walked back from the bathroom to the bedroom naked each morning at the same time and she made a point of watching.

On this Monday morning, with Marianne confined to bed, I had put Scamp, now 14-years-old, out and proceeded to feed our boy.

Once done I opened the front door to let Scamp in. She was not there. She was nowhere to be found. I put Howard in his warmest baby grow and went into the drive.

I found her collapsed in the Allisons' front garden. Pele, in a fit of desire, had mounted his much smaller love interest and she had had a heart attack as a result.

It was a mad Grand Prix performance to the vet in my TR6, find a parking place and then a mad dash with a four-week-old baby under one arm and a dying 14-year-old dog under the other.

However, I made it, and Scamp was still alive - just. But, yet again, I was forced to leave another loved one behind and wait and pray.

Again, God was with us, or so I told myself, as we all survived to tell the tale, with a very drugged dog back home in her basket that evening.

This Life In Death

Not even a three-day week, a bedridden wife, a month-old-baby and a serious ill dog to look after, while fitting in a 15-hour-work day did anything to dampen my enthusiasm. I even enjoyed experimenting to improve my cooking skills – although not always with the excellent results I set myself as I seem now to recall.

And, in time, this winter of lunatic national discontent started to thaw into a welcome spring and, despite England failing to qualify for the World Cup, most other things in my household were going according to plan, as spring turned into the summer of 1974 and the return of my mother from South Africa.

Her return to live in Poole, Dorset, with Peter was very welcome, and we would make the trek down from Manchester on a Friday night to spend the weekend with them as often as we could despite the 5-hour journey each way.

Howard went from a baby to become a toddler and we were very happy, even though England failed to qualify for the World Cup. However, there was a little consolation in that my England cricket hero Dennis Amiss, later to become a very good friend, was excelling on the World stage and Aston Villa were on the road to recovery and old 'First Division' status.

Soon it became Christmas time and 1975 was beckoning. This was to become a very significant year in my life. However, it started out with little to no indication that that was going to be the case.

Marianne and I were happy. I missed Birmingham but we had a very pleasant home and good friends. Work was hard as NWM was still struggling to recover from its difficulties of the previous two years, but we lived comfortably.

Then a series of bombshells exploded.

Michelle, my stepmother was arrested in Sainsbury's in Redditch just before Christmas charged with shoplifting.

This Life In Death

Obviously, my father had, unsurprisingly, ordered a cut in spending due to the poor state of his finances, caused by years of business neglect and Michelle spending cash which he no longer had.

She had decided that if she couldn't buy smoked salmon, prawns, and caviar then she would just steal them.

The shame of this exposure of her as a common thief and the prospect of no more money to lavish on herself sent her to her bed in the New Year, where she remained for two months while she refused to see anyone but her hairdresser just once a week when she would come to the house.

Then suddenly one day, she dressed, jumped into her new lemon coloured Triumph Spitfire sports car and left while my father was up the road having a drink in the Dog Inn.

He never saw her again. He was probably worth about half a million pounds when she had arrived in his life five years before, but he was penniless on this day.

Now that the money had gone so had she. He was a broken man. Alcohol and Michelle had turned a debonair, charming, and handsome man in his mid-forties into a hunched man with greying hair who had lost both his looks and his confidence before he was fifty.

Worse, it was also quite clear that Hodgson & Sons Ltd was by now in as poorly a state as its owner and neither could help each other towards recovery. Something had to be done.

I hadn't any savings and North West Mercantile wanted to get away from being 100% reliant on equity linked life assurance commissions. So, it was agreed that they would buy Hodgson & Sons Ltd and that I would run it.

I duly started negotiations with my father. He was relieved and took some heart that his nightmare might be resolved but, upon an initial due diligence investigation, matters began to look worse and worse.

This Life In Death

Meanwhile, back in Manchester the NWM Chairman, Peter Warburton had struck a deal with the Welfare Life Managing Director, one Alan Phillips, to try and improve our cash flow.

The deal was that if we supplied Alan with a Daimler Double Six, insured and with a free petrol allowance, he would act as a consultant and ensure our commission rates were increased and that payments were speeded up.

There was no FCA regulation to worry about in those days – but I seem to recall that the FSA did exist and perhaps might not have approved of such an arrangement if it had ever been told about it.

Nevertheless, David Meakin, his girlfriend – a delightful girl called Susan – Marianne and I were asked to take Alan out to the newly opened Manchester Playboy Club for dinner and be charming to him.

The Manchester Playboy Club was the new vogue in the city. Marianne and I had been before when we had dined with Pat Crerand and Denis Law, who had been charming companions and most interesting in giving me an insight to where Manchester United had gone wrong since the departure of Sir Matt Busby as their manager. It has always seemed amazing to me that the same club made all the same mistakes over 40 years later when Fergie retired.

The appointed day came, and Alan was invited to meet us all at our house for drinks before going on into town.

My father was staying with us at my invitation as I worried about him being on his own in 'The Woodlands' down in Warwickshire, now that Michelle had left, and we had been able to finish off the negotiation for the acquisition of Hodgson & Sons Ltd.

The price had come down to a miserable £14,000. He was grateful to even get that, and I think if NWM hadn't been so keen to have me add funerals to their financial service and printing businesses, I might have even struggled to get him that amount.

This Life In Death

He was to babysit Howard while we were out at the Playboy Club. Before we left, he had joined us for drinks and talked to Alan for a few minutes.

When we were seated at our table in the Playboy Club, I asked Alan what he and my father had talked about.

"Not much, he was rather boring and living in the past" he replied.

David, who normally drank tea rather than wine, downed a glass of Chablis in one, for he knew what was coming next.

I might be able to call my father what I wanted but nobody else should say a word against him. Not only is blood thicker than water but my father had given me so much love, kindness, and direction. He had made many sacrifices for me when I was as frail as he was now.

I exploded into a tirade of fury. David had another glass. Alan responded by saying that I was too loyal and sensitive. Marianne joined in on my side. David downed a third glass as he saw the new NWM commission deal sailing off down the Manchester Ship Canal.

Alan came back at her with a load of nonsense that families were not so important as oneself. This brought Susan into the discussion, or should I say 'punch up', on our side as David ordered another bottle of Chablis.

The more that I told Alan that my father was worth ten of him; the more Susan and Marianne extolled the virtues of family love; the more he stood his ground; the more David was exclusively enjoying the Chablis.

Then suddenly David exploded into the conversation with "Alan, I was brought up by two very fine Christian parents. If they had been here, they would have been horrified by your comments. So, if you don't want to do the new commission deal don't because we don't need to sell our souls to please you."

This Life In Death

Amazed silence at the table. However, this was topped by Alan. He announced that he wasn't offended, that everyone was entitled to their opinion, that the deal should go ahead, and that if he was me, he would have had the balls to buy my father's business himself.

The row was defused, and dinner finished with pleasant conversation coming from all quarters.

That night, I awoke at three in the morning, sat bolt upright in bed, put the light on, woke Marianne and announced, "Alan is right. I am going to buy Hodgson & Sons Ltd."

This statement was to change my life completely.

So, wherever you are today, Alan, I hope you read this and accept my heartfelt gratitude. You opened my eyes and let me see the 'bleeding obvious.'

You challenged my courage and threw down the gauntlet. I picked it up as I had become accustomed to. And so, you changed my life, that of my family, our business and its staff and, in time, the whole way the British funeral industry worked. Thank you.

This Life In Death

CHAPTER V

Our Finest Hour

(1975 – 1977)

I awoke and asked my father if I could purchase the family business instead of NWM. I promised to pay the same price. He agreed.

My fellow directors at Northwest Mercantile took the news that I now wanted to replace NWM as the purchaser remarkably well.

I believe that had quite a lot to do with the fact that I had uncovered the full extent, or so I thought I had, of the precarious financial health of Hodgson & Sons Ltd. This had clearly dampened their desire to proceed and now I was offering them a way out.

I moved fast. By noon, I had appointed the Manchester 'old school' solicitor, Aubrey Snowise, to act for me instead of NWM.

Things seemed to proceed remarkably smoothly to start with. The vendor/purchaser agreement was agreed without too much difficulty. After all, we were father and son. I adored him – and he had no choice but to trust me.

In late July, I drove to the Woodlands, where my father continued to live on his own, left Scamp and my XJ12 Jaguar with him and flew with Marianne and Little H to Marseilles so that Marianne could spend some time with her wonderful family before I had to return alone to start the salvation of Hodgson & Sons Ltd.

I was 25 years old, extremely confident that I knew what I was doing and believed that, thanks to my father's teaching, I was undoubtedly the best funeral conductor and indeed director in Birmingham. I really did not have an idea what life had in store for me next.

However, life was not going to keep me waiting too long to find out!

Taking advantage of the wonderful family atmosphere of Marianne's home in a tiny narrow little street in Pertuis, near Aix-en-Provence in the South of France, I expected to enjoy a rest, snuggled in the bosom of her adorable family.

Her mother was one of the only three saints I have ever met. We will come to the second and third, in volume II. I adored my parents as we know. However, as we also know, neither were saints.

I loved her father too. He was a wonderfully entertaining character who had taken a shine to me and somehow thought I was an English lord.

He certainly did not get that impression from me. Indeed, I found it most difficult to live up to, as he always wanted me to wear a suit and dress as a 19th century English gentleman in the middle of very warm French summer days so he could introduce me to the local VIPs of the town.

I was also very fond of Alex, Marianne's brother, and her two sisters Michele and Suzanne. All of them and their larger family had welcomed me and shown me love and affection at a time when, in my soul, I was still mourning the loss of my own family – not by death but by disruption.

It wasn't a rich financial environment there in Pertuis – in all truth, completely the opposite. However, it was extremely rich in love, affection, and plain wonderful genuine old fashioned Roman Catholic values and I basked in it all.

However, it wasn't too long before their only telephone on the ground floor of this narrow four floor house rang. It was my father. He had let Scamp out without a lead on and she had run off to look for me.

I was extremely worried and booked a flight to return to England. Scamp had been with me since my idyllic and cosseted childhood and then through all the rough days to now.

However, just before Alex was due to drive me to the airport, the phone rang again, and my father was able to announce that the police had found her dehydrated and exhausted. 1975 was an exceptionally hot summer in England.

She was now fine and when she went outside, he had attached her lead to a long washing line. Phew! Back to the holiday I thought.

I was wrong. A couple of days before I was due to fly home alone, leaving Marianne and Little H with her family, the phone rang again just after dinner and Alex and I raced down to answer it.

It was my father again; he was crying and clearly the worse for drink.

He had been to the Dog Inn, had a few vodkas with his mates, and on his way home had decided to test drive my XJ12.

He had pushed it to the limit on the new roads that were recently constructed in anticipation of the expansion of the Matchborough estate near Redditch.

He had lost control and had smashed it into a lamppost, which had been destroyed and, as you can imagine, the car was a virtual write-off.

However, it couldn't be as my father was not insured to drive the car and it was being paid for by me on finance.

I didn't shout or scream. Alex asked me why. I looked at him with a weary expression and announced that it wouldn't get the car fixed.

As I sat on the flight home alone, I felt that things were tough but that I could cope. But, then again, I had no idea what I might find out as more bad news crawled out of the woodwork. Perhaps, I hadn't seen anything yet!

The next morning, I arrived at the Oaklands Funeral Home at 8:30. I signed the purchase agreement which had already been signed by my father and was waiting for me on his old and my new desk along with a bank mandate.

This Life In Death

I was now the owner of Hodgson & Sons Ltd (est. 1850). My journey back from the horrors of my year of poverty and no hope seemed to be over for good. After all, I now owned the family business, was happily married and had a son.

In the last week, my beloved dog might have nearly been killed, my special Jaguar might lie in a smashed-up heap of scrap metal, and I had no money to have it repaired, but I now owned our family's version of 'Ewing Oil' and I would make a go of it.

This feeling of self-congratulatory euphoria was extremely short-lived. My father's secretary, a feisty but wonderful woman called Beryl Smith, entered my father's grand office, where I was now sitting behind his very 'Dallas' type big desk.

"The Midland Bank at Hockley want to see you" she announced with a troubled look.

"Why?" I asked.

"I don't know. But it is now!" she replied perhaps not quite telling me everything thing that she really knew.

I still lived in Manchester but had arrived from France into Birmingham Airport. So, I had to borrow an ill-fitting jacket and a car to comply with their order.

30 minutes later I was sitting in the manager's office. He looked like an angry man trying to resemble a very stern one.

"So, you are the young Mr Hodgson, are you?" he asked curtly.

"Indeed, am I Sir" was my polite reply – as in those days you always showed your elders the respect of calling him 'Sir.'

"Well Mr Hodgson, we have been trying to get your father to come into this branch for nine months. So now our patience is exhausted. We are going to foreclose on Hodgson & Sons today because we believe that you owe us more than the value of your assets that we hold and because you are making monthly trading losses. So, you have exhausted your security and have no ability to repay us."

Jesus Christ, I had given up a secure and extremely well-paid job, lost my car, the £14,000 paid for the business, and nearly lost my dog all for this!

Oh no. Oh no. No bloody way.

"Well, if you would just give me five minutes, I will explain how I plan to save all of us" I exclaimed in desperation and not really expecting him to listen, but what else could I do?

"Go ahead then" he said to my immense relief.

His face softened. He had got out of bed on the right side. He hadn't had an argument with his wife and the toast hadn't fallen marmalade side face down.

Perhaps, for once, God was going to be on my side. Perhaps fortune did favour the brave.

My five minutes request became a 45-minute monologue and then I left his office with a handshake and a £5,000 extension to the overdraft.

First crisis of the day, and a very major one, averted!

However, when I arrived back at the Oaklands, there were some new ones to deal with.

I got a call from my father's business partner in Barbados to tell me that yesterday their charter yacht had been lost at sea and would I deal with the Royal Bank of Canada who had a charge on it for the 90% mortgage taken out with them.

What! Shit, how could I possibly cover this huge $ debt. With the £5,000 overdraft extension I might just survive but not with this on top.

"You are his partner. You were skippering the boat at the time. Have you contacted the insurance company? It is insured, isn't it?" I said quite forcibly.

"Yes, it is and no I haven't yet."

"Well, you do that first and call me back."

I sat down to consider this latest ugly development when Beryl knocked on my door.

Was I aware of one or two things that had not come out in the due diligence as my solicitors had not asked the necessary questions.

"Like what?" I enquired quite tetchily as I could see a very bad day may be just about to get worse.

"Well, the Inland Revenue are very keen to see Mr Paul about his tax returns as he has been putting them off for some time."

"How long?"

"Five years."

"Five years! He owes tax for 1969/70?"

"Yes, and every year since."

"Jesus Christ!"

"And Michelle's Triumph Spitfire was purchased by Hodgson & Sons Ltd on finance and put through the books as a limousine. Oh, and we still have a company account at most big department stores for Michelle's use and a couple of credit cards."

"My father is self-employed, so we owe the Revenue nothing re him?"

"Correct."

"So, I'll ensure my father engages with his accountant and the Inland Revenue."

This Life In Death

"But he hasn't any money to pay them" pointed out a worried Beryl, who clearly liked my father.

"I'll cross that bridge when I come to it. As for the Spitfire, let the finance company know that Michelle has absconded to London with it and that we have cancelled the standing order for the monthly payments as it isn't her car and that we have reported it to the police as stolen. Tell them that they should reclaim the car as we can't sell it if we don't know where it is. And then cancel every single bloody charge account and credit card today," I said with increasing conviction that I was going to win come hell or high water.

"Then please send each member of staff to see me one at a time" I added as she left.

She turned, smiled back at me and said, "It feels good to have someone at the helm again."

I liked her then and that was never misplaced over the coming years.

Each staff member came to see me, except for my father's assistant manager, who was on holiday at the time.

There was now no one left on the staff that was there when I left five years previously.

These new employees were clearly not of the same quality. Their appearance was not up to Hodgson standards as I remembered them and while their manner was polite enough, they appeared to me to be a poorly led and dispirited little army.

I told them exactly what I had told the Midland Bank. They listened. However, I wasn't at all sure they believed me.

As the King was to say to me on many occasions years later "Seeing is believing." I knew that they would come to believe me in time.

However, I might not get time and I needed an immediate turn around in attitude and energy now.

This Life In Death

I was in luck. The embalmer was not at work. He had gone home. "Why?" I enquired. "Because there were no bodies to embalm," I was told.

I seized on the opportunity and sent for him. He was ordered back to work and eventually swaggered into my office with a slight little smirk on his face.

I asked him why he had gone home. He replied that there was nothing for him to do. He added that Mr Paul knew and didn't mind.

I knew that Mr Paul didn't know and that even in his current sorry state would have minded.

I did not like this guy. I could see that he not only had a bad attitude but that I would never mould the others into a team with him about.

Employment legislation was very different in 1975 to how it is in the UK now.

"OK", I said very calmly. "I'm going to do you a favour. You won't like working here anymore. So, I have decided to let you go."

"What? Are yow firing me?" he asked as his camp accent fell away to expose a Brummie replacement.

"Indeed, I am."

"Yow can't do that" he exclaimed indignantly.

"I just did. Good afternoon."

He left my office. After a few minutes I went down to the yard to inspect the garage, vehicles, mortuary, coffin fitting shop and coffin store.

The camp embalmer had left but not before he had entered the garage to announce that "the bastard has fucking sacked me."

It had had the desired effect. Every chauffeur bearer was hard at work waxing the fleet. I might have only arrived that morning, but I

This Life In Death

was now definitely master of this ship, and I was going to steer her away from the rocks and the crew already knew it.

The fleet consisted of one Rolls Royce Phantom III hearse, two Coleman Milne Ford limousines, a Humber Super Snipe hearse and a Ford Transit private ambulance.

The hearses and limousines were not in too bad a condition and would look good enough once I had re-introduced proper, washing, waxing and tyre blacking procedures.

However, the ambulance was in a very poor state. The sills were rusted through and patched up with mis-spelt metal coffin plates welded on to them.

The actual garage needed tidying as it was cluttered with the drivers' personal cars and various belongings.

I ordered all private vehicles out – and never to return. Moreover, I told everyone that anything that did not belong to the company must be removed at 5pm.

Everyone nodded in eager agreement. This was 1975 and at the height of Harold Wilson, Barbara Castle, Tony Benn, Denis Healey, et al, as part of the worst British government ever, destroying the country's economy with galloping inflation running at over 40% and unemployment rising.

The was already a clear uplift in morale and attitude. Everyone was keen to help and follow the new leader, rather than try and find another job.

I went from the garage to the mortuary, taking the garage foreman with me. The recently departed camp embalmer had lied. There were indeed four bodies to embalm in the fridges.

But at least the fridges were surprisingly working well enough, thank goodness in that heat, and by applying a little professional pride this whole area would scrub up to a decent standard.

149

This Life In Death

Next, we went to the coffin store. It was nearly bereft of any coffins. I looked in disbelief and asked where the coffins were.

"We have to go to Shenstone to collect them. We are allowed to collect a dozen as long as we pay for them and £50 off the old debt" obliged the foreman.

Christ this was not good news. In the Oaklands, there was a selection room where families would select a coffin or casket that they thought would be suitable and at a price to meet their budget.

There were ten selections available. Therefore, to meet clients' selections, we would have to drive the 20 or so miles several times a week, armed, on each occasion, with a cheque for what we needed and an additional £50 to pay off the old debt which was around £1,000. This was a huge sum in 1975.

My God could things get worse? Oh yes, they could.

I returned to my office, to do the garage orders for the following day's funerals – which I would conduct in my top hat and tails which had been mothballed in my old office for some five years but remained in excellent condition. Indeed, the tails were never even replaced over the next decade.

Next, I buzzed Beryl and asked her to come into my office. I told her I needed a daily notification of the debtor/creditor/bank position so I could judge how much we could pay out to the creditors.

I also wanted a detailed list of the debtors and creditors so I could see how much money we needed to collect, from whom and who should have priority in getting that cash.

Tight monetary control would be essential, if we were going to survive.

Beryl said I would have it all first thing in the morning. Then she asked if I was going to spend the night with my father. I replied that I was.

This Life In Death

She looked a little nervous and said she thought she ought to point out that he had had an unfortunate incident concerning the police while I was in France.

"The police?" Shit this day could not get any worse, could it?

She explained that my father had thought that he had seen a lion or a puma in the Woodland's garden while returning late one night from the Dog Inn.

He had rushed inside the house and returned with his shot gun and started firing - even though he could no longer see the beast.

In the process he had shot his own telephone wires down and alerted his distant rural neighbours to the fact a gun battle was taking place somewhere in the dark.

They had called the police. There was a bank robber, who had shot and killed a policeman in a bank robbery down south and was reported to now be somewhere in the Midlands.

The police had reacted by sending armed officers out from both Alcester and Birmingham. They had been deployed in the muddy ditch which ran alongside the Alcester Road which was adjacent to the Woodlands.

They made their way cautiously towards the gunfire from both directions.

Eventually, they burst into the ample Woodland gardens to find my father re-loading under a lamp at the side of the garage block.

As anyone could imagine they were not pleased. They then asked to see his licence for the shotgun. He had fetched it only for the officer, with all the spaghetti on his cap and pips on his shoulders, to explode as it was out of date.

My father then tried to explain that he was only trying to protect the community and that in 1942 he had won the 'Country Life Rapid Fire Award' as a schoolboy at Harrow.

This Life In Death

The furious policeman was not impressed. He had told my father that he was very lucky not to be arrested there and then but he would be facing prosecution for using a firearm without a current licence.

I looked at Beryl in complete disbelief.

Next my phone went, it was Marianne. Beryl left my office. However, before I could explain the terrible news that had been hitting me in waves all day; she announced that she had decided to remain in France as she didn't think living in the Woodlands, with my father, in the countryside and on only £63-a-week was a good idea. What's more, as Little H was so young, he would be staying with his mother. She didn't want to discuss the matter.

I explained that I couldn't force her to come but that I would not be giving up my son.

She put the phone down and now I felt like weeping. However, that British Empire upbringing ensured that I held it all in as Beryl came back in so I could sign a cheque to Olof Johnson, the ruddy coffin manufacturer out at Shenstone, who had us by the short and curlies.

I borrowed a limousine to travel the 18 or so miles out towards Studley in Warwickshire and the Woodlands in the then rural Mapleborough Green.

It was a beautifully warm summer's evening in late August, but I hardly noticed it as my mind kept drifting back to the day's events.

When I arrived, a shifty looking man, whom I instantly was suspicious of, opened the front door. Behind him was a fat, grubby looking woman hoovering the hall rug and polished wooden floor.

I entered to discover a third man hoovering the dining room.

I went into the drawing room. My father was sitting on a settee with his head in his hands. He was clearly in the middle of a serious nervous breakdown.

This Life In Death

The room was stuffy. All the windows were closed. It was very hot. There were at least 200 dead flies on the front bay windowsill. There were perhaps as many again on the sills of the other window.

The shifty looking man came in and announced they had finished cleaning and that my father owed them 3 hours x 3 people x £2-an-hour equalled £18.

That was a week's wages for one person then and clearly, they had done a very poor job and were ripping the 'Old Man' off.

I told the guy that there would be no money paid until every dead fly in the house had been removed.

They obliged and tried to claim another half hour each as a result. I informed them that they should have dusted the sills anyway; that they would not be paid a penny more and nor would we require them going forward.

"Well, there's fucking gratitude for you" announced the guy who reminded me of Uriah Heap.

"And who are you to fucking tell us", added the other equally dislikeable guy.

"I am the owner. Now get out before I call the police" I answered.

"You fucking stuck-up bastard" was the parting shot from the fat grubby woman, who looked as if her sagging braless 50-inch chest hadn't been exposed to a shower for some time and her lingering presence in the air in the hall suggested that my observation was not wrong.

I returned to the drawing room and opened all the windows. My father burst into tears. I asked him what was wrong. He replied everything was going wrong and that now his Dupont lighter would not work.

I sat next to him and hugged him, just as he had me on the road in Switzerland 11 years before at my moment of despair. He had not forsaken me then and I was not going to forsake him now.

This Life In Death

It had been a challenging day.

I awoke early, showered, shaved and dressed ready for my first operational day.

Upon my early arrival at the Oaklands, I took the borrowed limousine to the garage and waited for the drivers to arrive. All bar one arrived punctually and looked a lot smarter than the previous day.

It was a pleasant sunny morning and the limousine looked fine too as it had been waxed the previous evening.

Nevertheless, I asked them to watch me wash it and prepare it. I explained that all vehicles must be 100% prepared after the last funeral of the day and covered so that they were ready to go the next morning in any event and at all times of the year and however wet and cold we were.

I told them that they must follow the procedure that I was going to demonstrate of spray; soapy sponge from the roof down – leaving the wheels and tyres until last; spray again; leather; look for water marks; wipe and leather inside windows; panel dividing windows; and the entry chrome strips (where the manufacturer displays their name); take out and hoover interior well rugs; black the now dry tyres and cover.

In the morning, they were to remove the covers and dust the body work.

In between funerals we should wash again if necessary and if we had time to do so.

In the winter, when we might have seven services a day and so no time, we must always do the interior windows and rugs as mourners deserved to expect clean interiors even if theirs was the last funeral on a snowy and muddy day.

I explained all of this as I demonstrated it. The whole exercise only took me thirty minutes and the limousine looked brilliant.

This Life In Death

They looked shocked. This boss knew his stuff and could do their job better than them.

I allocated a vehicle to each chauffeur/bearer present and told them it was their personal responsibility to look after it.

I added that this was the 'Hodgson way', that it was part of a total procedure of ensuring that we arranged and conducted the best funerals in Birmingham. This is what we had always done until recently, and this is what we were going to do again.

There seemed to be a good response to this message and all present looked motivated as they busied themselves in preparation for the first funeral of the day – all that is but for the absentee and I knew where he was.

In all the mayhem of yesterday, I neglected to tell you that I had also inherited another responsibility when I acquired Hodgson & Sons Ltd – my 19-year-old brother Russell.

He had been totally neglected since being expelled from Malvern College. My mother had been in South Africa; my father was now in no state to look after himself let alone my brother; my sister had gone to live in New Zealand; and Michelle had never made the slightest effort to feed him, wash his clothes or even have his bedroom cleaned.

Russell had been allowed to run wild as an undisciplined youth, who had made no use of his considerable intellect, and had ended up working as a driver for Hodgson & Sons Ltd while sleeping on a camp bed in my old office at the Oaklands.

And that is where I found him. He was told that he was to set a good example to the others going forward. I had always adored my brother since his birth, but he could not be allowed to disrupt the planned recovery of our family business.

Having read the riot act to my half-asleep brother, who clearly did not like the sound of the new regime, I went to my new office and changed into my tailcoat. As I did the phone went and I was told that Marianne was on the line. I held my breath as I waited for her to be connected.

She sounded very remorseful. Her mother, the Saint Raymonde, had told her that her place was with her husband and that she could not stay in Pertuis with them.

She would be taking the plane tomorrow with Howie as agreed. I only showed a polite acceptance as I was still displeased by the extra stress her telephone call yesterday had caused me. Nevertheless, I was very relieved and delighted.

Next, I went downstairs to the front where the hearse and two limousines were waiting in an acceptable state with chauffeurs all as smartly dressed as possible, given the age of their livery and caps. They had now been joined by Russell, who didn't look too bad either.

I removed the ID ticket from the left head coffin handle and had Larry, the hearse driver, read the plate out to me. The two pieces of information told me that I had the right body, in the right type of coffin, going to the right address, at the right time, with the right number of limousines.

It also confirmed that the deceased was an Anglican and that a rota minister would be taking his funeral service at Perry Barr Crematorium half an hour after we were due at the house.

I then explained that we would be re-introducing the 'Hodgson way' of conducting a funeral.

We would be leading with the limousines on the way to the house with the hearse in the rear. This was so people in the street could see that we were on our way to a funeral and not an active funeral cortege.

Then as we came into the road of the family, we would slow and call the hearse through.

This Life In Death

Once at the address, I would contact the main mourner and establish which family flowers were to be placed on the coffin, with other wreaths going in the hearse and cut flowers wired on the hearse roof.

The chauffeurs would see to this and then return to their vehicles while I went inside to take the names of the mourners who would be travelling in the limousines and then get everyone into one room so I could explain to them the procedure.

This would put me in control of proceedings and would ensure 'a state funeral occasion' that would be seen by the masses in the street, rather than the disorganised affair dished up by our competitors.

Then I would return to the front door and nod. This was a signal for the hearse driver to move forward by the number of limousine places on the funeral and then return to open the first limousine's door as I led the first six mourners from the house.

Once that limousine was loaded, it would move forward slowly to be behind the hearse. I would return and read out the names of the family members in the second limousine and they would follow me as that car pulled into place outside the front door.

At the same time folk following in their own private cars would take up their position.

I would then inform any ladies remaining at home when we would be returning, in case they wished to put the kettle on for the family or, if no one was staying at home, I would ensure that someone had a key to get back in on their return.

Then I would thank the multitude standing outside on behalf of the family and inform them where the service would be taking place, in case they wished to attend.

Now we were all ready to go, I would place myself in front of the whole cortege and walk the funeral procession off down the street.

This Life In Death

In a working-class area, this would be as far as time would allow.

I would then step towards the kerb, slow my pace and slide into the front passenger seat of the hearse without it stopping.

I assured my chauffeur audience that this Royal Family funeral precision would be received as a mark of respect to the deceased and something they were only likely to get at Hodgsons.

I could now see from their motivated expressions that, apart from Russell, the rest were buying into this.

We had two funerals that day and both went off just as I had asked them to. I was absolutely delighted.

We had a mountain of creditors to pay. We had a mountain of debt to collect too. We had virtually no cash facility and we really needed new caps and livery to reflect the new staff attitude.

Moreover, we would need a new fleet before too long. We needed a new ambulance now and the Oaklands roof, with its seven peaks and surrounding valleys was leaking like HMS Hood.

So, Everest still had to be climbed.

However, I knew that I was already starting to win because we were already pulling together with a purpose.

I might not yet have the best footballers, they might not have the best kit, our stadium might be in need of repair, and we might be close to bankruptcy, but now they were my players and if they were loyal to me, I would be to them and together we had a chance.

A better day!

Marianne returned with Little H as planned and on her first morning answered the front door to the postman who enquired who she was.

"Mrs Hodgson" she replied.

This Life In Death

"Blimey, they are getting younger" he commented, having assumed she had replaced Michelle as my father's third wife.

I managed somehow to keep the peace at the Woodlands over the coming autumn months with more help from a patient Marianne than my father, who while appearing to recover on one day, could slip back into a depression or a drunken stupor without warning the next.

In October, tragedy struck. It was a Friday evening and I arrived home at about 21:00 hours having worked late on the debtors list.

I was driving my father's XJ6 – as my XJ12 was still being repaired and I was paying the garage owner off at £50-a-month on a massive £1,200 bill. This was due to go on for nearly two years as things stood but was hardly a big concern considering everything else that was going on.

As I drove into the car port, I felt the slightest of bumps. I thought I might have run over one of Howie's toys. I nearly didn't bother to look but decided to.

It was not a toy. It was Scamp. Marianne had let her out to welcome me as she was so proud of herself having been to the clippers that day and was looking great despite being now 17 years old. I didn't know she was there.

She was still struggling to get up despite her crushed head. I raced inside and grabbed by father's shot gun. But when I returned, she was dead.

My only connection with my idyllic childhood, my best friend through all the bad times was dead and I had killed her.

I am crying now as I write this as I can afford to. Indeed, I have been dreading coming to this part of my saga and have even debated whether I could bear to include it.

However, then I did not weep. I had to show my father, Marianne and Little H an example. So, I buried her in her blanket with her favourite chocolate and held my tears back. I had to keep going.

The next day I drove to Shrewsbury and bought a beautiful poodle bitch puppy for then the expensive price of £25. She was jet black and only eight weeks old. She was a beautiful, loving and happy little dog but for me she could never quite replace my most reliable and dearest friend of my youth. In fairness, it was too much of an ask for any dog or perhaps even person.

Marianne wanted to call her Grace. I vetoed this as you might expect, so we settled on Kelly instead.

As autumn turned into December and winter we were still surviving. We were keeping our creditors happy – just. We were collecting current funeral accounts orderly and making a dent in the mountain of old accounts.

Most people would usually pay up if I visited them to see why the account hadn't been settled – especially if I went to see them in the Rolls Royce hearse, which I did if a second visit was required. This less than subtle sign told the neighbours that they hadn't paid their funeral account.

The only real trouble I had was with a Hindu gentleman who had a grocer's shop on the other side of Birmingham in Longbridge, near to the old Austin factory.

I had been to see him on three previous occasions to hear broken promises. I timed my fourth visit when I hoped the shop would be full.

It was. He was busy and didn't want to talk about the outstanding account, although he acknowledged that the debt should be settled and would be.

I whispered that either he pays the £167 now or I would distribute £200 plus worth of food from his shelves to his clientele in the shop as I had no longer anything to lose.

This Life In Death

He banged open the till in an angry fashion and settled the account in cash and I gratefully smiled and gave him a receipt.

He was to use Hodgson & Sons again many times over the years and always paid in advance.

We were now very good at arranging and conducting wonderfully stage-managed funerals of any size or variety.

We were treating people from every race, colour, sex or religion as royalty. Our service was respectful, polite, considerate and above all efficient.

Slowly, and with some great word of mouth recommendations from the Anglican clergy, non-conformist ministers and Catholic and Sikh priests, all of whom were never offered incentives, and some nursing home matrons who often were, our weekly funeral numbers started to rise.

We were still having to collect our coffins from Olof Johnson at a dozen at a time and pay cash for them while reducing the old debt, but even that was coming down.

Indeed, the debtor/creditor bank position was improving and although we were by no means out of the woods, things were getting a little better all the time.

The Barbadian yacht's insurance company settled the claim in full and this paid off the Royal Bank of Canada. The problem with Michelle's Spitfire had been resolved and there was no longer the strain on the business that unproductive people like Michelle had created.

We were not yet able to invest in new livery, vehicles or the Oaklands roof but we were keeping the Midland Bank at Hockley happy, and I was being forced into awkward conversations with creditors less and less.

However, not before I had one with Avril Webb of S Webb, funeral directors of Wednesbury – a town just past West Bromwich on the west side of Birmingham.

We hired additional limousines when needed off S Webb. Avril was a very amusing buxom blonde. She called me one day to enquire where her cheque was. I told her it was in the post.

"That is the worst kept promise after I won't come in your mouth" she replied.

"What?"

"You heard. If you can't keep the second, we will have to see about the first", she laughed.

However, I was telling the truth, and the cheque arrived the next morning.

With crisis management under control, I started to make changes that I knew we could afford mainly because they cost little to nothing.

Having instigated a proper chapel check when I took over to ensure that we had the right body in the right coffin, in the right chapel, with the correct spelling of the names, and the correct age and date of death on the breast plate etc, I set about re-designing the 'flow' of the main Oaklands building.

I kicked Russell out of my old office, got it decorated by the caretaker over a weekend and changed it into an arrangement room.

Next to it was a large room that served as a family lounge for families who had services in the Oaklands large service chapel.

I brought the selection room, where people making funeral arrangements would select a coffin or casket, from downstairs up to be next to the new arrangement room and relocated the family lounge next to the service chapel, where the selection room had previously been. Very logical.

This Life In Death

The old arrangement room was then turned into an extra private viewing chapel, which gave me six in total. I decided to have one of these dedicated to Roman Catholic use and asked Father Fallon from St Francis's, the Roman Catholic church in Hockley to bless it.

He duly did and left me a small bottle of holy water on the altar for families to sprinkle on the coffin when paying their last respects.

"Father when it is empty do I come to the presbytery to get some more holy water?" I enquired.

"Be Jesus, no. Fill it up from the tap before the level drops beneath the crucifix on the bottle and give it a good shake and then it will all be holy water", was his reply.

Father Fallon was a large Irish priest who liked a drop of Irish whiskey and was a monumental character in his own right.

Over the coming years, I got to know and like him. However, he was not always easy to work with on funerals.

On one occasion, following a 7:00am mass, which had seen me up at 4:30am that morning, the cortege of a floral hearse, hearse and five limos was re-loaded and ready to leave St Francis's to make the trip across Birmingham to Lodge Hill Cemetery for the graveside committal service. But where was Father Fallon?

We had not seated him in the front of the lead limousine. He was not in the vestry nor the church. Where could he be? I had one eye on the time and the other on my mourners sat in the five limousines and the scores of private cars.

I asked the Polish ladies, who were arranging altar flowers, and whom he treated appallingly, where he might be. They nodded nervously towards the presbytery.

I went and was let in by a rather embarrassed housekeeper who showed me into the dining room. There was Father Fallon, tucking happily and quite unashamedly into bacon, sausages and three fried eggs without a thought for the hundred or so folk waiting or the fact that I had several following funerals to conduct.

On another occasion, we had set off on the same journey but without any breakfast delay. We were nearly there when the lead limousine informed me in the hearse, via the two-way radio telephone link – which came via the Oaklands - that Father Fallon had forgotten the holy water and his RC committal service book.

I paused the cortege at the lodge house by the entrance gate and where there were some public toilets.

There I found a cup and scooped some water out of a toilet as neither of the sink taps worked. I also collected a rhododendron twig with leaves and went back to the hearse.

Upon our arrival at the graveside, I passed both, along with a King James Anglican committal service order, which I kept in the hearse, to him secretly.

The committal proceeded with a mixture of a few Hail Marys, a little improvisation, a lot of protestant wording and all baptised with holy water straight out of the toilet which was sprinkled into the grave out of the cup by rhododendron leaves.

Nevertheless, Father Fallon carried it all off with great aplomb and in those days no self-respecting Roman Catholic would ever consider questioning a priest – Heaven forbade such behaviour.

Business was increasing apace as our regimental style of funerals and impeccable standards of service were helped by the fact that I was only twenty-five, had a slight resemblance to Robert Redford and was not sixty-five, with a beer belly and an ulcerated alcoholic nose like many of my competitors.

We finished 1975 on 400 funerals. This was down from 1,200 in 1960 before slum demolition hit the business and the bottle hit my father. But we had survived – albeit only just.

This Life In Death

In 1976 Hodgson & Sons was to conduct 600 funerals on its own account and I was able to afford roof repairs, order a new Ford Transit ambulance, two new Coleman Milne Ford limousines - all on finance, and I was also able to reclaim my XJ 12, which was now as good as new.

Moreover, I had finally paid off Olof Johnson, I could move to a coffin supplier where I could get credit terms.

However, I did not increase my £63-a-week pay packet – much to Marianne's annoyance.

Instead, I decided to speed up this recovery by making an acquisition. Initially, I had no takers to my advances, but then a funeral director from the Black Country took the bait.

His name was Hadley. He owned his own business out by Rowley Regis, as I recall, and a second in West Bromwich called Crowther Brothers. It was the latter he wanted to sell, and we agreed a price of £11,000 for a business conducting some 130 funerals per annum.

I insisted on doing my own due diligence much to his surprise. I quickly discovered that the vehicles were worthless. They were 1950s Austin Princesses with manual column gear changes and most of these gear levers came off in your hand.

So, no vehicles were to be included in the sale and the price dropped to £9,500. Then I wanted to see every one of the 130 funeral accounts for last year.

These were duly supplied. However, Mr. Hadley must have thought that I had just got off the last ship to dock in Liverpool from the US.

I saw immediately what I was looking for – where these funerals had come from. Some 90 came from the West Bromwich area and the rest from the Rowley area.

Yes – you got it, he was attempting to sell me funeral numbers from the business he was keeping.

Now I had a problem. Tell him what I knew and risk him calling off the deal or paying him for funeral numbers that I was not going to get.

I decided on a third way. I told him that I would pay him £6,000 now and £3,500 on the first anniversary of the sale. He accepted.

I took copies of the invoices and after the deal was done confronted him with the evidence. Initially, he denied that they were Hadley clients. So, I proposed that we visit them to ask them. He conceded that they were and so we agreed that the £3,500 was no longer owed.

As the Hodgson numbers were growing, I decided to strengthen the Oaklands team.

Stuart Scott, my father's old assistant manager was to remain as embalmer and my number two. As Russell had left to return to college, I needed a new chauffeur/bearer, while Beryl now needed some help with arrangements and the administration thereof as she needed to concentrate on the accounts – due to the increased activity of the business.

I went to the old NWM office in Digbeth and recruited John Taylor You will recall that he was my first manager at Tri-Star Investments some six years before.

I gave John his own office next to Beryl's and mine, where he would administer the funeral arrangements he had made in the new arrangement room next to the new selection room.

I could only afford to offer him £35-a-week, but this could be topped up by a generous commission on coffin or casket sales.

Therefore, he was quick to realise where this potential additional income would come from. He had been given strict instructions that he was not to sell coffins but allow families to select one of their choice in line with their budget.

This Life In Death

As a result, his commission income relied on the clients' choice and soon he could, with a high degree of accuracy, pinpoint what coffin was to be selected by the sort of car that pulled onto the Oaklands forecourt.

If it was a Jaguar, it was likely to be a well-off family from Edgbaston or Handsworth Wood who wished to save their money and hide their grief. Therefore, the coffin selected would be the cheapest – usually with the words, "Well, it's only going to be burnt isn't it?" Most of these people already had a second house, car, wife and mortgage and so needed to save their inheritance. They had the money but did not want to spend it.

If it was a battered old Austin or Morris, it was likely to be a family from somewhere like Aston or Smethwick who wanted to put on a show for the rest of the street to demonstrate both their grief and that they had money to spend when they didn't. This would usually result in them selecting a much more expensive solid oak double raised lid – even if it was to be cremated.

But it was always the powder blue Ford Zephyrs, complete with zebra skin cushions on the back shelf which delighted him the most. Such cars were owned by Afro-Caribbean families, and this meant they would select a casket and JT, as I Christened him, knew that this meant an extra £7.50 in his wage packet on Friday.

In his book, 'Undertaking in the Fast Lane', Timothy Penrose's description of JT is both unfair and inaccurate. JT was, along with Beryl Smith, to provide immense effort, loyal help and vital support which enabled me to transform Hodgson & Sons Ltd over the next decade.

As soon as I bought Crowther Bros, I recruited his wife, Joan, to run it as a branch office operation, moved the office to West Bromwich High Street and the funerals went up to 175 per annum immediately.

This Life In Death

Although just a branch office, we retained the name and had hearse and limousine plates made so that we could replace the 'Hodgson' nameplates with them when conducting a Crowther funeral.

Hodgson & Sons now had the Oaklands Funeral Home, Lozells and Erdington branch offices and one for Crowther Bros in West Bromwich.

In 1977 funeral numbers grew to over 800 per annum and so double the 400 that we had finished 1975 on but all conducted with the same number of staff and vehicles.

Then I decided, at least a decade before anyone else in the industry would, to take disbursements in advance.

There were four reasons behind my thinking: firstly, if an account was not paid, we would lose not just our fees but the disbursements too. These amounts payable for the cremation or burial; doctors' fees (in the case of a cremation); the clergy fees; obituary notices and flowers etc. amounted to circa 33% of any funeral account and had to be settled by us irrespective of whether we had been paid or not.

Secondly, by collecting them in advance we not only avoided this risk, but we were able to demonstrate to the client that that a large part of the account did not go into our coffers.

Thirdly, it improved total account payments as, by paying a good portion before the funeral, the client was not left with such a mountain to climb after it and so was less inclined to risk a county court judgement for non-payment.

Lastly, there was a considerable additional benefit to our cash flow.

All in all, this last addition to this area of the business meant that along with our confirmation letter of the arrangements and the price of the funeral before the funeral, plus the discount if our detailed account was settled within fourteen days after the funeral, and our minister's confirmation to ensure he couldn't wriggle if he failed to turn up, that matters were now as watertight as I could make them.

This Life In Death

Therefore, if we did and charged what we had written, we would not only be providing excellent standards of service and facility, but we would be protected from unfair and unjustified criticism too.

These were tiny baby steps to what was to lie ahead. However, they should never be underestimated because, as with a baby, such steps were the hardest and nothing else would have resulted without such steps being taken and with the fortitude and dedication that they were taken with.

At this time Hodgson & Sons Ltd was still a very small private business. However, the all-important foundations had been laid and would be replicated over and over again, as we expanded, in the future.

So, despite the great accolades that we were to receive and were then still a long way off, this was perhaps our finest hour.

1917, Robert Ward, perhaps of noble birth, serving in Egypt.

This Life In Death

1927, my mother with her grandmother.

My mother at 17 and growing up in World War II.

This Life In Death

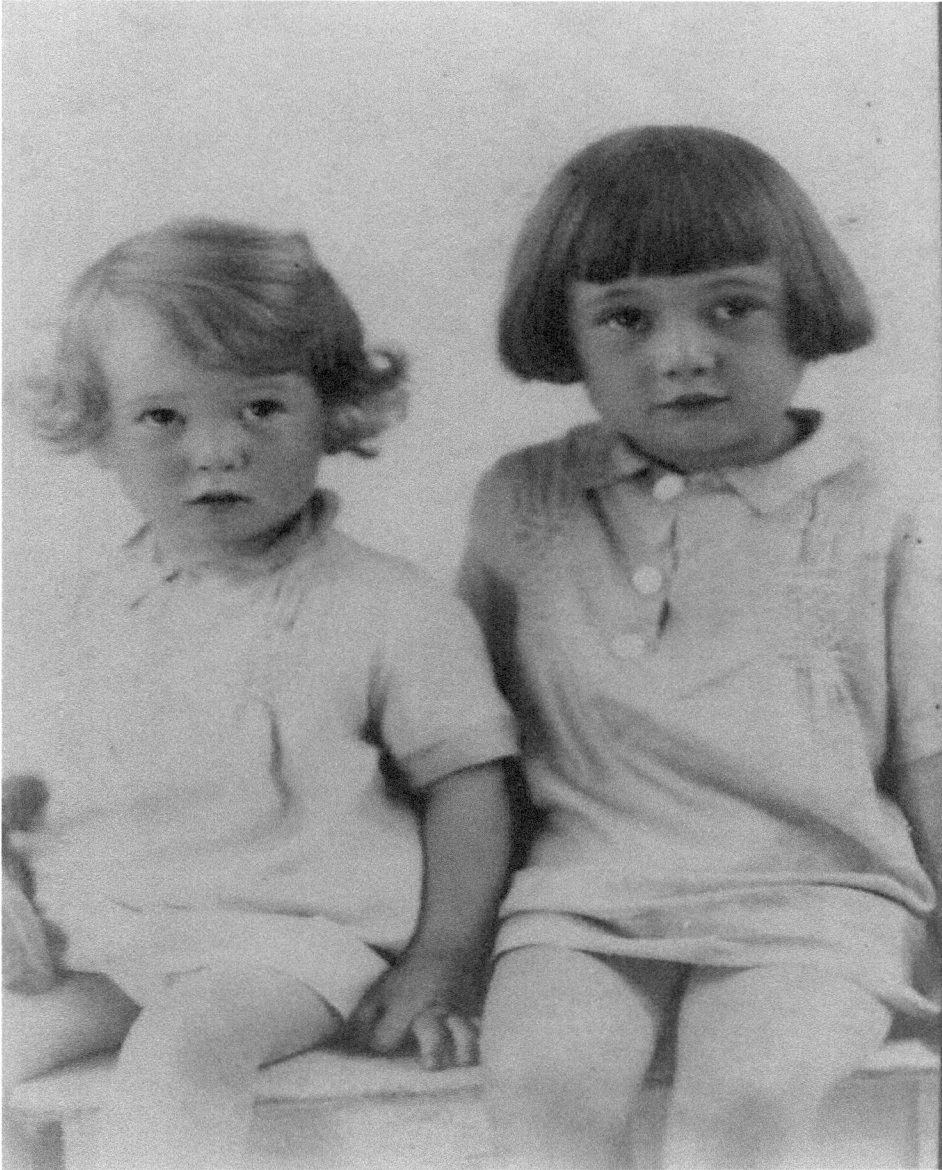

1927, my father with his sister June. He died at 58. She lived until she was well into her '90s.

This Life In Death

1949, my parents started 21 years of marriage. The first half was as blissful as the second half was traumatic.

This Life In Death

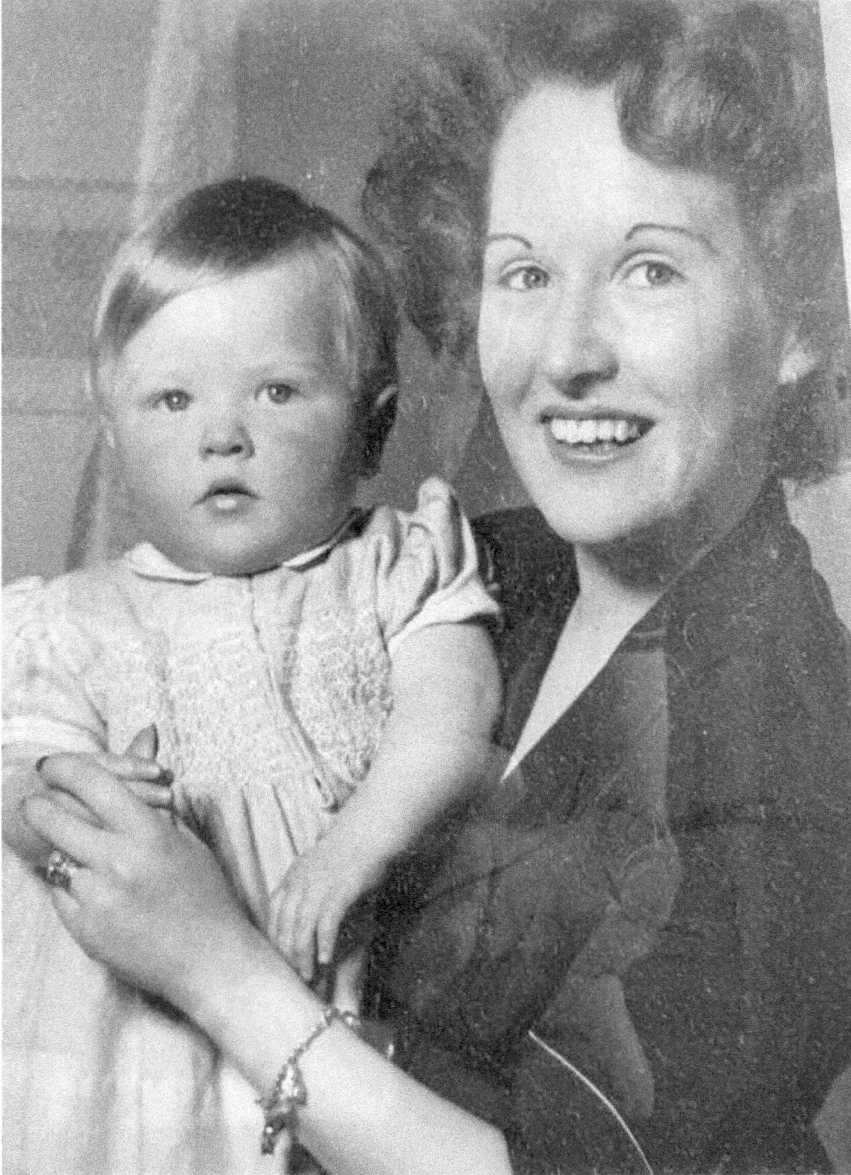

1951, My mother with her first born.

This Life In Death

July 1953, my father and me in Bournemouth. My father was patient and kind to his placid son.

The old Hockley office that I remember as a little boy. Families often queued up outside to make funeral arrangements during the winter flu epidemic.

This Life In Death

1954, I'm the one with the awful haircut.

This Life In Death

The Milky Bar Kid? No that's me.

The real Milky Bar Kid.

This Life In Death

1960, at home with my brother and my best friend Scamp.

1961, my sister and I at Sandbanks with sweet cigarettes. Hard to imagine those being given to children today.

1964, Aiglon 1st XI soccer. That's me in the back row, second from the left.

1972, 'Report Room' in N.W.M. Altrincham. John Firth (right) and I could spend 20 hours a day there sometimes.

This Life In Death

1975, I now own Hodgson. The topper and tails may be nineteenth century, but the shirt and tie are horribly '70s.

1979, and the dedication of Oaklands Funeral Home, The Bishop of Birmingham, who was sweet when in front of the camara, and a pain when not.

This Life In Death

1980. Our unique and much-loved son Charles. He is never far from my thoughts.

1981, France. A happy trio.

1982, Now only two of us – heartbroken and it shows.

This Life In Death

1982, A Sikh leader's funeral. I led 10,000 people on a six mile walk to the crematorium. It was only weeks after my son Charles's death.

This Life In Death

1983, Eden Wood, me on Macca.

This Life In Death

Graham Hodson (second left), John Taylor, Michael Hackney (far right), Sue Miskin and I pose outside the London Stock Exchange.

1986, Once inside and on the floor of the exchange, we know we have done it, and it shows on our faces. Hodgson Holdings plc was the last company to be floated on the floor of the exchange.

This Life In Death

1986, Business magazine's Top 40 under 40 ceremony with Richard Branson on the piano.

Barry Lewis's photograph in the Sunday Times magazine gets me noticed as does the 'Mr. Death' headline.

This Life In Death

1987, Now every photographer wants me to wear the trademark hat and coat-even inside.

1987, the Ingalls deal press conference.

1988, at St James's Palace being presented to Her Majesty.

1988, photograph taken for Maxwell's Daily Record, on the main lawn of 'Eden Wood'.

1989, The Savoy launch of 'Dignity in Destiny'. This was the subject of another TV programme about Hodgson Holdings plc.

1989, just after the really big deal.

1989, A six-year-old Jamieson with Marianne and me at Port Grimaud.

2024, me in Positano at the Il San Pietro Hotel. Older and hopefully a little wiser.

2024, having a drink with my 'brother Alex' by his pool.
If I'm 'Mr. Death' then he is 'Mr. Rent-a-car'.

This Life In Death

Chapter VI

Happiness & Destruction

(1977 – 1981)

Besides JT, I had three new additions to the cause.

Firstly, my father had decided to move out of the Woodlands, much to Marianne's relief; but to my great joy, also wanted to earn additional cash as a chauffeur bearer.

I made him hearse driver and my assistant conductor. He was a great addition and was much more responsible, loyal and talented than Russell had ever been. He might be older, less confident and not in the best of health, but he was so knowledgeable and completely embodied the Hodgson dedication to putting bereaved families first.

Secondly, we had a new full-time chauffeur. I can't sadly remember his name. However, I will never forget him. On his first funeral, I put him on the lead limousine so I could keep an eye on him and explain again what was expected on the way to the house.

I told him that he should memorise a landmark in the road so that I would be able to recognise the house on our return after the funeral. This was because we were in Kingstanding and all the houses, which had been built by the Birmingham City Council in the 1930s, looked the same as each other.

He nodded his understanding as I called the hearse through as we approached the house.

On our return, after the funeral, I whispered, as the family was in the back of the limousine, to ask if could see his landmark.

"No" he replied.

"What was it?" I asked so I might help him.

"A large black dog sitting outside the house" he replied.

This Life In Death

Unsurprisingly, he did not survive the week.

Thirdly, Howie joined me at work aged three. Marianne had taken up an appointment to be Head of French at my old prep school – West House. She was to become a brilliant teacher and no student ever failed their French common entrance exam as she literally terrified them towards successful results which would have the Woke Society screaming their disapproval today.

This meant we had nobody to look after Little H and so a play school was found on the City Rd in Birmingham.

I took him on the first morning and had to peel him off me to leave him as he screamed the place down. The lady assured me he would be fine, that this was quite normal and that tomorrow he would be happy to be left.

However, the next day's episode was the same as the previous day, I was leaving down the garden path and feeling very uncomfortable, when I heard a loud slap and the words, "Shut up you naughty boy."

I swivelled on my heels and ran back, plucked my son out of her arms with a "you're lucky that I don't hit you" and was gone.

As a result, Howie was brought up by 'Auntie Beryl' until it was time to go to West House aged four.

He became a mine of information and would tell me about any rows Stuart, Beryl, or John might be having while I was out conducting funerals.

He also used to line up his pedal cars at home, sit in the last and push the others forward. A visiting friend asked the three-year-old what he was doing.

"I'm playing funerals" was his reply. Good lad!

xxxxxxx

This Life In Death

January 1978 was cold and icy as usual. Nobody was listening vaguely to Prince Charles about the possibility of global warming then.

And, as usual, the death rate soared. One Monday evening at about 18:30, Keith, the Oaklands caretaker, who lived in an apartment in the funeral home with his partner Jenny and her young children, knocked on my door.

We needed to do a coroner's removal in Handsworth just off the Soho Road. The deceased was a large West Indian lady. The police were at the address, but both of our ambulances were still out with four staff and there was only him left – and he was supposed to be doing the viewing.

I asked him to ask Jenny to change her clothes and do the viewing and told him that he and I would take the Super Snipe hearse.

Luckily, one of the ambulances was still out on hospital removals which meant we had the luxury of being able to use its American stretcher that had wheeled legs which were collapsible as it entered the hearse deck.

Keith was a very skinny man. He needed to run around in the shower to get wet. Jenny was a very nice lady, but quite the opposite. Indeed, Marianne would often comment to me, in her very frank French way, that sex would only be possible if Keith was on top.

Therefore, Keith, although a dedicated and hard worker, would not be one's first choice to be your partner on a house removal to collect a large West Indian lady.

We arrived at the address. There was a policeman waiting. The street lighting was fine but as he showed us into the house by pointing his torch into a dark hall, I realised that there was no electricity supply in there.

"Where is the lady?" I enquired.

This Life In Death

"On the fourth floor I believe mate", replied the young officer.

"Aren't you certain? Haven't you been up there?" I asked.

"Not my job mate and I'm not going up there now either".

"Well can we borrow your torch then?" I enquired as we were in a hearse rather than an ambulance, which carried them.

"No, the torch stays with me" he snapped nervously.

Keith and I placed the American stretcher at the foot of the stairs and took the body bag, affectionately known to funeral staff as the cricket bag, upstairs with only the streetlight coming through the front windows to guide us.

We made our way with some difficulty up to the fourth floor and eventually found the lady on the floor of an unfurnished room with her naked body wrapped in an old British army coat.

The room was very dark but there was just enough light coming in from the hallway to make her out. I noticed what I thought was an enormous breast protruding from the coat. It wasn't, it was a huge tumour on her side.

How very terrible. This poor woman had died alone in an unheated, unlit, and unfurnished room.

Suddenly, Keith said in a shaky voice, "What are all of those red lights on the floor behind you?"

I turned round and moved a step towards them. They squeaked and started to move. They were rats.

We moved the lady carefully and with great difficulty towards the 'cricket bag.' We put the label on her toe and wrapped her in a clean white sheet, before securing the buckled straps.

We carefully edged back towards the steep staircase as the rats squeaked their disapproval that we were stealing their banquet.

This Life In Death

I was dreading the descent. It would have been very difficult with three strong men and well-lit stairs, but in the dark, with just two of you and one was Keith, the chances of getting down to the ground with the lady, Keith and me in one piece seemed very slim.

I knew Keith would be unable to hold on if he had the upper head end, so I determined that he should descend first with the foot end.

Each step gave birth to increased agony in my back and terrible pain in my fingers as I knew that come hell or high water that I must not stumble or let the 16 stone that I was holding go as this would send the lady tobogganing over Keith as she crashed to the bottom of that flight.

Nearly 40 minutes after we had ascended, we completed the descent. I was shattered and the base of my spine felt terrible. There should be little wonder that a decade later I was to lose two discs because of this kind of abuse. And there was no 'Health & Safety' in those days to forbid such activities.

And talking of 'Health & Safety', our helpful young policeman was waiting for us with his torch by the front door as we carefully placed the 'cricket bag' on the American stretcher before lifting it up so that the legs dropped down.

"You took your time then. I should have knocked off and been having my tea by now" he complained.

"Just fuck off", I growled through gritted teeth with by best Clint Eastwood impersonation.

I was furious but expected some trouble for my outburst. However, he said nothing but meekly closed the front door once we were through it and on our way back to the hearse.

I used this true story in my 2002 fictional book 'Exhumed Innocent', the sequel to the 1999 'Six Feet Under'. Both books were full of true stories woven into the fictional life of the hero Stillion Sloane. Writing about the experience of what really happened is so much more authentic than trying to invent it.

In the years from 1968 until 1971 and then again from 1975 until 1984, when I hung up my top hat from conducting daily so I could build 'the empire', I was to conduct several thousand funerals. 99.9% of these were to be perfect and led to the considerable growth of Hodgson funeral numbers.

They are all a hazy memory now. However, I can still remember in minute detail when anything went wrong. Difficulties often featured Stuart Scott.

Stuart was a very decent man and a great embalmer. However, he had a short fuse, would panic easily and could be become defeatist when you needed him to stand up and be counted.

He told me that I was asking too much when I wanted a fleet vehicle completely prepared from a muddy state inside and out in 45 minutes. I took my tailcoat off and did it in 41.

He told me he couldn't wheel the coffins through the snow across the yard and up into the Oaklands in time for viewing on his own – as the others were either on removals or washing the fleet. I came down from my office and in a fury pushed six up on my own in some fifteen minutes as he trotted behind telling me that he could have managed.

He backed one of my first two new limousines towards a lamp post, whereupon I instinctively put my left hand down to stop him damaging my pride and joy. The result was a broken little finger – which is still bent today.

He was driving the second limousine, when I was backing a hearse and three limousines into a cul-de-sac near Handsworth Cemetery. Having guided the third in, I stepped to the front of it to guide Stuart, I did it perfectly, but upon my signal to stop, he kept coming.

This Life In Death

He trapped me between the two limos. I tapped the boot. He panicked and slammed his boot down on the accelerator, motoring my knees about a foot into the boot of his limousine.

Luckily, this limousine was part of a second new fleet of Ford limousines and due to a combination of rolled over finance, very good exchange pricing with Coleman Milne, I bought three new models to replace the outgoing two that were only a year old.

Why luckily? This was because the bumper heights on these new models was different from the front to the back and so my legs buckled and my knees were able to take the strain rather than my legs being broken.

Nevertheless, I was in a great deal of pain and my temperature went through the roof with the shock. I remember walking towards the front door of the house and praying to God to prevent me from vomiting over the chief mourner when introducing myself.

We all carried on as if nothing had happened and we all believed we had got away with it as nothing was said even when I asked if everything had been conducted to the family's entire satisfaction upon our return to their home.

It was a typically busy Friday; it had been the first funeral of a cold winter's day and I continued to conduct five more funerals before returning to the Oaklands in the late afternoon.

As I hobbled up the stairs, JT asked me if my legs could be broken, before telling me that the family had phoned to ask if I was okay – as they had seen everything from their lounge window.

I went to the Birmingham Accident Hospital later that evening. It was nothing more than bad bruising. I was clearly made of tougher material than Ford cars. I even made it out to dinner that evening.

That was important as Marianne and I balanced this tough working life with a very full social life from Friday evening to a Sunday afternoon each weekend. I still remember these weekends, especially the Sunday lunches in the Cotswolds with the warmth associated with a loving family life.

xxxxxxx

1978 also saw me make my third acquisition to follow that of Hodgson and Crowther. This was A Hamer of Oldbury. Oldbury is a small Black Country town west of Birmingham and just south of West Bromwich.

It had been a reasonably sized firm but was now conducting only 50 funerals-a-year. However, it would be another addition to the cluster that all were run from the Oaklands hub. We now had five branch offices – as I had also opened a green field site in Witton next to Villa Park.

These additions and the strong growth of the Oaklands funeral numbers in general and with the Sikh and West Indian communities in particular meant that we surpassed the 1,000 funeral per annum mark in 1978, 250% up on just 3 years ago.

Now I could put my salary up and we moved to a new home in Harborne in Birmingham. I even bought a Rolls Royce, upon which I was able to claim 100% capital allowance, as a wedding limousine. However, when it wasn't being hired for a wedding, I was happy to drive it. Most importantly, and as a sign of better trading results, the Rolls was not bought on finance.

I was still running away from being poor, but I felt I had done enough to allow Marianne, Howie and me a few indulgences.

Arthur Hamer was a caricature of a 19th century undertaker. He was a little overweight, had a slightly ulcerated alcoholic nose, a receding hairline, thinning black hair which was greased back and greying at the temples.

This Life In Death

He was in a downward spiral of drinking which was causing business failure, which was causing more drowning of his sorrows in beer.

He wanted to sell badly but really had next to nothing to offer – no vehicles, a rented property, which although in a good position was in a poor state of repair and falling funeral numbers due to his fallen reputation.

I can't exactly remember what I offered him, but I seem to recall that it was £5,000. He accepted it and asked for a job.

I told him that he would hate Hodgson & Sons Ltd, we were perfectionists and that the partaking of alcohol, even when offered by grateful clients after a funeral, was absolutely forbidden during working hours.

He begged for a chance and promised not to let me down. I knew him from my days at Hartland & Son nearly a decade before. He was a rogue – but a very likeable one.

I granted his request. He was extremely grateful. Moreover, he was as good as his word, and worked through all weathers for Hodgson & Sons as number one hearse driver until he retired at over 65 nearly a decade later.

He struck up an immediate and lasting friendship with – yes you guessed – my father. They became inseparable and while they obeyed the no alcohol rule during the working day, they would delight in each other's company over a pint when the working day was done.

They had both seen better days, but equally they were now both enjoying life with a purpose and restored self-respect.

In the June, my father then decided that perhaps he deserved a little indulgence too. I jumped out of a limousine on the Oaklands forecourt and was about to dash upstairs to my office when a man stopped me in the reception with a bouquet of flowers. I enquired whose funeral the flowers were for.

This Life In Death

"No, Mr Hodgson they are for you and come with your new MGB Sports car."

"What? There must be some mistake" I replied in some confusion.

At that moment my father popped his head round the door into the hall and asked if he could have a private word with me. We went into the hall together, leaving the chap with the flowers behind.

"I ordered the car. I probably won't live too long, and it will be my last car", he said with a true ring of sincerity.

"You will live for years if I have anything to do with it" was my reply as I went back into the reception and accepted the flowers graciously.

That night after work, my father, with the hood down and Arthur in the passenger seat, accelerated into the Holyhead Rd to turn right up the hill and on the way to a little pub by the West Bromwich Albion ground.

I was watching from my office window as they went. An ageing rocker on a large motorbike was forced to brake and hit his horn. My father stuck two fingers into the air to indicate what he thought as he sped away.

The next day Arthur told me that the first set of lights up the hill were on red and the brand new MGB had to stop. The older rocker had pulled up alongside Arthur, who had pointed to my father as the culprit. However, the would be 'Hell's Angel' did not attack.

xxxxxxx

For at least two years I had been trying to persuade Marianne to have a second child. Initially, she was not keen as she had suffered so much giving birth to Howard.

This Life In Death

However, in 1978 she agreed and immediately fell pregnant. She was terribly sick and starving throughout and then in December fell over on some spilled petrol on a garage forecourt in Bristol Street and broke her leg when eight months pregnant.

I carried her upstairs to bed on the first evening. This is not to be recommended, as an eight-month pregnant woman with a leg in a very heavy plaster of paris cast was about as heavy as the West Indian lady that Keith and I had taken from that bleak place. It nearly killed me. So, I taught her to go up the stairs backwards on her bottom in future.

We spent Christmas in Dorset with my mother. We then returned to a very cold, icy and snow-covered Birmingham to deal with the expected huge rise in the death rate.

On the 10th of January 1979, having conducted seven funerals for the day, my father and were returning to my home on snow covered and icy roads.

I had invited him to stay the night with us as we had an early start the next morning, the weather was awful and his apartment was in Henley-in-Arden, some twenty miles to the south of the Oaklands.

We were in Bearwood, when a car overshot a halt sign in the appalling conditions, and rammed into the car we were in, which I remember was Marianne's, because it would drive in the snow. The Rolls was with Evans Halshaw for a service. They had lent me an Austin Marina to drive as a result. Unfortunately, this Marina would not drive in the snow.

The young lady driver of the out-of-control vehicle was very upset. So was I. Marianne's, car was very seriously damaged and had to be towed away.

My father and I walked the last quarter of a mile home to a fabulous beef bourguignon. We had worked late and by the time dinner was over it was nearly midnight. So, it was about 12:45 when I crawled into bed exhausted.

This Life In Death

I was drifting off into a well-deserved and much looked forward to sleep, when the light was back on, and Marianne was announcing that her waters had broken.

"No, you are imagining it" I replied hopefully.

"I'll call a taxi" she countered.

"You will do no such thing" I commanded as I dragged myself out of bed and got dressed.

We had nothing to drive but the Marina - a wonderful advert for the decline of the British mass-produced car made by a lazy union dominated workforce in Longbridge, Birmingham.

Their communist leader, one Red Robbo, was nationally famous for calling strikes and British Leyland cars were gaining a worldwide reputation for being the most unreliable made anywhere.

This was the 'winter of discontent' that would burst into the Thatcher spring revolution and a national fightback against unions, strikes, inflation and a growing international reputation for the being the 'sick man of Europe'.

But that was still a few months away, and for now, I was having to face a more immediate problem of getting my expectant wife to hospital in a car that would not work in the snow.

I managed somehow to get it down Lordswood Road and into Knightlow Rd. But then we had to go up a hill and we came to a standstill. We still had three miles to go to get the Queen Elizabeth II Hospital in Selly Oak.

Marianne, quite rightly, looked very worried. I put the car into reverse to have another attempt. It seemed to work quite well in reverse. So, I managed to turn it round in someone's driveway and we made it up the hill and beyond and all the way to the hospital in reverse gear.

This Life In Death

We dashed into the hospital, where the staff acted very swiftly to get her into a delivery ward where she joined some six or so other ladies who were all closed off by green curtained screens.

Things had moved on a lot in the five years since Howard was born in Manchester. Firstly, she was offered and happily accepted an epidural injection to ensure a painless birth. Secondly, a nurse wired her up to a machine to monitor the baby's heartbeat.

Neither of these things had been available in December 1973 but were now in January 1979.

The nurse then asked Marianne what sex she would like the baby to be, as despite the above-mentioned improvements, scans were not yet available, and nobody knew the sex of a baby until the birth happened.

Marianne replied that she would like a little girl. I already knew this and had kept my preference to myself over the nine months. I wanted a second son as I didn't believe I would be able to talk her into having a third child. But I had decided that Marianne's wish should have priority as she had gone through another pregnancy to please me.

In the end I was to have six children over a 32-year-period – five boys and one girl. My daughter is very precious to me and just as loved as my five sons. However, back in 1979 I was secretly hoping that we would have another little Aston Villa supporter and Beatle fan and somehow couldn't get my head around the idea that this could be a girl.

The nurse told her that she was having a little girl. I couldn't help myself and blurted out the obvious question.

"How do you know?"

"I can tell by the heartbeat" she replied with a smile as she left the cubicle.

I was up and off and went into all the other cubicles.

This Life In Death

"Please excuse me" I said to each of the ladies who were in various states of undress and labour.

One was in the stirrups about to give birth with two nurses in attendance.

"What are you doing?" asked one.

"Just looking at the heartbeat" I replied and beat a hasty retreat.

I went back to Marianne and told her not to be 100% certain of having a girl.

"It's all bollocks or all of you are having girls" was Doctor Hodgson's new-found medical advice.

Mr Day, the private gynaecologist, duly arrived and this delivery was relatively swift, easy and painless compared to that of Howard.

The baby's head appeared, at around 6:45 in the morning I think, and I thought any second we will know the sex. Then in a flash there was the cord and then, I couldn't be certain or was I imagining it, was there also a fairly large willie there too?

I hadn't imagined it. Charles Alexandre Howard Hodgson had made his entrance. Marianne might have wanted a girl a second earlier, but she was now besotted with her new son and so was I.

I left mother and son because I had to go to work. I went back to Lordswood Rd, with some difficulty in the Marina, had a shower and dressed for the next seven funerals. I hadn't had any sleep, but at only 28 I could deal with it.

I arrived at the Oaklands, for Angus, Keith's replacement, to congratulate me on the birth of Charles and then add that he had more good news – we had had five house removals overnight.

I was shattered but had to smile to myself as I considered that only at the rarefied competitive atmosphere of Hodgson & Sons could anyone mention five house removals in the same breath as the birth of a son.

Charles was to develop into one of the most fascinating and captivating people I have ever met. He was to become enchanting, wilful, strong and a unique personality.

However, on this day, he had only just been born. He wasn't quite as perfect a 'Beatle Paul' baby as Howie had been and even had half an ear lobe missing.

Notwithstanding this he was to grow into a wonderfully handsome toddler, with the natural deep auburn hair of his mother, worn in a Rolling Stone bob style, almost black almond shaped eyes and the handsome smile of my father.

xxxxxxx

It was at this time that Howard also started at West House, where my father, my brother Russell, and I had been to school and where Marianne now terrified pupils into French language success.

He was to make friends immediately with another new boy called Daniel. His surname was Fewtrel and his father, Eddie, owned a string of nightclubs in Birmingham.

He was the head of the much-feared Fewtrel family, which boasted many brothers and who had stopped the Krays expanding their gangland empire up the M1 from London to Birmingham – or so local legend had it.

At this time, in the late 1970s, Birmingham boasted two families who liked to be thought of as hard, very tough and liked the common folk of Birmingham to both fear and respect them.

This Life In Death

I had been brought up on the genteel side of the tracks. These two families had not.

One was the Fewtrels, the other was the Broadhursts, who had made it very big in scrap metal. I vaguely knew the Fewtrels but I knew the Broadhursts much better as I had conducted many funeral services for them.

The first that comes to mind was a very sad and tragic death. A young girl in her late teens or perhaps early twenties had committed suicide. The funeral was a huge affair as you might expect.

The cortege left the house in Kingstanding, once the largest council estate in Europe, and known locally as 'Little Russia' for its cold weather rather than its politics.

Its real name, Kingstanding, comes from the fact the Charles I stood on the high ground there to watch the siege and attack by the Roundheads on Aston Hall in the lower ground towards the southeast.

The Hall had been set in rural countryside in the 17th Century during the Civil War but was to be surrounded by terraced housing and the magnificent Villa Park in the 19th Century as the Industrial Revolution exploded in Great Britain and Birmingham became known as 'The Workshop of the World.'

The Broadhursts were a very large family. Some of them were very rich but they bred like rabbits and those less close by birth to the matriarch, Jean Broadhurst, still lived in council housing in places like Kingstanding.

The young girl had been born a Broadhurst but had married. It seemed, perhaps unfairly, that the younger male members of this 'Shelby' style family had decided that her death was her husband's fault. He had been barred from attending the funeral as a result.

This information quite naturally had been kept within the family and so had not been shared with their funeral directors.

This Life In Death

The funeral cortege was typical of a young death in a working family that had become wealthy. There was a floral hearse, a hearse to transport a solid panelled oak, double raised lid coffin and six limousines. It was a visual demonstration of Broadhurst power.

Hodgson & Sons were in their element. We had loaded the limousines individually, as each pulled into place, with the usual 'state funeral' precision and I was walking the funeral as far as time would permit. In Kingstanding, the rule was the further the walk, the greater the respect.

We had come some way from the house and were descending the steep terrain of 'Little Russia' towards the Kingstanding Road, when the silence of respect was broken by raucous yelling. I paused and turned.

Young men from limousines four, five and six had got out of these slow-moving vehicles and were racing over an expansive piece of grass towards one council house while screaming that they would "hang the bastard."

I was quickly there and asked them to return to their limos.

"We're going to lynch the fucker."

"Yeah, string the bastard up."

"Gentlemen, please return to the vehicles immediately or I'll be forced to cancel the funeral" I interrupted a second time.

"Shut the fuck up you posh prick or I'll…" the young man's voice died.

"Get back in the cars now" commanded a deep woman's voice from behind me. It was the matriarch speaking. She didn't have to repeat herself. They were gone.

Jean Broadhurst apologised to me, smiled pleasantly and the funeral cortege proceeded without further incident.

Over the next decade I got to know the family much better.

This Life In Death

Firstly, I ended up playing football in the same football team as two Broadhurst lads and got on very well with them. Indeed, I really liked them. The three of us made up a very uncompromising centre back trio who didn't take prisoners. My brother Russell was also a talented midfield member of this team.

Indeed, we even got to the final of the Cup of the North Birmingham FA Cup in 1981. We were going to play a brilliant 100% Afro-Caribbean team from Lozells in this big game. They had reached that stage by murdering their opponents by often 10 goals or more and in one case by 17 - 0.

We had the odd girlfriend or parent turn up to see us play them. They brought over 250 fans.

Their supporters very quickly caught on to my 'posh' accent barking defensive orders and began making fun of it. This was out of need because we were defending well under fierce pressure and while the game was being mostly played in our penalty area, we had not conceded a goal and their supporters' frustration was growing.

They won yet another corner, one of their two strikers went up for a header as it floated across, so did I and we clashed heads with both of us landing in a heap as a result.

I got up. He didn't. He was out cold. An ambulance arrived in about four minutes – unlike today – and he was stretchered off to hospital to chants of the "The Voodoo man did it." I was by now even less popular with their supporters.

Eventually, they got a goal – but our talented striker, another posh chap called Simon Davies, scored a second half equaliser.

Now it was going down to the wire.

Then in the last five minutes, their other striker, who looked and played like Thierry Henri, turned me brilliantly. He was 18, I was 31. I bust a gut to catch him. I slid in just as he was going to shoot.

This Life In Death

I missed the ball but got him. He went down heavily. His collar bone shot out of his skin in a horrible compound fracture. Another ambulance arrived to take him to hospital as their frenzied supporters screamed "Voodoo Man off."

Referees always ignored chants like this and sendings-off were rare. However, he did point to the penalty spot. They scored the penalty and won the match amid scenes of near riot.

A month later I went to the prize giving evening. I was the only one of our team who did. The whole winning team turned up – including both badly injured strikers.

We had a beer together and laughed as the one with the broken collar bone told me that I had 'massive balls' to turn up.

In all of this I had come to realise that, while the Broadhursts might have liked, and even promoted, their 'hard' image, they were deep down nice guys.

Secondly, and later again, when in his teens, Howard was to go out with a Broadhurst girl called Luci Mae and through her became very friendly with her brothers – a generation down from my footballing comrades.

I think that on balance the Fewtrels held the Broadhursts more in awe than the other way round.

I had met Eddie on the odd occasion and had no reason to dislike him – indeed, rather to the contrary.

However, he and his family were to become propelled into the centre of our lives, and the result was to be terribly disruptive to all of us and of absolutely no credit to me whatsoever.

Howard was now at West House. Marianne taught there. Howard had become 'best mates' with Daniel Fewtrel. Soon Marianne and Daniel's mother Hazel were to become friends too.

This Life In Death

As a result, Hazel was invited to Charles's Christening in March 1979. She was a dark haired and attractive woman of 42 years of age. I noticed her smiling at me and hanging on my every word. I was very flattered and instantly thought of her as a 'real woman.'

Philip and Sandra Dunn, who we had reunited with on our return to Birmingham in 1975, and Marianne and I were soon to be invited to Eddie's new night club Boogie's. We were made to feel like star guests.

I believe that Hazel had always been faithful to Eddie. I don't think that he had always been to her. But whatever her motive, she now quizzed Marianne about what I liked and didn't. She now would always manage a few words with me alone on a Friday or Saturday night at Boogie's – where she could tell me that I was the best-looking man in Birmingham and that it was so wonderful that I just didn't know it.

I was becoming totally infatuated with her. My whole body ached for her. I couldn't think of anything else.

Gone was the discipline that had got me away from asthmatic spastic, saw me through the tough Switzerland years, my family's destruction and the re-building of Hodgson & Sons Ltd.

Worse, I should have remembered that Marianne had not wanted a second child; that I had persuaded her to have one and now three months after that I was about to embark on a wholly destructive and irresponsible love affair.

Of course, I was aware of all of this, and I didn't let it affect my running of Hodgson & Sons. But I was also struggling with internal demons as well as a passion for this raven-haired temptress.

In reality, the gene that the Hodgson male is either blessed or perhaps cursed with, of having a gigantic libido erupted into a double whammy of lust and a sudden need to make up for a loss of freedom that had been denied me as I had struggled through the last decade into the relatively sunny uplands of now.

This Life In Death

As a result, I should resist here the temptation to lay all the blame at Hazels, door as I write. It takes two to tango and I was a very willing dancer.

Hazel changed her family Easter holiday to co-inside with ours with the Dunns in Tenerife. We all stayed in the same hotel. By the time that was over I knew I could not resist her any longer.

The affair was very physical and mixed the elation of passionate sex and infatuation with the trauma of realising you were not the great man you thought you were.

Marianne was never an idiot and after less than two months realised what was happening. She told Eddie and of course the shit hit the fan.

Hazel, accompanied by her lovely younger daughter Abigail, left home and together we set up home in various hotels, leading a ridiculous, nomadic life.

On the first night, Howie fell off his slide in the garden at home and broke his arm. I wasn't there. He cried for me all night. I felt a completely terrible father who had turned his back on everything he had been building when I found out. But, despite this I remained wholly infatuated.

My parents reacted with some surprise that their virtuous son, who had saved the family business could behave so badly.

Nevertheless, they reacted typically once the news had sunk in. My father counselled me very sensibly, but I did not listen. My mother attempted to run Hazel over with her car and by me pushing the latter out of the way prevented her from injury and my mother being arrested as a result.

All the time I was getting messages from Eddie that I would not look so good when he had had someone throw acid in my face. This just made the pig-headed me more determined not to be thwarted in my desires.

This Life In Death

However, Hazel and I eventually decided that we had to both return home. Neither of us wanted to at that moment but we both had come to realise that the whole business was bound to end in a tragedy of some kind.

Then, one Saturday at about 5:30 in the morning in late July, Eddie turned up drunk on my front lawn demanding to be let in at the top of his voice.

He had come straight from Boogie's where a few brothers had told him he needed to sort me out. He was staggering around and yelling at the top of his voice so half Lordswood Rd could hear him.

I had no choice but to go down and open the door. I did and received a good right hook to my nose, where his wedding ring made a small scar that I still have today.

The fight progressed through the hall and into the kitchen. He was a much heavier man than me, but I was some fifteen years younger and much fitter. I punched him back and wrestled him to the floor by the oven. I sat on top of him, pinned his arms down and started to throttle him. I was very angry - just as I had been with Charles England some fifteen years, and what seemed like a lifetime, earlier.

Then I noticed the fear in his eyes. He must have thought that I was going to kill him. Suddenly, he looked old and frail.

My blind rage gave way to reason. He hadn't asked me to have an affair with his wife. But I had had one and had disrupted his family's life and made him a laughing stock with his peers in his macho world.

Marianne was screaming for us to stop, the children's nanny came downstairs, and I jumped off him and he left – but not before he uttered his parting speech that I would never see another Christmas.

The affair was now over, and Marianne, the children and I left for France for our summer holiday. Once there her mother noticed that she was cooler towards me than previously and warned her to treat a good man like me better.

This Life In Death

To Marianne's eternal credit she never uttered a word about the affair in her own defence. So, her parents were spared the story of my abysmal behaviour unlike mine, whom she had appealed to for help.

I asked her why her mother seemed so pro-me. She explained. I told her that I would own up. She pleaded with me not to do so. This was, as she explained, because she wanted her mother to be protected from what had happened. She said, "She loves you so much, I couldn't break her heart." My God, I did not deserve this act of generosity.

However, this was not the end of the story. There was an extraordinary postscript.

While I was away in France, one morning there was a knock on the Fewtrel front door in Fitzroy Avenue, Harborne, Birmingham.

Eddie opened the door. In front of him stood a man in a yachting reefer jacket, a RMYC skipper's cap and tie, an old Harrovian scarf and grey flannel trousers.

Behind him was a blue soft top MGB GT sports car with the hood down.

"Good morning, Mr Fewtrel I presume? My name is Paul Hodgson. I have a letter for you. A copy of the same has already been lodged with my solicitors, Messrs Cartwright & Lewis. It instructs them to inform the police that if anything untoward happens to my son Howard then you will be to blame. So, you had better pray that he doesn't slip under a bus, or you will be going to prison for a very long time. I bid you good day."

With that he turned got back into his MGB GT and roared away.

Eddie stood there speechless. He was frightened of both licensing magistrates and the police as either could close him down. He also suspected that the police would believe a 'toff' like Paul Hodgson over him any day of the week. He believed the police were part of a conspiracy to keep folk like him where they belonged, which was below the Paul Hodgsons of this world.

My father had saved me. Moreover, he never told me what he had done. So how do I know the story then? Because Eddie's wife was standing behind him and Hazel told me in vivid detail.

The affair, although only of a few months' duration, had been intense and although everyone suffered, I think Eddie was to suffer more from its effects than anyone. 'For No One' was now his song. For this I'm truly sorry for the pain I caused him.

In 1997, Abigail, now a young woman, got in touch with me to say her parents had separated and her mother really needed to see me. She now lived in the same apartment block in Edgbaston as my mother. I went to see her.

In 2004, Abigail contacted me again. Hazel was terminally ill with cancer. I went to see her in hospital and sat there chatting with her and Eddie. She was serene and very brave. Eddie was gracious and charming. I was extremely glad that I went. There is no black and white in life and I was happy that we shared that afternoon.

I also went to her funeral and stood at the back of the Oratory on the Hagley Rd. It was a very well attended affair. I was happy for Eddie and her that it was. I crept in and out. I wanted to pay my respects but not to draw attention to an affair which had been a Birmingham society scandal of twenty-five years earlier.

xxxxxxx

With this disruption behind me, I determined to re-double by efforts to build Hodgson into an empire. I was no longer so frightened of being poor – because I wasn't.

This Life In Death

However, now I had discovered another ghost in my locker. I had realised that if I took my foot 'off the gas', I was likely to fall into the same bad habits as George, Ossie, Les and Paul. Surely, this was just the same as going back to the completely useless child I had been. Therefore, the efforts of the last twenty-five years would be in vain. Going forward, I needed to think with my head and not my penis.

If I needed other women, then this was in my character make-up and not Marianne's fault. My drive and determination must be focused on building Hodgson and not on being some Brummie Gigolo who drove a Rolls Royce.

I resumed my acquisition strategy with great gusto. On my return from France, I drove immediately to see the owner of funeral directors in Brierley Hill in the West Midlands. John Taylor had tipped me off that he had answered our advert in the NAFD magazine.

The firm was JT Brookes and the owner, a very pleasant man of the same name, must have been very surprised to see a chap arrive at his funeral home that evening in a Rolls Royce and dressed more like Rod Stewart than a funeral director.

Nevertheless, we got on well, had a cup of tea and then he showed me round. After that we went to his sitting room, as he lived on site, and had a glass of sherry.

He proved to me that he owned the premises and vehicles and did 450 funerals a year. I offered him, I think, £45,000 and we shook on the deal.

In those days your word was really your bond.

Now we were conducting around 1,500 funerals a year – an increase of some 375% in four years and had seven outlets. However, JT Brookes was too far away to be run as a branch of the Oaklands.

Therefore, with Mr Brookes retiring, I needed a new funeral director and manager over there. I chose Sandra Dunn's cousin. His name was Graham Hodson, without the 'g' as in my surname, and I had been sailing with him that summer in the South of France.

He had no funeral directing experience, but, while the lawyers were busy exchanging contracts, I personally trained him in the 'Hodgson way' and he became a good, if somewhat reluctant funeral conductor, and a very willing and useful business manager. He will figure in this story from 1979 to 1991, and like JT and Beryl, as a key player.

In 1980, I was approached by a Black Country funeral director named Stephen Downing. I knew his father from my JH Hartland days of a decade before when I had attended the North Worcester & South Staffs National Association of Funeral Directors meetings in Dudley along with other FDs such as Vernon Kendrick, Arthur Hamer and others from the Black Country area.

Stephen was an outgoing and charming chap and quickly explained that he and his father wanted to realise some cash but wanted to stay in the funeral business and had hit on an idea.

They owned Downing, their family business which conducted some 200 funerals per annum, but they also owned a much larger business called FW Collins in Bilston near Wolverhampton and that conducted over 750 funerals-a-year.

They needed more income than Downing could provide but needed to sell something, as I recall, so that they could buy a house that Stephen wanted.

Their idea was to swap FW Collins for JT Brookes plus cash to cover the additional 300 funerals per annum that I would be gaining. Was I interested?

Yes I was, so JT Brookes became the only funeral business that I ever sold. I can't recall the cash amount now over 44 years later, but it was not large enough to worry the Midland Bank at Hockley who by now were willing to lend me anything I wanted.

This Life In Death

With this transaction and organic growth occurring at Hodgson, Hamer and Crowther branches, Hodgson & Sons Ltd were now conducting over 2,000 funerals per annum.

This was phenomenal growth in the staid family or Coop owned funeral industry of 40 years ago – where there were only various Cooperative operations, a handful of larger companies of conducting circa 2,000 funerals or more per year and the rest of the market was operated by family-owned businesses which ranged from 150 to 1,000 per annum.

Little had changed in the 20th Century, and nobody expected it to in the future either. The Birmingham Funeral Directors Guild and The North Worcester & South Staffs NAFD might becoming alarmed, and somewhat jealous of our success, but other than that we were still below everyone else's radar.

However, what happened next was to change all of that. Following that eventful cup final in Birmingham at Easter 1981 involving the Broadhursts, I went sailing in Southern Spain and found a boat there that I wanted to buy. I put down a £6,000 deposit.

Not long after, the NAFD magazine advised a company for sale. It turned out to be Ann Bonham & Son of Northampton. This was a business conducting some 1,100 funerals each year.

I was interested. The business was the best funeral directing business in the town and all the funerals were mainly conducted out of one premises.

It was run by two brothers, Denis and Cyril Bonham. Denis's son David Bonham was also employed by the business. It was a good traditional British funeral director with good standards of service and facility. It was not in the same league as Hodgson & Sons, but not even all NSM members were apart from James Summers of Cardiff.

I went to see Denis. We got on well. I offered him, with the Midland Bank's approval, £250,000. I didn't buy the boat and forfeited the £6,000 deposit. I wished that I hadn't just bought a new house which

I will refer to shortly. He said he would consider my proposal but needed time to consider it.

He told me that he would like to sell to me as he believed that I was the only real funeral director he had met who was interested in buying his business and that he believed that I would keep on his son, David, and his manager, one Don York, and give them a chance in the expanding Hodgson business.

However, he had to get the best price for the family and there was also interest from the mighty Co-op Wholesale Division in Manchester, which owned a high percentage of the UK Coop funeral businesses, and two larger private firms than me.

One was Lodge Brothers, who conducted some 5,000 funerals a year in the northern 'Home Counties' and the other, a much larger business, was a property business situated in southern England. It was called the Great Southern Group and owned several sizeable funeral directors, crematoria and cemeteries south of the Thames.

The result would be decided on putting a final offer in a 'sealed bid' process. This is where the highest bidder wins.

Denis was candid when he told me that I was, as a result, unlikely to win. I talked to the Midland Bank and agreed what I could go to. This figure was £350,000. I duly entered my sealed bid.

One morning, I was about to pick up my top hat to go out on the second funeral of the day, when my phone went. JT told me that there was someone on the line about Bonhams. I told him to put him through. He did.

The man introduced himself and told me told I had bought Ann Bonhams. I was 31 years of age, we had been going out of business less than five years earlier and yet I had won this prize. I had just beaten the biggest and the best in the industry. I had intended to win, and I had. I had intended to be unstoppable and now I knew that I was.

This Life In Death

The elation was short lived. By the time I put the phone receiver back down I was in panic mode. What had I done? I had just borrowed a fortune and risked Marianne and the boys' quality of life and especially a new wonderful house that I had only just bought for them to live in.

So, I had just risked everything I had worked so hard to gain. What happened if the death rate dropped alarmingly as forecast in the coming winter busy period? What would I do?

I felt like phoning the bloke back and saying that the deal was off. However, I had to go and conduct a funeral instead. By the time I had, I had also composed myself. It would be OK, and I would deal with it.

We signed up Ann Bonhams. Graham Hodson, his wife Wendy and their two daughters Abigail and Amber, were moved from their Stafford home to Rugby so that he could manage the place. Don York and David Bonham were retained as promised and we got ready for the winter rush – which was still common in 1981.

It came early and thick and fast. The Midland Bank at Hockley purred with pleasure. All trading names – Hodgson, Crowther, Hamer, Collins and Bonhams were very busy. The death rate was high, and we were getting organic growth too in all trading names.

We had started to send out a review sheet with our final account in 1978, over 40 years before Trustpilot existed, and these were coming back by the hundred praising our services.

What about the new house that I just mentioned? Six months earlier, in the autumn of 1980, Marianne, the boys and I had a Sunday lunch in Streetly by Sutton Park, near the Borough of Sutton Coldfield, just north of Birmingham.

Afterwards, I showed her the famous Roman Road, which was a private drive on a private estate, where the great and the good of Birmingham industrial wealth lived.

This Life In Death

We were by now very happy again and our only domestic concern was how to contain our second son Charles, Howard was, by now, a model young man of seven, Charles was a two-year-old maniac who knew no fear. You will learn more about him shortly.

She asked me to stop outside one house. It was a mock Jacobean mansion that had been built in 1931 and was situated just down from the Little Aston Golf Club, which was very 'old school', exclusive and where David, HRH Prince of Wales, had flown in and landed on the course in the 1930s to play golf. This was before he became Edward VIII and created the abdication crisis of 1936.

She told me that she had never seen such a beautiful house. It was aptly called 'Eden Wood.'

By a heaven-sent coincidence, it became available within a fortnight. We were having drinks at a friend's house in Sutton when Marianne saw it advertised in the local Sutton Coldfield paper. Her face lit up.

I knew I owed her for the pain and humiliation the Hazel affair had caused her, and I also knew how well we were doing at work.

So, I bought it for £175,000. This was a lot of money in 1980 and when I had agreed to do this, I had no idea that the Bonham business would become available within months.

I needn't have worried. The loans from the Midland Bank in Hockley for FW Collins, Eden Wood, Ann Bonhams and everything preceding these were all repaid by spring 1982. We were now well and truly on our way.

So, 1981 was a very happy year. Marianne and I had put the Hazel affair behind us. We were as one again. In addition, Marianne was now living in the home of her dreams and drove a brand-new Jaguar XJS. I had bought the latter for her from PJ Evans, (today Evans Halshaw), on Bristol Street, Birmingham, and had received two free Austin Metros thrown in free of charge – such was the state of the British car industry then and their desperation for a sale.

This Life In Death

We had also bought two horses, mine a 17 + 3 gelding 2-year-old from Ireland, who had hardly been ridden. I called him McCartney. He was very dangerous to start with.

He reared up at old lady who fell into a ditch. He kicked a hole in a corporation bus. He jumped over a six-foot hedge and galloped around a well-manicured lawn after being spooked by a JCB; there was nothing I could do initially to stop him much to the house-owner's horror.

He reared up on a bridge and nearly deposited both of us onto electric train lines below. He got annoyed when the Chester Rd lights turned red, and he got left behind by the other horses. A woman driver got too close him at the same time. He kicked her headlights out before completing the demolition of her car by sitting on her bonnet which forced the front wheels off – one of which went through a Clark's shoe shop window and set the alarm off.

Indeed, only an attractive stable girl called Kerry and I would climb up to ride him. All my horse-riding friends sensibly declined to mount him.

Even the three 'hunting and shooting' sisters, whom I nicknamed 'the Mitford sisters' due to their spoilt 'landed gentry' attitude to life, where they all fiercely rode both men and horses with great gusto and thought of little else.

Indeed, when I first met the eldest at a cocktail party and she discovered what I did, she called over her sisters and asked them to guess.

"An actor" said the middle sister.

"A singer" said the youngest.

"No. No – completely the opposite" replied their older sister.

"A rubbish man" exclaimed the youngest.

"Well nearly!" Replied the eldest.

This Life In Death

So much for the regard the local nobility held funeral directors in!

Kerry and I managed to tame Macca over the next two years so much that I could jump him as high as six feet and 'rock canter' him at the speed of a companion horse trotting next to him.

Marianne's horse was called Mistral. He was much tamer and a lot smaller. However, he often managed to throw her off, usually while jumping brush wood in Sutton Park.

Charlie would say, "Have a nice ride, Daddy. Don't fall off, Mummy". In the end Marianne decided Mistral had to go.

Most important of all, our two sons were growing into two wonderful and yet completely different boys who looked very similar and usually were dressed in identical outfits. Howard, envied by all his friends as the perfect looking and perfectly behaved young man their mothers praised and Charles a fearless and very determined child with a cheeky smile that hid an iron will to get his own way, while living on the wild side.

As a family we could not have been happier. We seemed so blessed. It is perhaps just as well that we don't always know what lies round the corner.

In addition, Hodgson & Sons Ltd had done far more by now than escape bankruptcy. It was now in training to become the company that would become a major force in British Funeral directing before completely changing the sleepy UK funeral market forever.

Lastly, I can't leave 1981 without recording a dollop of double cream on top of all this icing on the cake that I have already articulated.

Aston Villa became Champions of the First Division, today's Premiership. They had used only thirteen players under the wonderful management of Ron Saunders and his superb captain Denis Mortimer to push everyone else, including Liverpool, aside.

This Life In Death

Howard was to record at the time that, on the day Villa were crowned as champions, he had never seen me look so happy.

He had been coming to Villa with Russell and me since he was four years of age. I had introduced him to Ron Saunders and the whole team at the Bodymoor Heath training around that time, and he became completely speechless when Andy Gray said hello. It was all too much for him.

Life was as good as it gets in 1981.

This Life In Death

Chapter VII

My The King of China

1982

From being nothing like the perfect looking baby that Howard had been, Charles had grown into a similar looking boy to Howard.

They boasted the same haircut, a neat long-haired page boy cut. Howard's hair was darker and Charles's redder. They had the same complexion and similar coloured eyes. The main difference was that while Howie had large round Paul McCartney eyes, Charlie had almond shaped eyes.

As already recorded, their characters were very different, but as is often the case, they got on very well as a result. That was as long as Charlie didn't think that Howie might be usurping his position as Daddy's boy.

"My Daddy's boy", he would tell his mother when she would buy him a cornetto ice-cream and ask him if he was now Mummy's boy as she passed it to him.

"No, Howie's Mummy's boy. My Daddy's boy."

He never referred to himself as 'I' or 'me' but always 'my'.

The stories of his balmy single-minded bravery are too many and too repetitive for you, and too painful for me to record them all here. So, I will just restrict myself to just one typical example.

In October 1981, the four of us along with Philip and Sandra Dunn and their two sons, Adam and Jacob, went to Malta for the October half-term break.

We decided to take the children to the Popeye film set which had become a tourist attraction once the film had been shot. This was because the houses built for the film were so spectacularly perched at various stages up and down the very high cliffs.

We were all listening attentively to the guide's commentary, when a man's voice behind and above us screamed out.

"There's a little girl on that roof over there."

We turned round and followed his arm pointing out the direction. This was no little girl. This was a long-haired boy called Charles. He was standing with his feet either side of the apex of the house's roof and looking down. He was inches from the end which dropped over a hundred feet, perhaps over 200 feet, into the sea below.

I raced to it and shinned up the ladder that he had. He had his back to me. I said as calmly as I could, "Hi Charlie, come to Daddy."

He turned round to face me. My heart was pumping as if it was going to come through my chest.

"Don't run. Just walk to Daddy."

He did. It seemed like a lifetime was passing as we edged towards each other. Finally, I grabbed him.

Did I hug him? No.

"What the hell are you doing?" I screamed in an explosion of anger instead, as I carried him back down the ladder. I probably smacked him too. I can't remember but I could have done. Forty years ago, we did smack our children, just as our parents had smacked us.

The boys would usually be allowed to wait up for me to come home from work and I would then read or make up a bedtime story.

However, on this holiday I re-wrote the lyrics of McCartney's Lennon/McCartney composition Rocky Racoon so that the story was about them. Howie was Rocky and Charlie was Dan – because Charlie wanted to win the gun fight and because I thought Howie ought to be the star. He deserved as much for allowing his little brother so much of the limelight.

My father even got a bit part in the Hodgson version. The verse 'The doctor came in, stinking of gin, and proceeded to lie on the table' became, rather irreverently, 'Grandpa came in….' etc., much to the boys' amusement.

I would sing our version each night in my best Bob Dylan voice before I went down to dinner in the hotel only for them to beg for it again and again.

xxxxxxx

1982 started off as 1981 had finished. We were a very happy family, Charlie was drawing constant attention to himself by his antics, the business was booming, bank debt was paid off and more Midland Bank cash provided to buy SA Bates, a funeral director conducting 400 funerals-a-year, 350 in Dunstable and 50 in Tring.

We are now getting out of the Midlands and closer to London.

This also meant that we were conducting some 3,600 funerals per annum – a 900% increase in six and a half years and I still owned as much equity as I did the day that I had bought by father out.

How had Hodgson & Sons Ltd achieved this remarkable recovery? There were three main ingredients to its success. Firstly, we offered very high standards of service and facility which led to high levels of client satisfaction and therefore organic growth by client recommendation. Secondly, we offered a wider range of choice. This allowed for every family budget. Those who wanted to spend more could. Those that didn't needn't. However, the average income per funeral ended up much higher than our lowest price. This increased overall margin and thus profits. Thirdly, by rationalisation of capital equipment, we could get much higher usage and thus 'sweat' the assets. A funeral business has around an 80% fixed overhead ratio. This means that 80% of cost is going to be paid irrespective of how many funerals were being conducted. For example, by rationalisation we were able to get as many funerals out of a fleet in a day as other funeral directors got in a week.

These three reasons gave us a major financial advantage. As a result, success gave rise to even greater success.

Moreover, business was conducted very differently in the 1980s. There was no quick and sweat free way to become a billionaire overnight then as there is today.

That was because the invention of software for folk's hardware to propel one to stardom overnight didn't exist - because mobiles, tablets, laptops and even desktops didn't exist yet.

Neither was there an easy access to a world market keen to log on to the next fashionable social media trend as there was no internet.

And even if there had been, 90% of the world wouldn't have been able to afford a mobile let alone a computer to tune in and turn on.

Business was usually done locally, verbally, or by post or occasionally by some new mode of communication, which few had or trusted, called a fax machine.

Moreover, there were fewer 'venture capitalists,' known today as 'private equity firms', then either. These are the guys who promised then, as they do now, to help you gear up to expand your business to make your fortune in exchange for you agreeing for them to provide you with high interest mezzanine debt and granting them an equity stake in your firm.

They usually leave you five years later with less equity in a poorer company once they have asset stripped it and left you with a range of overpriced products that are now of a lesser quality too.

This Life In Death

They tend to be good for their investors by passing on high returns to them. This has usually been achieved at your company's expense. So, it is bad for your clients, your employees, your company and so you.

However, none of these routes had had or would have anything to do with our progress for some years to come.

We were still not on the big competitors' radar, but we were starting to annoy other National Selected Mortician members, the elitist funeral directing club imported from the USA that my father had joined in 1963, as well as the Birmingham Funeral Directors' Guild, the North Worcester & South Staffs NAFD and the local NAFDs in Northampton and now Dunstable.

xxxxxxx

When in Malta in October 1981, Philip, Sandra, Marianne and I had discussed over dinner how great it would be to visit the Far East. This was far less common in those days. Most working English families still took their holidays either at some English seaside resort, on the Costa Brava in Spain or perhaps the islands of Ibiza or Majorca. Richer folk went to the Cote d'Azur in the South of France.

The Scots either stayed at home or ventured as far south as Blackpool where some would spend their fortnight re-tarmacking the streets there in multi-coloured puke while running the gauntlet of those fierce Lancastrian guest-house landladies.

We wanted to go to Asia, so we booked a weekend together in the Lake District in early January 1982 to ride horses and then to Thailand for a fortnight in early April three months later.

Just as we were leaving to go to Thailand, news of the Argentinian invasion of the Falklands was announced.

This Life In Death

Margaret Thatcher had been struggling to stop the express train decline of Britain under successive Wilson, Heath and then Wilson again before Callaghan governments.

She had been elected on the back of the desperation of the British public's alarm of how we had become the laughing stock of Europe and a by-word for poor quality and unreliable goods across the world.

The various British governments since 1964 had continued to ignore the basic rules of economics and in the social revolution of post-war Britain, by 1979, matters had gone so badly wrong that even the 'man in the street' realised that we would have to take some rather nasty medicine to recover our economic health.

Thus arrived the 'Blessed Margaret' as was one of her nicknames – along with many less flattering.

However, in the first two years of her administration, the nation had experienced both pain but continued economic strife and so her popularity had fallen but had recovered enough after two years in power that a national opinion poll put out a 33% level pegging for her Tory Party with Labour and the Liberals a few days before the Falklands crisis exploded across the world newspapers' front pages.

Before this, President Ronald Reagan in the US had appointed a Mrs Kirkpatrick – a lady of Irish decent – to develop American relations with South America.

When the CIA had warned the President about their fear of a forthcoming invasion of the Falklands, Mrs Kirkpatrick, who had little love for Britain or the Anglo/American special relationship, advised the President to keep out of any ensuing conflict as it would damage US/South America relations.

Caspar Weinberger, the US head of foreign policy, and others in his administration told him differently.

Weinberger, like the President admired and wanted to help Mrs Thatcher. On the other hand, the US did not want to alienate the huge

This Life In Death

South American market on its doorstep. Reagan elected to phone the Argentinean President, one General Galtieri, and try and dissuade him from the invasion as the best course of action.

Once the polite small talk was over, Galtieri explained that his military dictatorship was not popular with the Argentinean people due to inflation and economic failure. He further explained that he intended to take back all British territories in the area and rally the people behind him in a moment of national passion and pride. As a result, he and the military would be popular once more.

He went on to explain that as the British were no longer powerful enough to respond, they would be forced to go the UN and complain bitterly instead.

The UN would impose economic sanctions on Argentina – but that these would not work as they never had ever before anywhere and so he would remain in power as a national hero.

Reagan listened in silence. When Galtieri finished, he just issued these few words. "I don't believe you have met this woman, have you?"

The rest is history and blasted away over the next two months which were also easily the worst months of my life to date and now I'm faced with reliving them here – which is something I have refused to do for over 40 years.

So please forgive me if the next episode of my life is not as fully detailed as the rest. This is because I'm afraid I'm still too fragile to relive it in the written word even now.

The day before leaving for Thailand I had a morbid mood of impending danger come over me. That night before leaving work, I wrote a detailed letter about what was to happen in the event of my death, including leaving my horse Macca to Kerry (the stable girl) and our dog Kelly to my mother. I put it in my office safe marked 'In the event of my death.'

This Life In Death

Nevertheless, telling myself that I was a complete idiot and to pull myself together, I was ready to go on the 5th April 1982 with the usual attitude that I must set an example to all.

Four Hodgsons and four Dunns left Birmingham for Heathrow on our way to Pattaya in Thailand. Philip drove us down to SA Bates in Dunstable, where we left his car and got one of my chauffeurs to drive us on to Heathrow Airport.

Philip had a Marina estate car. The four boys were in the boot. Howie and Adam started to sing 'Prince Charming' a song which was a 'hit' at the time by a guy called Adam Ant.

Charles beat them up because he mistakenly thought they were singing 'pinch Charlie' instead. We all laughed. We were very happy.

We then flew overnight to Bahrain to refuel and on again to Bangkok. It was dark when we arrived at our hotel. We had dinner and afterwards strolled outside in the humid atmosphere with the children.

Charlie kept singing, "Pong King Kong. My The King of China." We laughed because of his almond shaped eyes.

Both boys were sleeping with us. Howie in a bed and Charlie in a cot. In the morning Charles woke us all up with his continued assertion that he was the King of China.

We took the boys to breakfast where they had scrambled eggs. Then we all elected to go to the pool area rather than the beach.

Howie and Adam were playing in the pool in front of us. Philip and Sandra Dunn decided to go for a walk with Jacob. Charlie wanted to go too. Marianne and I agreed and said that we would keep an eye on Howie and Adam while they took Jacob and Charles. They went.

Marianne had become suspicious that I was having an affair with Kerry, who looked after Macca. This was not the case. However, I had proved very unreliable over the Hazel affair and so she had good reason to doubt me as a result. Moreover, I did fancy Kerry, and she knew me well enough to see it.

There followed an argument about this. Suddenly the Dunns arrived back after their walk with Jacob but not Charles. Apparently, he had wanted to come back to Daddy and Mummy, and they had let him go.

I raced round the hotel grounds with my heart pounding while begging God to keep him safe.

Then there was a shout from a hotel balcony.

"There's a child at the bottom of that pool."

This was a different pool to where we had been lounging. It was him and he had drowned.

The next few days are a blur of emotion even now. I was far too destroyed to cry, and I knew that it was my duty to get Marianne, Howard and Charles's, body home.

I was in deep trauma, up on the ceiling looking down and could see myself as I dealt with the police, the coroner, the BA rep and others.

Marianne had dressed our son in his best frilly white shirt, grey pantaloons, white socks and black patent leather shoes while his body was still in the hotel. She had also put his gold cross around his neck and his gold ID chain on his wrist. These were stolen as soon as he got to the public mortuary.

I noticed this immediately when I asked to see his body there. They had also placed him in a fridge on top of an old man.

The attendant had his radio blaring. I told him to turn it off or I would kill him. When he did, I also told him to move my son onto a tray of his own. This he did but with a begrudging look on his face. I was still tempted to kill him, but Philip persuaded me otherwise.

This Life In Death

On our eventual arrival back home, I had Charlie placed in a specially commissioned casket and had one of my staff, a good man called John McManus, destroy the wrecked coffin that my son had come home in.

Our families rallied round. Marianne's parents came to stay along with her brother Alex who slept in Charles's bed to keep Howard company and played football all day with him. My mother and Peter came up from Dorset to be near to us. My father was very helpful and loving, my sister came up from Kent, and even Russell, not known for his thoughtfulness, bought tickets for Howard and I to go and see Aston Villa play in the semi-final of the European Cup in Brussels – even flying there with the team. I sat next to Brian Little on the coach to the ground. He was very kind and thoughtful and has remained a friend since.

Villa won and were through to the European Cup final. Gordan Cowans, Villa's star England International midfielder, kept his promise and waved to Howie.

This should have been a joyous occasion and I tried very hard to put a brave face on. However, I was just hollow and empty inside.

Someone had arranged for Howard and I to go to Villa Park the week before and meet the team. Cowans, Morley, Evans, McNaught, Shaw, Withe et al were wonderful to Howie. Denis Mortimer gave him his sweat bands. Howie was to wear them until they literally rotted on his wrists.

The world and his wife came to pay their respects and then attend his funeral. It was a huge affair with perhaps as many as 500 folk in attendance. An Afro-Caribbean choir came from Lozells to sing in the posh Edgbaston Old Church. Two Church of England ministers, a Roman Catholic priest and one Jamaican pastor presided over the service in a very unusual, for those days, act of unity.

Charles was then committed in Handsworth Cemetery, as his mother is a French Roman Catholic and did not want him to be cremated.

This Life In Death

I can still see my father and Marianne's, holding on to each other as they peered down into the new brick grave for four internments next to the gothic chapel there.

Over the next forty years none of us have ever once visited his grave, whatever the weather, without the sun bursting through – even on very cloudy and rainy days.

I am not an atheist, rather an agnostic, nevertheless, as this happens on all occasions, whether it is me or any of my children who visit him, I must confess that the thought lingers that perhaps I have got it wrong and that we don't know everything just because we can't read about it on our laptops.

We very quickly realised that it would be impossible to talk about 'Pong King Kong' outside our family and immediate circle of close friends. Death always glorifies the deceased. Charlie was both glorious and unique when he was alive, we knew it then and we didn't need him to go out of sight to realise it.

So, we also knew it and that those who hadn't known him would never understand by our second-hand explanations of who he was. So, we just didn't talk about him to the outside world.

Instead, we set up the 'Charles Hodgson Foundation'. It was to donate over a hundred thousand pounds to various charities over the next decade thanks to the tireless efforts of Marianne and many friends, but one Shirley Wooley in particular.

All children are unique and over the next 40 years, I was lucky enough to be blessed by having another four children and three grandchildren. I adore them all. They have their own individual characters, and none are vaguely like 'the King of China'.

None that is until the birth of my third grandchild, a girl called Alexandra. She looks like Charlie, she is mischievous and wilful like Charlie, she talks like Charlie, and she even refers to herself as 'my.' Marianne and I both are amazed by who she is, but we don't talk about it outside our family.

This Life In Death

Once the funeral was over life changed. The crowds had gone and with them a lot of acquaintances. People were genuinely very sorry for us, but they didn't necessarily want to ruin their dinner parties by us turning up and the evening turning into a maudlin affair as a result.

People were praising my stoic courage. I had gone back to work announcing that I had a wife and son to support and that I must not forget that. They thought that Marianne was lucky to have such a strong man.

The truth was somewhat different. Marianne, as a French Roman Catholic, had enabled herself to cry, talk about her grief and show any emotion that helped her.

I, as an Anglican middle-class British Empire boy, could do no such thing. My persona was a façade. I went to work. I did a very good job with even more conviction to 'do unto others as you would have done unto you.'

However, at night I was staring at the wall with no appetite for life anymore.

Many years before, in 1969, I had conducted my first Hodgson funeral at Perry Barr Crematorium. There I had come across a young organist who was even younger than me. We were just kids in an old man's world. We liked each other.

He was still there when I bought my father out in 1975 and we would chat if he came out of the chapel while the service was on.

He was a very talented musician. He thought it funny to develop hymned up versions of various popular songs and play them as entry, committal or exit music during services.

His selection included 'He Ain't Heavy, He's My Brother' by the Hollies; 'Fire' by Arthur Brown; 'Come On, Baby Light My Fire' by the Doors; 'Carry That Weight' by the Beatles and perhaps the most irreverent 'It's All Over Now' by the Rolling Stones.

This Life In Death

No one ever suspected what he was doing, and I even got asked occasionally by families what was the name of the beautiful music played at the crematorium.

Years later when appearing on 'Loose Ends' on BBC Radio 4, Ned Sherrin asked me about this, as I had borrowed the story for my fictional novel, 'Six Feet Under.'

The very intelligent Stephen Fry was also a guest on the show and doubted that it was possible. Roy Emerson, another guest, then got up and hymned up a song on the studio organ and invited the live audience to identify it. They couldn't.

Nevertheless, back then in the late 1970s, I determined to talk to my friend and tell him that his little prank would get spotted sooner or later and that he would end up in a lot of trouble.

"Listen" I lectured, "If you are that talented, make music work for you. Every day but Sunday, you get up in the morning come here, play all day, give piano lessons in the evening and play in a band all night. Despite this you can't afford a decent car. Start writing songs."

"Can't." He replied.

"Why not?"

"Can't write lyrics."

"Yes, you can. Any fool can. It's the music which is hard."

"Not to me."

After Charlie's death in May 1982, as the Falklands War was coming to a very bad end for General Galtieri just as President Reagan had predicted it would, I was sitting in the Eden Wood drawing room one evening on my own and staring into space.

Then I noticed a battered old Vauxhall Viva coming up the long drive. The doorbell went. I answered it and there stood my friend.

This Life In Death

He passed me a cassette and said, "I wrote the music. Now you write the lyrics" and left me standing there.

I went back to the drawing room. I played the cassette piece by piece throughout the night. I wrote the lyrics to 'A New Day' before having a shower and going to work.

Michael Sullivan had just saved my life. We were to write eight songs together over the next two months and are still writing them today 42 years later – with well over 50 in our Hodgson & Sullivan catalogue.

He will never understand how much I value him and his wife Elspeth. He will never know how important that one act of kindness was in 1982. He allowed me to find a channel to release all that crushing grief from my body and start a process of recovery which saw me burst into tears one morning a year after Charles's death.

These were the first tears I had cried, and I knew that they meant that I was on the mend.

About a week after his death, I was sleeping and dreamt that Charlie was lying on my chest asleep and that his drowning had been nothing but a very bad nightmare. I awoke and the reality was almost too painful to breathe. I was never to dream of Charlie again until a night in April 2024. I got up and sent an emergency email to the whole family warning them to be very careful. I told them I had dreamt of Charles and that this could be a warning.

At midday, I received an email from Russell's girlfriend. He had liver failure and only days to live.

xxxxxxx

Before I went away to Thailand, I had commissioned a builder, who did work for Hodgson at the Oaklands, to carry out some work at Eden Wood. He and his builder's mate were to knock down a huge

245

greenhouse in the spacious grounds and replace it with a stable block for Macca and Mistral.

We were away and they were working on the project on the 7th of April. Suddenly, during an early morning tea-break the mate said casually, "I thought they were all in Thailand."

"They are", said the builder with his back to the house as he supped his tea.

"Well which one is that in the window then?" asked the mate.

The builder turned round and saw Charles in an upstairs window. This was on the 7th April at the time that he had drowned.

He didn't tell me until a few days later when I returned for fear of upsetting me further needlessly.

Over the next few weeks, following Michael giving me his wonderful cassette gift, he and I are worked tirelessly on our new songs.

I wrote the lyrics and sometimes the melody, so I would sing the song to him and then he would write the music. Other times I would give him the lyrics and only be able to tell him the style of the song – ballad, twelve bar blues or rock etc. The hardest for me was if he wrote the music first and I had to make the lyrics fit his tune.

When I was not at work this became my focus and therapy.

One Saturday afternoon we had turned the Eden Wood drawing room into our recording studio and were jamming away, when Marianne came in to see how we were doing. She went to do something and then returned to collect her car keys which she had left on the back of one of the settees. They weren't there. Michael and I stopped playing and helped her look for them. They could not be found despite being a very large bunch including not only the keys to her XJS but all her Eden Wood keys too.

A few days later she was putting silver away having had it cleaned in a cupboard in the dining room. She saw Howie behind her out of the corner of her eye and asked him to pass her some cutlery from the table. He didn't. She turned round and he had gone. She went into the kitchen to admonish him for this, and he looked up from his work very surprised and told her he hadn't moved from the table there for the last hour.

This was followed by Betty, our wonderful housekeeper whom we had inherited with Eden Wood, starting to complain that things were being moved or even hidden from her.

Then one night matters came to a head. Howard and Marianne were already upstairs in bed. I was on my own downstairs finishing a new lyric. I put the alarm on and started to ascend the back staircase with a glass of orange juice in one hand and my shiny black funeral directing shoes in the other. I had 30 seconds to press the button at the top of the stairs in order to prevent the alarm from going off.

As I jogged up, I suddenly knew Charlie was in front of me. I didn't see him, but I knew he was there. I put the juice and shoes down and pressed the alarm button to prevent it from going off.

Then I sat down on the top step and spoke to him. I told him that we would be OK. I told him that although we missed him and couldn't wait to be reunited with him, we would survive. I told him that he must be lonely here on his own and that he should go to where he should be. Then I got up and went to bed.

The next day as I was leaving for work something compelled me to go into the drawing room as I crossed the great hall. Why? I have no idea. I went in and there on the same settee were the keys. I picked them up. They were so extremely cold that they stuck to my hand.

Charlie had gone.

xxxxxxx

This Life In Death

Before leaving behind the biggest tragedy faced by me in my life, I should address two questions which I imagine might have occurred to you.

The first is did we consider suing the hotel for not have an attendant lifeguard or even a warning sign about deep water?

Yes, we did even though society was not so compensation culture minded in those days. However, we knew it would not bring Charlie back and we were frankly struggling enough without having to live it all over again a hundred times in a court case against a hotel on the other side of the world. So, we decided not to.

Secondly, why were we not angry with Philip and Sandra Dunn? After all, he had gone off with them and they had returned without him, having sent a three-year-old back on his own through water and so he was destined to drown as a result.

I honestly don't know is the truthful answer. I suspect that it was because I blamed Marianne for wanting him to go with them in the first place so she could argue with me about Kerry.

I kept this inside me, but it burst out on a plane ride to Cyprus in June 1982 when I laid the blame firmly at her door. This was both unfair and unkind. She had been no more guilty than me in the circumstances of his death and was just as desolated as me by it.

However, me pointing the finger of blame in her direction, her resulting guilty feeling and then our silence meant it was years, and more acts of disregard towards us by Philip Dunn, that Marianne and I finally realised that Philip and Sandra Dunn's irresponsible neglect had played a significant part in Charles' death. However, by that time Philip was, as we shall see, behind bars and we didn't see Sandra any more.

This Life In Death

Chapter VIII

Battles Everywhere

1982 – 1985

In a moment of almost empty happiness in the year from hell, Aston Villa won the European Cup on 26th May 1982.

We were in Cyprus at the time. Mike came too and we composed every day. I was now addicted to writing songs with him.

In late June, and now back in Birmingham, we spent the whole night with several excellent session musicians in Phil Savage's recording studio. Phil did the vocals and we walked out with eight good compositions recorded at 6 o'clock the next morning. I went back to Eden Wood, showered and set about conducting four funerals.

Tony Barton and his Villa team were to bring this magnificent trophy to the official launch of the Charles Hodgson Foundation later that year, where those first eight songs written by Hodgson & Sullivan were performed by Mike's band in front of a large and kind audience of well-wishers.

In August we rented a villa in Corsica. I also rented a piano and Mike came to play it. Alex, his fiancée, a delightful girl called Beatrice, and Marianne's sister, Michele, came too.

We were starting to feel a little more alive, when we got a message that my father had been rushed to hospital with pneumonia.

I managed to speak to him via a Corsican pay phone to a mobile ward telephone in the atrocious Dudley Rd Hospital in Birmingham. I told him we would never fall out again. I told him how much I loved him and that I would see him the next day.

On arriving at Birmingham Airport, I went straight to the hospital. They showed me to his ward. His bed was empty and had no bed clothes on it. A nurse told me that sadly I was too late and that a doctor would come to talk to me. I waited in a little room off the ward. I was in total shock. Completely numb. How could I be asked to face the death of my beloved father just months after the loss of my beloved son?

Eventually, the doctor arrived. He explained that they had been forced to insert a tube through his back and into his lung to drain the fluid in order to save his life. The wound had got infected.

"So, was it the infection or the pneumonia that killed him?" I asked.

"Oh, I'm so sorry. He's not dead. We have moved him to East Birmingham hospital."

The bloody useless NHS was nearly as bad then as it is today.

I visited him every evening. He was very drugged and hardly knew me. He usually was rambling out loud. In his mind, either back at the 'Fleet Air-Arm' training camp during 1944 and very frightened of crashing his plane or on a train back from Harrow to Birmingham in 1942 praying to God to let his mother live when she was already dead.

Eventually, he recovered, was released from hospital and went to share a flat in Selly Oak with my brother. This was not to be a happy experience.

Then in October my mother's husband Peter died suddenly. She had loved him dearly but was very brave, continued to go to work in Fox's Estate Agents in Canford Cliffs, near Poole Harbour, and despite now being on her own, to give her weekly cocktail parties.

In many ways she was like a Victorian Dowager. She had a very stiff upper lip and acted as if nothing had happened that she couldn't take in her stride – the show must go on.

The weekend following Peter's death, the Dunns and the Hodgsons were due to go riding in the New Forest in Hampshire. I ensured that mother joined us. She looked just as she had when her mother had died twenty years earlier. She was a grey shade of white and looked very tired but there were no tears nor outward signs of emotion. I knew who she was, and I knew that I was her son.

Macca had been supposed to have joined us in the New Forest so that I could ride him. The stable in Streetly had managed to get the 17/3 gelding into a horse trailer – as he was too big for any horse box – with some difficulty.

However, by the time the stable owner had got as far as Gloucestershire on the M5, Macca was having a fit and throwing himself around and stamping his hooves on the wooden floor.

Part of it gave way and his front left leg plunged into the hole and only stopped a few inches above the road while the trailer was doing 55 miles an hour.

He had gone lame in the process and had to be taken back to Streetly. But luckily, those inches of grace between his hoof and the road meant that he had been spared being shot due to a broken leg. My God what next would go wrong in 1982?

Marianne and I decided that we needed to have another baby. We both wanted a boy. This was not to replace Charlie. It was to give us a new purpose, a new focus and thanks to my selfish and unfair outburst she thought that she 'owed' me a son.

She immediately fell pregnant, but the strain of the bereavement meant that it was too soon, and she lost it at three months.

Just as 1981 had been the perfect year, 1982 had been desperately terrible and unbearably awful. It had taken every fibre of my strength to hold everything together.

I had had to draw on every bit of my mother's stubborn strength and my father's Empire principles to come through it. But Howie, Marianne, and I had. We were battle scarred and bleeding, but we had not been sunk and nor would we be.

This Life In Death

In the late summer Marianne fell pregnant again. By now it was common for pregnant women to have a scan. So, we were able by the late autumn to dispense with old wives' tales about predicting the sex of a baby.

Marianne had a scan and was asked if she would like to know the sex of her baby. She answered that she would. She was told that it was a boy. When she told me the warmth of the joy I felt ran through my veins and was unfreezing my soul as it went. Suddenly, I felt alive and able to look forward to happier times ahead for the first time since Charlie's death.

The pain of his death had not gone. Indeed, it never would and still hasn't forty-two years later. But I did feel with some certainty that I would now gain back some zest for life in place of mere grim determination to win my battle.

We engaged the brilliant gynaecologist Joe Jordan, who was a reserve for Mr Pinker to the Royal Family and was also famous for his treatment of cancer at the Women's Hospital in Birmingham.

Joe and Val Jordan were to become great friends of ours and along with other members of Edgbaston society we started to rekindle a social life as things returned to some sort of normality in our lives.

However, this pregnancy was to prove, perhaps unsurprisingly, very difficult. Nearly every week, Marianne had a little 'show' of fluid or felt that she was losing the baby. For some inexplicable reason this nearly always happened on a Saturday morning when I was riding Macca.

There were no mobiles in those days, so as I rode into the stable yard someone would rush out of the office and tell me that there was an emergency. I would leap into my new XJS, which was now an excellent car under the leadership of Sir John Egan, and race home, collect Marianne and Howard and we would then take off at breakneck speed for the Queen Elizabeth Hospital in Selly Oak, some 25 minutes away from Streetly.

This Life In Death

This happened so regularly that the nursing staff there actually thought that I was either an equestrian rider or an instructor as I always turned up in white riding breeches, riding boots and a riding 'bone dry' coat.

Meanwhile, the expansion of Hodgson had continued at a full steam ahead pace driven by my grim determination to carry on as normal.

We were to add Fox of South Elmsall Yorkshire, Bramley's of Doncaster, and S.A. Evans of Hereford in 1983 which added another 1,000 funerals a year to the total in 1983. With organic growth we were now approaching a figure of 5,000 funerals on an annualised basis.

This success brought with it some nasty attention from the National Selected Morticians UK wing and one member of the Birmingham Funeral Directors' Guild as we shall see.

During the Whit Bank Holiday that year, Howie and I were playing snooker in the old staff quarters above the garage block at Eden Wood. These had been converted into both offices for Beryl Smith and Velma, my PA, and a snooker room for Howard.

Suddenly, the internal phone rang. It was Marianne. She had been resting but had awoken feeling that things weren't right. She was sure something was wrong and was upset.

The three of us made the usual dash to the QE Hospital. By now I had a car phone, which were front runners to mobile phones, and so was able to call Joe Jordan at home. He met us there.

Marianne had a scan. The baby had caught himself up in the placenta and was becoming angry. Joe explained that Marianne had held on for long enough but now we could allow the baby to be born. He advised that he would perform a caesarean section immediately.

Marianne smiled at Joe happily. I realised that she hadn't understood what he had just told her.

This Life In Death

Indeed, she had thought he was going to give her another epidural injection rather than a caesarean operation.

I explained to her the reality of what was going to happen. She sat bolt upright in bed and told everyone to keep away from her and that her body was not going to be scarred.

Joe explained that the scar would be very small and below her bikini line. Therefore, if anyone saw it other than me, she would have some explaining to do.

The operation went ahead and within an hour we were a family of four once more. The sense of relief that our new son had arrived safely after giving us so much worry over the preceding eight months was also immense.

We had not told anyone, including Howie, that Marianne and I knew that our new addition was a boy. When Joe appeared to tell Howie and me the joyous news, it was a delight to watch his joy at having a new little brother.

Looking back now, I know how close we were then to Howie and how much we loved him. I had even written a song for him in the aftermath of Charles's death.

However, I don't think either Marianne or I really quite appreciated that his pain at the loss of Charles was quite as great as ours and that now he would have to face having to share our attention with a son that we had wanted so badly. He had coped and was to cope wonderfully with both events.

Marianne had wanted to call our new son Charles. I had refused on the grounds that I didn't see why a child should be bought into this world as a substitute for another. Moreover, if both boys had the same name, then in time, the identity of the original Charles would be lost.

This Life In Death

As a result, the question of our new son's name had not been settled when he was born, although Marianne had always referred to him as 'Baby Raphael.'

However, I was not convinced. I had named my first two sons and proceeded to take matters into my own hands on this third occasion too.

I liked the royal Stuart name James. However, Howard was already Howard James Paul. I was Howard Osmond Paul. My father was Osmond Paul Charles. His father Osmond George. Our beloved Charles had been christened Charles Alexandre Howard.

Therefore, while I wanted something original, I still wanted it linked to the Hodgson family and especially Charles.

So, I chose Jamieson Charles Alexandre Howard and with this became an ongoing tradition of us christening Hodgson males with four Christian names.

The announcement was put in the Birmingham Evening Mail, and I raced round to the hospital with a copy to show master Jamieson and his mother. Luckily, Marianne adored the name.

So, soon we were able to take Jamie home and become a normal family again by delighting in the arrival of our wonderful new baby son, who looked like both of his brothers but had blond hair much to Marianne's delight.

She dedicated his very existence to me, and he and I were joined at the hip for at least the first 12 years of his life and were to do so many things together for the next 28 years thereafter.

The death of Charles in Thailand and the activity of the Charles Hodgson Foundation for Children had attracted quite a lot of local press attention over the last year.

The Birmingham Evening Mail called and asked if they could send a journalist and photographer to the hospital to photograph us and get a comment from me. I saw no reason to say no. This was joyous news and a ray of hope for anyone else mortified by a similar loss.

The result was a front-page photograph of Marianne, Jamieson, and me under the title 'Son For Tragedy Couple.' The story was repeated in the Wolverhampton Express & Star. This sent a funeral director from Birmingham and another from Wolverhampton into orbit with fury.

The Birmingham funeral director was one Tommy Furber of Thos. Furber, funeral directors of Harborne in Birmingham. Tommy had taken my mother out to dinner a couple of times when in 1968 she had become temporarily separated from my father as he had gone to live in Majorca in the first of his mid-life crises.

Tommy had served in World War II, without winning any medals in an undistinguished campaign. Nevertheless, he had been caught up in the damn thing for six years of his life defending his country. That was enormously to his credit.

However, he was a mean and small-minded man who was jealous of my father's looks, charm, Harrow education and Aston Martins. So, he had loved the Old Man's fall from grace in the late '60s and early '70s.

But then, when a mere 25-year-old started ripping up tree trunks in his industry, who also happened to be Paul's son, it meant that he could hardly contain his jealousy and hatred for me.

This newspaper article was a bridge too far for him. He started to tell the whole of Birmingham society that I was using my son's death to promote my funeral business.

When I first heard this from Philip Dunn's mother, who moved in the same circles as Tommy, I doubted it was true. But then the same story came back from another source and although flabbergasted that any compassionate person could even think, never mind say such things, I had no option but to decide that it was true.

This Life In Death

I knew that I would not be able to sit in the same meeting room with him ever again. I needed to act. I went to the next Guild meeting and waited for 'any other business' to come up on the agenda.

I told the meeting that one member of the Guild had been telling anyone who would listen that I was using my son's death to promote Hodgson & Sons Ltd. I did not name Tommy Furber. But he went a darker shade of magenta as I spoke. He looked very frightened that I would name him. But I had no intention of acting as poorly as him and so I didn't.

Instead, I explained that I would not like anyone in the room to lose a child forever like me, but perhaps for just one minute, to see just how one would never ever contemplate using that loss for gain.

I said that I would never attend the monthly meetings again but would abide by the rules of the Guild nevertheless and expected to be treated as a member that did not attend the monthly meetings. The other Guild members tried to persuade me to stay but as I was adamant, they eventually agreed to my terms, and I left the meeting.

I did abide by the rules as I had promised. However, the Birmingham Funeral Directors Guild was not as honourable as I had been brought up to be.

Soon I noticed that we were not getting any coroner's removals. I enquired from the Birmingham coroner's office why this was and was told that Hodgson & Sons had been removed from the Birmingham Funeral Directors' list of participating firms.

I was furious. I informed the Guild that they had 24 hours to put Hodgson & Sons name back on the list or I would offer to do all Birmingham Coroner's removals free of charge from anywhere in the Birmingham area. We were back on the list by lunchtime that day.

Then, at the next meeting of the National Selected Morticians in London, I was told at the start of the meeting that Jennings, a large firm in Wolverhampton, had complained about the fact that I had bought FW Collins in neighbouring Bilston and that they wanted

This Life In Death

Hodgson & Sons removed from the NSM as they no longer felt comfortable discussing their business openly with me present.

I was amazed as we had bought Collins nearly two years before in 1981 and they had never raised an objection then or since. Moreover, I also knew that the NSM back in the US would hate a firm to be removed on the grounds of protecting another firm who wanted to uphold a restrictive practice.

I did not see that NSM membership held many advantages for Hodgson & Sons Ltd, but my father had been very proud to belong to this 'by invitation only' exclusive club and had always lived by its rules in a way that several other members hadn't.

Indeed, at this time, Hodgson & Sons were only matched in facilities by James Summers of Cardiff and even they fell well short of our standards of Hodgson service.

Moreover, I didn't see why Hodgson & Sons Ltd should be drummed out of a club for no other reason than someone's jealousy.

Nevertheless, the members voted to support Jennings and we were out - only to be immediately invited back by the US head office out of fear that I would sue.

I declined to either sue or return to the NSM. Instead, I determined that our success would grow so high that it would hurt their necks to look up at us.

On a happier note, J was christened in Edgbaston Old Church in July 1983. We booked the whole dining room at the prestigious Plough & Harrow Hotel on the Hagley Road and invited close to 100 guests to celebrate this wonderful day with us.

Philip Dunn, who had recently left Sandra for a man called Roy, turned up in a bright yellow Rolls Royce, which he had bought for the new love of his life. Maybe I should have picked up on this as a warning sign of what lay around the corner. However, I was frankly too happy to notice much other than my wonderful new son.

This Life In Death

1983 had been a struggle to find a positive route out of the dark mental abyss of 1982. However, we had kept the family on course to follow a bright light at the end of the darkest tunnel. We had not walked alone but together, and we had rewarded by the birth of Jamieson.

The business had continued to expand driven by my obsession to make it successful which had been hardened by the atrocious behaviour of the Birmingham Funeral Directors' Guild and the UK branch of the National Selected Morticians.

However, my hurt and anger towards them in general could never be directed towards one George Rose of Lymm Rose Funeral Directors of Nottingham. He was the one NSM member who always showed me sympathy and was a very decent human being. I was extremely sad when he died some thirty years later.

xxxxxxx

As the months of 1983 passed into 1984, J was developing from a baby into a little boy with his own personality. He was cautious compared to Charlie, but we weren't complaining about that.

Worryingly, he started to develop asthma as I had as a child. Therefore, the damp Birmingham winter months put him at risk.

About this time, I had bought back one of my father's old branch offices on Kingstanding Circle, re-opened it as a branch office and moved Beryl and Velma there so that they could make funeral arrangements as well as do their jobs. I also moved my own office there and put JT in charge of the Oaklands with John McManus as his number one conductor.

One foggy morning my private line rang in my new office. It was Marianne. Sheila Cleverly, J's nanny, was worried as he was having

This Life In Death

an asthma attack. We agreed that we would take him to the QEII hospital. I said that I would drive him there. She agreed to bring him to my office as it was on the way.

Something told me not to wait in my car but to drive back towards Eden Wood to meet her on the way. I will never know who or what put that notion in my head, but it was to prove to be a vital thought.

I drove towards home and flashed her down. I crossed the road to her XJS. Sheila was in the back with J on her lap. He looked lifeless and his lips were going blue.

I told Marianne to take my car and follow me. I said we were diverting to the Good Hope Hospital in Sutton Coldfield instead as it was closer.

I told Sheila to keep slapping his face and talking to him to keep him awake. I drove like a madman over red lights and round a roundabout the wrong way. I had already lost one son and I was not just about to lose another.

I screeched to a halt at the hospital, grabbed J and ran inside. I banged on a frosted glass hatch in the reception. It opened.

A woman poked her head out.

"This child isn't breathing", I screamed.

She responded by taking out a white card and said, "Name?"

I lent inside the hatch with J in one arm and with the other I grabbed her hair and banged her head hard on her desk.

"I said this child is not breathing."

This time she got the message, and we were rushed through to emergency where he was given oxygen.

This Life In Death

He had survived the ordeal, but these were desperate moments when I really feared lighting was going to strike twice to blight our lives again.

Next it was my turn to be ill. My back was very painful, I had pain in my legs, and I felt dizzy. A top consultant was engaged, and I visited his very smart consulting rooms in Edgbaston.

I'm afraid I can't recall his name now over 40 years later, but I can still see him most clearly. He had silver grey hair; a British Empire air of the 1930s with a white starched shirt, grey tie, black waistcoat and jacket, grey pinstripe trousers, shiny black shoes and a red carnation. Indeed, he looked much more like a funeral director than I did.

He could not come up with a diagnosis and so decided that I should spend 5 days having tests in the Priory Hospital, which was like a 5-star-hotel in Edgbaston and situated between the golf club and the world-famous cricket ground.

Once I was in my specially purchased white night shirt, as I didn't own any pyjamas, and established in my very comfortable private suite, he would visit a cheerful me each morning and explain that he believed that I could have cancer of the spine, a brain tumour or MS. It goes without saying that, after each briefing, I felt a lot less cheerful.

One of the tests was a myelogram. As I recall this meant I was injected with various coloured fluids and spun upside down and around and around to see where they went in my body. I remain surprised even now that the Gestapo didn't use this form of torture during World War II.

Now I felt much worse than before and looked it. Even the eminent cancer surgeon and great friend Joe Jordan looked worried when he visited me that night.

However, the next day I felt much better and determined to be positive and cheerful. Indeed, that evening there were two very pretty nurses on night duty.

This Life In Death

They transferred the other private ward calls to my room and stayed with me. We got on like a house on fire. One was a very well-to-do girl from Worcestershire, the other a local Jamaican girl from Aston. Inevitably, this all ended in one hell of a game of 'doctors and nurses' which started with a bed bath and a 'topless' vs. 'bottomless' competition before all hell let lose. I fell asleep at around 6:00 completely shattered.

The next day I was sent on a stretcher and by ambulance to the Birmingham Eye Hospital, placed in a dark cubicle, and given a button to press as soon as I saw a red dot appear on the screen in front of me. Following these tests, I was taken back to the Priory.

Once there, I was immediately sent back again to the Eye Hospital. The tests had failed. They had to be redone. I kept very quiet about the reason for the failure was that I had slept through the entire thing – perhaps unsurprisingly given the previous evenings feast of activity.

Eventually, I was released and given the 'all clear' on all the three horrid illnesses. However, I now had terrible headaches periodically which I had not had before.

Marianne, Howard, Jamie, his nanny Sheila and I went immediately to Madeira for Easter. My headaches persisted. However, if I lay down, they disappeared.

One morning, I was lying by the pool reading a most amusing book called 'The Henry Root Letters'. It had me roaring with laughter continually. At one point of such hysteria, I sneezed, and a load of boiling hot pink fluid shot down my nose. It had been injected into me during the myelogram and had sitting on my brain ever since.

As a result, the headaches disappeared completely, and I now also knew that I didn't have a brain tumour, MS or cancer of the spine and despite everything had managed to participate in the 'local hospital three-in-a-bed Olympics'. However, most annoyingly, the symptoms were to continue for another decade.

This Life In Death

Looking back, I seem to have become increasingly schizophrenic – a pious and perfect professional at work and completely irresponsible child at play.

In the Spring of 1985 Doug Ellis and I jointly organised a charity evening at 'Celebrities'. This was a very smart Club on the Hagley Rd in Birmingham. He was raising money for diabetes and I for the Charles Hodgson Foundation for Children. I seem to recall it was a Sunday – and I believe that it was the famous one when Denis Taylor beat the vastly more talented Steve Davis in the World Snooker Final of that year.

Celebrities had been set out like London's 'Talk of the Town' with tables being banked steeply from the stage to the rear, so that all dinners could see the cabaret acts while eating.

Doug had reserved his personal table near the stage. I thought that we should give priority to the folk that Marianne and her fund raisers like Shirley Woolley were selling tables of 10 to. So, ours was at the back of the room.

There were various cabaret acts, a question-and-answer session with a couple of Aston Villa players, a raffle and an auction.

Doug had put a week's holiday at the Hotel Villamil, Majorca in as the star item to be auctioned. The auction had been a success until this last bid. However, with this and perhaps because people had spent a lot already, bidding was slow.

From the back of the room, I tried to get things moving. It worked and bidding started to go well. However, I was a little too clever and, much to Doug's amusement, got left with the holiday – and at a premium price.

This was towards the end of my funeral conducting career. I had struck up a friendly relationship with a young lady who worked in the Witton Cemetery administration office for some time. I would have to go in the office at the entrance to the cemetery to hand in the 'green' certificate and collect the grave deeds for the family.

This Life In Death

One day in the early summer, she asked me where I was going on my holiday. I told her about the holiday I had got left with at the auction and that I would be going to Majorca the following Saturday as we were going to France as usual later in the summer.

She told me that she had been there last year and went topless on the beach.

"Got any photos?" I asked.

"No but I can show you", she smiled.

She came to my office after work the following evening when I was the only one left. She bought a bottle of wine, and you can guess the rest.

This wonderfully unemotional, uncomplicated and pleasure-seeking relationship was to exist spasmodically for many years.

xxxxxxx

In the late autumn of 84, we went to Paris for the weekend to stay with Uncle George and meet up there with Marianne's brother Alex and his lovely wife Beatrice.

George's wife had died a few months earlier. He looked much older than the last time I had seen him, and the once gracious apartment felt tired and in need of a spring clean. However, he seemed very pleased to see us and offered to look after Howard and Jamieson while the four of us went out to dinner at Maxim's on Saturday evening which was only walking distance away.

Alex and I dressed in a black tie, white wing collared shirt, dinner jacket and finished the look with a white silk scarf hanging loosely over our shoulders as was the fashion of the time.

This Life In Death

After dinner we danced. We had been seated next to a very large and extremely noisy party of some 20 or so French North African Arabs. The head of their party was a distinguished looking man in his late '60s.

While we were dancing, he too was with his partner for the evening, a young French woman in her early twenties. Everyone was dancing cheek to cheek. He clumsily bumped into Marianne and me, as he uttered the words to his young desire, "Mais tu es la rose de la rose."

He had stepped on Marianne's foot in the process but did not bother to apologise even though he clearly knew what he had done. I was infuriated.

We danced on and I could not wait until they passed us on the cruise round this very privileged dance floor that shook every time a train on the Paris Metro passed underneath us.

When we did meet up again, I didn't stamp on the young French women's foot, instead I said in a very audible voice to Marianne, "Mais, tu es la rose de la rose, de la rose, de la rose".

This visibly seriously annoyed the patriarch. I suspected he felt that he had lost face and he looked furious.

When we came to leave, it was at the same time as his party. They were glaring at me, but I was not intimidated and when a young male member of their group could not get his partner's coat over her puffed sleeves, I could not resist commenting, in a loud voice, "He has a problem getting it up."

The whole exit group stopped and stared. One of them, perhaps the patriarch's son, approached me and said, "You are a typically arrogant upper-class Englishman. We will be waiting for you outside."

I turned to Alex and said, "This is my quarrel. Look after Marianne in here."

This Life In Death

Alex said, "No. I'm coming with you. This is France, you are my family, and do you think I would let you face over ten guys alone?"

So, we went together out and faced ten of them. I came face to face with the guy, in his John Lennon specs, who thought that I was so objectionable.

He said, "You are such an arrogant English arsehole coming here on your own. There are ten of us."

"There are two of us actually, and that is more than enough" I replied.

I smashed the Lennon specs back into his face with a left hook to his right eye. The fight was on.

Alex and I did very well and, with the help of Marianne and Beatrice at the back of the ensuing circular fight using their handbags to bash guys on the head, we were holding our own.

Then, the Maxim security staff arrived, and our opponents ran away. Alex and I were very proud of our Anglo-Franco effort. We had been out-numbered, held our own and neither had suffered any damage – except me, but that was because I had punched the wall in the flying fist fight and broken two knuckles, which meant that I was unable to open a bottle of Champagne for two years.

We were congratulating each other how great we both were, when an onlooking Australian, who had witnessed the whole punch-up with his wife said to me, "Hey Pom, I suppose, you think you are great, with your Queensbury boxing rules!"

"We did OK", I replied.

"You wouldn't have lasted two minutes in Sydney. You never used your feet once!"

When we got back to Uncle George's, we were met by the eleven year old Howie who reported Jamie had developed a temperature. He had indeed and I sat up with him all night in a tepid bath to keep it under control as we hunted for a French doctor to come and see him.

Marianne and I were so scared in case lightning was going to strike twice. However, we got the poorly Jamie home the next day to Eden Wood and safety. Phew!

xxxxxxx

Meanwhile, Mrs Thatcher had been basking in the warm sunlight of the glorious victory over Argentina in the Falklands War. Our leader appeared courageous, our armed forces professional and Britain had looked to be a winner again.

The US magazine 'Time' boasted 'Britain Is Back' on its front cover – a headline which reflected that Britain had stopped being about tea breaks and strikes and had returned to become the Churchillian nation that the world so admired once more.

It had been a turning point for the country and suddenly Mrs Thatcher's ratings in the opinion polls soared as her tough monetary medicine, as prescribed by her two financial advisers, Sir John Hoskyns and Alan Walters, had started to work.

The nation had been forced to swallow this medicine since 1979 and it had got worse with the 1981 budget cuts of £3.5 billion in public spending.

Hoskyns and Walters knew that the government had to show the nation, the financial markets and, indeed, the world, that Britain was determined to deal with its enormous insupportable borrowings and get inflation under control.

However, if the financial markets were quick to applaud these courageous acts, understandably, the British public, which were either out of a job at worst, or subjected to a severe squeeze on their living standards at best, were less sure.

Nevertheless, Thatcher held her nerve then and by 1983 this policy of 'sound money' was paying off. The economy was recovering quickly. New small economically profitable businesses, helped by economic grants, were shooting up on newly created industrial estates built to replace old, unionised lame ducks which had been demolished when she had refused to support them artificially unlike previous governments.

So, she now took the opportunity to go to the country and won a landslide victory. The Iron Lady had turned the economy around by being brave and refusing to do a U-turn that both parties had continually done ever since the Second World War.

Now that she had also beaten the enemy across the seas and, with a huge working majority in the House of Commons, she was to focus her guns on her enemy at home – the trade unions.

1983 had seen her take on the Steelworkers' Union and crush them. However, she had declined a 'punch up' with the National Union of Mineworkers (the NUM) in the same year as she was advised that coal stocks at the power stations were not high enough and so she declined a 'show down' until she had ordered them built up.

She had not forgotten that she was leader of her party because Edward Heath had taken on the miners in 1974 and lost.

However, by 1984 she was ready, and war was declared. The NUM strike lasted nearly a year. It was brutal and caused great hardship and bitterness in mining communities all over the country.

This was a political fight rather than an industrial dispute.

In the red corner, the leader of the NUM, a communist, with an eye for personal gain as well as a hatred of capitalism, Arthur Scargill, backed by fanatical communists.

This Life In Death

In the blue corner, Margaret Hilda Thatcher, a grocer's daughter from Grantham, who believed that an individual, a family, a business, a multi-national company or a nation had to make money before they could spend it.

So, this was a civil war of ideological hate rather than a pay dispute.

Scargill, perhaps buoyed by his earlier victory against Heath, was easily provoked into this war. He made the massive mistake of declaring a strike without first having a national ballot of the members of the NUM.

He was loyally followed by his own South Yorkshire Miners. However, other areas, notably the Nottingham miners, were affronted by this lack of a ballot and continued to work.

Initially, Scargill was holding his own with the media, and public opinion was split. Perhaps the majority were in favour of the government, but this was by no means an overwhelming majority.

Then Thatcher moved McGregor, her Canadian Chief of the Coal Board, who was good at his job but a PR disaster, to one side when dealing with the media in favour of her only 'Tory wet' in the cabinet, Peter Walker.

Walker's sensible, logical and very reasonable approach night after night on BBC and ITV news came across brilliantly compared to the Scargill caricature of a character out of George Orwell's 'Animal Farm'.

Slowly, the vast majority of the nation was won over and even the striking miners started to lose support in the very communities where they lived.

This was down to the government campaign in part, down to the government appearing to be winning the war in part, but also down to the intimidation tactics used by the miners themselves, who tried to force local folk not to go to their jobs in support of them.

This Life In Death

We had a business in South Elmsall, Pontefract, as previously mentioned. There, our chauffeur bearers had to crawl through neighbour's gardens to get to work and hope that they would not be confronted by striking miners as they would be beaten up.

This attitude lost the striking miners a lot of sympathy from their own communities. Funeral workers not being allowed to go to work and thus causing a loved one's funeral to be cancelled smacked of a Soviet dictatorship and most folk disagreed with that.

Then one day in 1984, as miners were drifting back to work, I was at Fox's in South Elmsall, doing my usual monthly surprise visit to check on the standards of service and facility. A call came through. It was a removal. Everyone was out on a funeral bar one young apprentice in the coffin fitting shop.

It was a coroner's removal. A young miner, who had drifted back to work, had been bullied and ostracised by his friends and colleagues as a result. He had blown his brains out in by putting his dad's shotgun in his mouth and pulling the trigger.

I organised the apprentice and we went. We removed him to the ambulance. Then I went back to his bedroom and washed his brains off the wall, cleaned up the room, took away soiled bedding and folded the rest.

As I did, I knew that downstairs there were parents who were suffering as much, if not more, than we had with the loss of Charles. I knew that this had been a needless death caused by a ridiculous political struggle, and worse by man's inhumanity to man. This boy should not have died and his mates' fanaticism had caused it.

Years later, I was to visit Reid's Palace in Madeira at Easter. There I met Sir Peter Walker, by then Lord Walker.

He was a Tory wet, a compassionate and caring Conservative; a man who believed in capitalism as long as it promoted a meritocracy which created wealth to look after all in society in the process.

This Life In Death

He was a very decent and likeable man of a not dissimilar age to my father and with much the same attitude to life's need to be fair and caring.

I must confess that I liked him in the same way that I liked James Callaghan, the Labour Prime Minister before Mrs Thatcher came to power, and whom I had also met.

Lord Walker shared this story of the 1984 miners' strike. One Sunday evening his landline phone went at home.

A man said, "You won't know me."

"How did you get my number?" enquired Lord Walker.

"It's in the phone book" answered the man, much to Peter's surprise.

The man cut to the point quickly. He told the government minister that he was a signalman on the main line out of Nottingham that was used to get the coal to the power stations.

The NUM had encouraged other unions to support them by striking or at least disrupting coal distribution. As a result, some National Union of Signalmen were not willing to signal a 'green' to allow the trains to pass.

"I will send you the times when I'm on duty. You send the trains then and I will ensure they get a green signal."

He was as good as his word and the already high coal stocks at the power stations were kept high as a result.

"He did this out of the goodness of his heart?" I enquired at the end of this amazing tale.

"He did it because Scargill had denied the NUM membership a vote" was the peer's reply.

"So, he wanted nothing for himself?"

"Correct. However, he unexpectedly got an MBE in the New Year's Honours List" chuckled Lord Walker.

By the end of 1984 the strike was over, and Thatcher had won. This victory signalled the end of trade union power, which had dominated industrial life since the end of the Second World War, and which had come close to destroying the UK's economy in the 1970s.

Now the stock-market sensing a political and economic recovery, started to move up. The US was also on the move. The price of oil was declining from $40 a barrel in 1979 to only $10 in 1986 and this led to a decline in other commodity prices too.

None of this was to help the third World. But the US/European and especially the Anglo recovery certainly allowed the industrialised countries to enjoy several years of strong non-inflationary growth. With it came massive advances in technology which was to allow the west to invent, produce and then consume new gadgets such as mobile phones which kept this boom alive.

In Britain, those companies that had survived the severe recession of the early 1980s were leaner, fitter and the fittest started to expand by gobbling up the weakest of the survivors.

A takeover boom began to take place as ambitious companies suddenly saw growth by acquisition as a much quicker route to success than organic growth.

Now the whole market was taking a leaf out of Hodgson & Sons book. So, this new climate was perfect for us and gave me much to think about.

We had been making acquisitions for the last ten years. These had been made partly by retained earnings and partly by bank borrowings, where I had had to commit my children, my wife, my home and the very shirt on my back to the bank.

This Life In Death

This route to growth had made us successful but was painfully slow in this new environment. Whereas a stock market quotation opened the prospect to much faster growth.

Nevertheless, I was nervous. If this bull market was to end or if Mrs T was to lose the next election, then I might have floated Hodgson & Sons to see its share price fall and my percentage of the same be of a considerably lower value than it was under private ownership.

Moreover, there had only been one funeral company floated on the Unlisted Securities Market previously and that was Kenyon Securities in 1983. It hadn't been a huge success. Therefore, I remained sceptical that a flotation was a viable option for Hodgson & Sons Ltd.

There was no reliable evidence to suggest that in these heady times of high-profile flotations, which brought masses of publicity and so increased investor interest in a feeding frenzy, would suit us going forward.

Nevertheless, I thought we should take a closer look and so I took our accountant Steven Heathcote's advice and retired from conducting funerals in late 1984 to concentrate on the business's expansion.

Then, in early 1985, I asked to see Grindley Brandts, a very famous British Empire Bank in Asia and the Indian sub-continent, which operated as a merchant bank in the UK.

They sent a man called Robin Walker to see me. He thought we would be ideal to float and that I would be a stock market star. He said that I looked like a footballer or a rock star, and this was completely unique given that most people thought that funeral directors were ageing men with greased back thinning hair, an ulcerated alcoholic nose, who only smiled when the death rate went up. My looks were our USP according to him. I remained unconvinced.

This Life In Death

Also, in 1984 my father decided that he wanted to retire. I gave him a deserved and decent pension and he decided to go and live with his sister in Southbourne near Bournemouth.

His life of sharing a flat in Selly Oak with my brother had not been a success. My brother Russell had wanted to look after his father, but my father had ended up looking after him. Worse my father's finances, which I had got in order, were once more plunged into debt.

I transferred money to him to put this right and he left for Southbourne in good spirits. However, he and his sister did not get on and soon I was obliged to visit him at her home at her behest.

I explained that she was being most welcoming and that his flying off the handle at her was not going to ensure that he continued to be a welcomed guest.

He responded by telling me that I had completely wrecked the family business by over expanding it.

He added that his last year in charge might not have been too successful but that had been down to the 1974 oil crisis. I decided not to argue that point.

However, by 1985 Auntie June could no longer cope with him and so we found him a very pleasant residential guest house with a great sea view.

In May, the landlady called me to say that he was not well. I was going to drive from Birmingham to see my mother in Poole, only about 10 miles away, that weekend. I said I would come over and see him.

On Saturday 5th May 1985 Marianne, J and I went to see him. Howie elected to stay with his grandmother and her new boyfriend, a very kind chap called Alan Baker.

This Life In Death

We were shown upstairs to my father's room with a fantastic sea view looking over Poole Bay towards Old Harry Rocks. He was in bed, and looked very smart in his pyjamas, but did not look well in himself.

I had taken him a gift to boost his bank account because he had continued to be worried about his finances since he had gone back into debt when he had lived with his younger son. He looked at the £500 cheque with pleasure.

He turned to me and said, "Don't ever throw your life away and lose it."

I smiled and said no Hodgson would ever be poor again. I then pulled out a brochure of a QEII cruise and told him that in August we would all go; that he would need a new dinner jacket as he had lost weight etc.

He listened and then interrupted me when I was in full flow.

"Did I ever tell you what a good-looking boy you are?"

I was struck dumb. I had spent my whole life trying to impress him. I had always felt that I had failed. I was sitting on the end of his bed and turned to look at him in sheer shock. He had a tenderness and serenity in his eyes which was wonderful to behold.

I managed to continue to describe our plans but later, as the little bundle of energy called J was tiring us all out, we left. I kissed my father on his forehead before I went. It had been a wonderful afternoon.

The next morning at my mother's apartment, overlooking Poole Harbour, the phone rang at six o'clock. It was for me, and it was the landlady of his residential home.

She told me that my father had been rushed into hospital later that evening and had died during the night.

I was overcome with despair. My hero; my beacon; my funeral directing guide; the man who had sat up with me as a poorly

275

asthmatic child; the man who had hugged me on that road in Villars when I was so unhappy; the man who had risked his life to tell Eddie Fewtrel to let me go free, was no more.

I had craved his approval. I had never achieved it but for one silly sentence about my face within hours of his death.

There was an immediate empty abyss. I missed him so much. I even questioned, in those initial minutes, how I was going run my life without him.

He had died on the 6th May. This was my sister's birthday and so very unfair on her.

We arranged his funeral to be a service in Edgbaston Old Church, followed by a cremation at Perry Barr Crematorium. The same clergy who had attended upon Charles, three years earlier, would officiate.

My mother agreed to come in the lead limousine with the close family, although she declined to attend the wake afterwards. We did not know why at the time that this was because she was to be married to her third husband later that day.

As the impressive cortege made its way to the church, my mother announced that there would not be many people in church as my father had fallen from grace many years ago.

I bit my tongue as there is nothing more inappropriate than a family row on the way to a funeral service.

John McManus, whom the Old Man liked, was conducting, and his pal Arthur Hamer was driving the hearse. Eventually, we came round the corner on the Calthorpe Road to get a view of the church, and I couldn't see a pavement, kerb stone or grass for parked cars.

The great and the not so great had turned up to pay their respects to Osmond Paul Charles Hodgson. My eyes filled with tears then as they are now as I write this.

This Life In Death

I had, I think understandably, pre-recorded a eulogy for Charles. But for my father, I climbed the steps into the pulpit to give it live and with every ounce of love and gratitude that I could without breaking down.

I didn't make him out to be a saint because he wasn't. I did make him out to be my hero because he was and I loved him so very, very much.

On that last afternoon with him, my father had also made me promise that, in the event anything happened to him, that I would always look after my brother Russell.

"Russ will never make it alone. You do know that."

"Well, he got great 'A' levels."

"You didn't, but that's not the point."

I promised and, as God is my witness, I was to keep that promise for the next 40 years.

In the late summer of 1985. I took a table at a large private function in a grand house on the way to Henley-in-Arden owned by a successful local businessman called Norman Gidley. It was organised as a part of Dennis Amiss's benefit year. Dennis had played for Warwickshire since the early 1960s, had been England's most successful batsman in the mid 1970s and was soon to retire as he was now in his mid 40s.

I bought some raffle tickets and luckily won first prize – two return tickets on Concorde to New York. A friend at the table, Alan Carter, grabbed them and, thinking that I was wealthy enough, announced that they should be auctioned off.

However, Jimmy Combes, the Aston Villa goalkeeper and Worcestershire bowler had other ideas. He took them from Alan gave them back to me as he told Alan that Dennis did not want that sort of thing. Well done Jimmy and Dennis ,I thought.

This Life In Death

However, I refused to go without Howie and J and so had to buy two more tickets on Concorde and get a suite in the Waldorf Towers for the four of us to stay in. As a result, the weekend cost me a fortune.

While there, the Hotel organised a driver to take us sightseeing in a large black Cadillac.

"Where would you like to go?" The Chauffeur enquired.

"Harlem" I responded.

With which he passed me the car keys and said, "In that case you will have to drive yourself sir."

New York was still a very rough place then.

This Life In Death

Chapter VIV

Flotation

1986

Not long after my father's funeral in May 1985, Robin Walker came to Eden Wood one sunny evening. He had told me previously that I needed to pay Grindleys an annual retainer of £15,000 per annum. We had previously agreed on £10,000.

Now he was asserting that it should really be £15,000.

"How would you like £5,000 instead" I replied.

"What?"

"We made a deal. It was for £10,000. Now you want £15,000 so I'm offering you £5,000."

He said he would have to think about it. He was going to have dinner in Birmingham with another client but would return tomorrow with his answer before taking the train back to London.

I told him that he should also consider something else at the same time. That was that if he wanted to secure Hodgson & Sons Ltd as a client with the view to it being floated on the USM then he would have to offer my brother a job.

Robin returned the next morning with the news that Russell was to be offered a job with Capel Cure Myers, London Stockbrokers who had been bought by Grindleys in preparation for 'Big Bang' which was to happen in the following year.

I was delighted. I had kept my promise to my father and Russell had been handed a very good job and a great career opportunity.

I thanked him and enquired about the retainer.

This Life In Death

"Oh that. We'll stick with £10,000. I stuck the extra £5,000 on to the client's fees that I had dinner with last night" smirked Robin, who really could show some of the less acceptable faces of capitalism.

Therefore, the preparations for flotation on the USM the next year were started with Grindley Brandts and Capel Cure Myers. It would not be easy. Hodgson & Sons Ltd still only made a relatively small £200,000-a-year (1983) and enjoyed a nil net asset value thanks to all the goodwill sitting on the balance sheet as a result of its acquisitions over the last decade. Intensive work would be necessary.

It was decided the first requirement would be to replace the Midland Bank. Replace the Midland Bank you ask. Hadn't they supported me every step of the way?

Indeed, they had, and I was grateful. But now they were suffering from the 'Jesus of Nazareth Theory." What is that? It is a theory of mine that Jesus might have been the son of God to millions of people down the centuries but to the folk of Nazareth he was but the carpenter's son.

I might be intending to go on to become a stock market star to the investors of the UK but to the Midland Bank in Hockley, I was but a local funeral director that they had saved a decade earlier.

We had outgrown the Midland's perception of us and that became obvious when they were became increasingly nervous of our acquisitions in 1984 which included Preedy of Bristol.

With Robin's help we switched from the Midland to Lloyds in 1985. However, by the end of that year our new bankers were even feeling a little exposed too, as we had acquired AV Bands of Worcester too.

Their 800 funerals per annum meant that we were entering 1986 with 24 outlets now conducting 5,600 funerals a year.

This might have been a long way from the 400 that I had bought a little over a decade earlier but Lloyds Bank could see that they had lent a lot and that there wasn't too much on the balance sheet to support their borrowings.

Therefore, they were keen on a flotation or us raising some form of long-term capital flow from a financial institution to lower their risk.

I approached Albert E Sharp, Birmingham Stockbrokers, who had an investment arm called Sharp Unquoted Midland Investment Trust – known as SUMIT.

They were pleased to buy the shares that I had bought off my brother, by cancelling all his debts to me. This equalled 8.3% for £396,000, which came to me. They also subscribed a further £350,000 for a combination of convertible preference shares and loan stock, which went into the company.

At the same time Grindleys, who were also desperate to be in on this exciting story, had asked me to sell them a similar stake. I declined but referred them to my sister who still had her inherited 8.3%.

They bought her out and that meant that Hodgson & Sons Ltd now had just three shareholders. SUMIT with 8.3%, Grindleys with 8.3% and me with 83.4%.

To oversee their investment, SUMIT put a non-executive director on the Board. This stabilised the financial situation at the end of 1985, but it was not enough for my financial ambition. I was determined not to miss this express train to growth which I perceived was a game changer.

I could see the possibilities of growth through acquisition, and only a public company would provide me with the vehicle to take advantage of these opportunities before someone else did.

Despite my fears of a stock market bear-phase or a Thatcher electoral defeat – the first was to come in 1987 while in the same year Thatcher romped home to a huge third term win – I knew that conditions were perfect for this funeral bloke from Brum to have a go.

This Life In Death

In the City, many banks and stockbrokers were selling themselves to larger, often overseas, financial institutions as they prepared for their own Thatcher inspired revolution known as 'Big Bang.'

As with the unions and many companies, the City of London had become a nice cosy cartel. Like them it needed shaking up to keep London as the European leading Stock Exchange.

Now that my mind was made up, I wanted it done quickly. We motored from February to May 1986. We worked 20 hours a day. I had some appalling sessions with drafting people which made me allergic to them, as I am sure they were to me.

However, by the end of May the work was done. Moreover, in the process, the head of the Grindleys team, Michael Hackney, and of the CCM team, Chris Callaway, had become and would remain two of my three best friends ever. We had bonded.

Michael had replaced the Machiavellian Robin in 1985 and was to be welcomed into the Hodgson family as we shall see later.

Chris and I were to graduate from 'entrepreneur to corporate client adviser' to many other corporate adventures before spending over 20 years watching England play test matches in foreign parts with, a by then, adult J.

We now needed to fix the flotation price and set the ball rolling with a few press interviews. I accepted a price of 85p. This was high enough to value the company properly, but not too high for investors not to see an upside for them.

However, I was very coy about press interviews. Funeral directors were usually seen but not heard. I said I would only do one. This turned out to be with John Jay of the Sunday Telegraph. He treated the flotation seriously and this was to open the flood gates.

Neville Boyd Mansell of the Birmingham Post was first in and very supportive:

This Life In Death

'Just a year after Ingalls was taken over by the House of Fraser, Birmingham is going to have another publicly quoted undertaker. Hodgson Holdings (for this was to be our listed title) still based in Handsworth where it was founded in 1850, is bringing 32% of its shares to the Unlisted Securities Market this week, though a placing arranged by ANZ Merchant Bank (they had bought Grindleys while all of this was going on) who are the owners of Capel Cure Myers.

The plan is to raise about £3million for the company to enable it to continue a policy of expanding by buying up what it perceives as less-efficient funeral businesses – a policy which has carried its own profits from £113,000 in 1981 to £484,000 last year (1985) and £442,000 for the last six months to April 1986. Existing shareholders will collect £1.2 million, among them SUMIT, which will be left with 8.5% of the enlarged equity after selling 3%.

But why invest in him? Well, his market is never going to collapse. You could argue that he is the funeral industry Lord Hanson. The ANZ Bank believes that his shares are worth 14 years' earnings in the present stock market, linked to a yield of under 4%.

Now Mr Hodgson says he can buy another undertaker for one year's turnover or five to six times earnings. From day one, those earnings will be reflected in his own much more highly rated shares. And he has a very specific formula for increasing them ('we go in with a 155-point hit list when we acquire a company').

In all, he has 24 offices, none so far in London or the South, which they expect to do 5,600 funerals a year, about 1% of the total deaths in England and Wales. The nearest he comes to a monopoly is with something like 60% in Northampton and 20% in Northamptonshire. The Co-op has about 25% of the market and the House of Fraser 5%.

Much of the rest of the work is done by 2,000 small family businesses. Mr Hodgson believes many of them are hopelessly badly managed – and ripe to be taken over during the next ten years.'

This Life In Death

Mr Boyd Mansell had got this more or less right as he had listened intently to what he was told and was keen to report that correctly. Unlike many more lazy and less dedicated journalists of today.

The Times also compared me to Lord Hanson. However, neither they, the Financial Times or the Guardian recommended readers to buy. However, the Daily Mail said that the shares should do well, while the Investors Chronicle described the shares as fair value.

Ironically, more importantly, Robin Walker had been right about me looking like a rock star, because as soon as my photograph was printed in the financial press, so increasingly was non-financial press alerted to this story and they alerted the rest of the British public to Hodgson Holdings plc as a social interest rather than financial investment story. This gave it a much wider investment audience as a result.

I became a celebrity overnight and my mother adored every moment of it.

In the event, the shares, launched at 85p on June 16th 1986, as Hodgson Holdings plc became the last company to be floated on the floor of the London Stock Exchange before electrification and 'Big Bang.'

They immediately moved to a modest premium of 7p – which indicated that we had judged the flotation price perfectly.

I wasted no time in making use of my new war chest to make a flurry of takeovers in the autumn of 1986 and the early months of 1987.

By March 1987, on the back of this and a strong bull market, our shares had risen from 85p to 185p within less than ten months of launch. Fair value? Oh yes and I was being treated like a sort of 'David Beckham of funeral directing' as a result.

In the previous year The Great Southern Group had joined Kenyon Securities PLC and Hodgson Holdings plc on the USM and the USM magazine noted that the bull market was becoming fascinated by the funeral sector in general, and its new 'enfant terrible' Howard Hodgson, in particular.

The review went on to say that Hodgson's 'acquisition led tenfold increases in funerals conducted per annum and consistent profit suggest it is a well-managed concern with a sound future,' while it noted that both Kenyon and GSG, while also appearing to be well managed, had only enjoyed modest growth by comparison.

So, a combination of investor adviser praise and the start of my whirlwind romance with the colour supplement press, Hodgson Holdings shares were pushed up higher and higher.

However, because of this business acclaim and 'rock star' glamour, one fact was now being lost on everyone and would remain so to all except those who knew the real story.

I was the only person who had ever been a practicing proper funeral director. Moreover, it was that grounding in two very good funeral businesses and my experience learnt doing a funeral director's job, that had made me the best entrepreneur in the field rather than my 'rock star' looks or my apparent general business ability.

I actually knew what I was doing and how to do it to maximum effect. This was not always true of my competitors. However, this all seem to get lost in this period of Thatcher super star entrepreneurs and looking back I did little to dispel my new celebrity image. Instead, I preferred to bask in the attention it engendered - especially from the opposite sex.

Throughout this period, I was continually running up and down from Birmingham International to Euston Station in London on British Rail Inter-City trains. I would rise at 5:30 and, having showered, shaved, suited and booted, would set off for the station – a fifteen-minute dash in my 5 litre XJS. Once there I would catch the 7:00 train.

If I had to take a train in the middle of the day from the head office in Sutton Coldfield, the journey would take longer due to the traffic, and

This Life In Death

I often cut it fine due to pressure of communication done by landline phones in the days before effective mobiles and computers.

On one such occasion, I was dashing to make a 14:00 train. I had Graham Hodson in the front and my PA Timothy Penrose in the back as we roared out of the car park with head lights on full beam.

We sped down the middle of the road forcing cars going in either direction to pull over, we then cut at high speed through a garage forecourt to avoid a red traffic light in Erdington as we wanted to do a left turn there.

Graham laughed as he noticed a guy pouring petrol over his feet with his mouth open at this spectacle. However, by now Penrose was screaming and begging to be dropped off. He seems to have forgotten this incident when writing 'Undertaking in the Fast Lane.'

I completely admit that this was very irresponsible behaviour by me. However, a combination of continual work pressure to deal with the City of London, while running Hodgson and the instilled belief that, as a City super star, I could do as I wanted, was to blame.

xxxxxxx

During the period before flotation, I had received some 'old money out' from SUMIT as already reported.

Marianne and I decided that, as Eden Wood had been bought by me off Hodgson Holdings plc by a succession of very expensive bonuses, tax wise, to prepare for the flotation, we should invest in a French property so we could spend more time with her family without putting them to the trouble of looking after us.

However, this proved to be easier said than done. But, after an extensive search, eventually one was found in Port Grimaud next door to the very pleasant, as well as famous, actress Joan Collins. I duly handed over the cash to Philip Dunn, to facilitate its purchase.

However, during the actual flotation legal meetings in 1986 with Grindley and CCM, Philip's attendance became inconsistent without warning and his advice therefore, at times, was non-existent.

Luckily for me, the CCM lawyer, a very decent man called Dick Towner, refused to take advantage of us because of our solicitor's absence, and with the full support of Christopher Callaway and Michael Hackney we agreed each point fairly and openly.

About the same time Graham Hodson popped in to see Philip at a hotel that he had bought in mid-Wales because his boyfriend Roy, liked the idea of owning one.

Graham reported that the quality of the hotel's refurbishment was truly unbelievable and more akin to the Ritz Hotel in London rather than a small Welsh hotel used by travelling salesmen mainly. I thought Graham was exaggerating and reminded him that Philip had secured a government grant from the Welsh Office to do the work needed.

So, I had had enough warning signs but had steadfastly refused to see any of them by some sort of blind loyalty to Philip and Sandra Dunn.

Then at Christmas in 1987 the queue of acquisitions that Hodgson Holdings were completing virtually at a rate of one a week came to a sudden stop due to the Christmas recess and I was faced with a huge problem when we returned to work.

Some of the money Hodgson Holdings plc had been depositing for the acquisitions with Philip's client account to our order to settle for acquisitions had been stolen by him and he had been using money deposited for a previous acquisition to pay for the current one, and thus disguising the missing funds.

This Life In Death

Therefore, the Christmas recess had created a gap and meant Hodgson Holdings had no need to send further funds. Therefore, the chain was broken and when the most recent payment became due for, as I recall a company called Stone and Ham of Cardiff, the money was not there.

I was horrified, shocked that Philip as a solicitor, friend and gentleman could do such a thing, and extremely angry as Lloyds Bank were both our bankers and those of Stoddard Taylor (Philip's firm).

Luckily, we had enough cash to cover the deficit. But, Lloyds, as banks always do, tried very hard to absolve themselves of any responsibility, despite the fact that they were negligent in not advising us that funds we had deposited to Phillip had not been used for the purpose that we had intended.

The Bank tried to intimidate me. I stood firm and eventually the account manager was demoted and moved to a small branch in Small Heath.

The bank became nervous as everything was immediately open to a police investigation, and soon they also discovered that the cash that I had personally also deposited into Philip's client account for the purchase of the French property in Port Grimaud had also gone missing.

So, he had stolen circa £1 million pounds from us, about 40% of which was from me and 60% from Hodgson Holdings.

It was also discovered that he had stolen another several hundred thousand from his father's elderly lady clients who had deposited cash with him for various reasons.

Philip's father, who was also elderly and had recently retired, had served honourably in World War II, was a very honest man and was rightly horrified by his son's actions.

This Life In Death

The Law Society called him out of retirement and unfairly held him initially accountable. However, once the police case was proved against Philip and he was sentenced to a prison sentence, the Law Society paid Hodgson Holdings, me and the old ladies out in full and Mr. Dunn senior was once again allowed to retire, I believe.

So, a man who had received nothing but love and kindness from his father; nothing but love and admiration from his wife and children; and nothing but friendship and copious legal fees from me had betrayed us all.

When asked why by Marianne, he replied, "I did it all for love."

Indeed, the love cause of this vile behaviour, Roy, was to make most of his illiteracy, claiming in his statement to the police, that he knew nothing of Philip's actions and signed the same with a 'X'. He was to face no charges as a result.

Here ends the association with Philip Spencer Dunn and this saga.

A man who had been born to a childhood friend of my mother. A man that I had met when we were both poor but had both come from kinder childhoods. A man who had been an usher at my wedding. A man that I had trusted with my son and my money. One had died in his care and the other had been stolen by him.

I have thought long and hard about writing this piece for the sake of his two sons Adam and Jacob . However, I decided it would discredit the integrity of this memoir to leave this element of my life out as the experience speaks volumes about my stupidity as it does about his dishonesty.

This Life In Death

Chapter X

Fame, Flirtation & Ingalls

1987

Shortly after the flotation, I received the surprise accolade of being voted one of the 'Top 40 Under 40' Businessmen in the country by the glossy magazine 'Business.'

The 40 were mainly male and Richard Branson and Alan Sugar were the most famous. We all appeared in page upon page of colour photographs in the magazine before gathering around a piano, not being really played by Richard, as we sang, 'Hi Ho, Hi Ho, it's off to work we go' for ITN's News at Ten.

Corny? Absolutely! But completely in keeping for a period when entrepreneurs were replacing footballers as the bedfellows of rock stars as sex symbols. I had always wanted to be a 'Beatle' and this was probably the closest I was going to get and so I lapped it up.

Richard was exceptionally pleasant and sociable for a man who was so clearly shy, and I can't recall Sugar being there. Although our paths were to cross some three years later when John Major invited us, along with other entrepreneurs and a mixture of Tory politicians, to 10 Downing Street for drinks.

Sugar and I struck up a conversation, and then, from behind us, the kindly and surprisingly tall then PM put his arms on my, and the midget Sugar's, shoulders with the words, "I bet you two are hatching a deal!"

"What's your game then", barked the furious Sugar as he shrugged Mayor's arm off as he swung round with the words, "We were talking football if you must know."

Over the next few years some of the 40 were to fall from grace. A few by association with the Guinness/Distillers scandal but most caused

This Life In Death

by their companies falling victim to having heavy borrowings when there was a huge hike in interest rates towards the end of the decade.

Others hit hard times then too, staggered but recovered. These included the famous Alan Sugar of Amstrad and Michael Green of Carlton Communications.

Some, like Richard Branson, Nigel Rudd, Bruce Oldfield and me, continued to prosper.

The 'Top 40 Under 40' had come as a complete surprise. I had never even read Business Magazine, did not expect to be selected and really didn't believe that I deserved the accolade.

However, my inclusion did no harm at all, as Robin Walker's prediction seemed to be increasingly coming true. The media's escalating fascination with a blond long-haired (grown since retiring from funeral conducting) funeral director was keeping my profile high and our share price even higher.

And the acquisitions were still coming thick and fast. By the end of 1986 the company was arranging 50% more funerals than it had when it floated just six months before. The NSM members were now getting the neck ache from looking up that they deserved but this only increased their jealousy.

Boyd Mansell in the Birmingham Post continued his support:

'Yesterday, he had to deliver, in hard figures for the year to October. Sure enough, his £840,000 profit was 15% ahead of his forecast in June and 65% of his last year as a private company.'

The Birmingham Post was backing an Aston Villa fan and local boy made good. I was both proud and grateful. However, now the Financial Times was also weighing in on my side and this is the pinnacle of any entrepreneur's career and a serious compliment as this publication is not easily impressed:

This Life In Death

'The death rate may be static but that presents no problem for the expansion of Hodgson. A few years ago, undertaking was very much a family affair, but as the money spent on funerals has declined more companies have come up for sale. Hodgson and others have therefore been able to buy up competitors and then introduce classic economy of scale policies. This is one reason for pre-tax margins in 1986 of about 30%. Another has been the company's growing success in selling ancillaries such as flowers and memorials. The year ahead should see profits in the £1.2m range, putting shares of 196p on a prospective p/e of 22. The high ratings will put some investors off but the shares, which traded at just 85p when the company was floated on 1st June represent reasonable value for those prepared to take the long view.'

Not all the analysis was quite right, but they were backing me, and I was extremely complimented and happy.

Long term view? I think not. The shares were to rise even more rapidly and were to reach 304p on a prospective p/e of 70. Wow! This heady combination of our ability to be better funeral directors, work harder than the competition at acquisitions and ensure profit enhancement by understanding the business better was clearly invincible.

However, the Sunday colour supplement massive desire to follow me was also a big reason for the success. They wanted to photograph me at work, playing cricket, sailing, riding, swimming or being just with the kids at home.

This was huge because it not only attracted a mini-David Beckham media fascination, which flattered my ego, but, more importantly, it meant that every Monday morning our share price jumped as new investors instructed their stockbroker to get them a piece of the Hodgson cake.

Therefore, our market capitalisation grew and grew and that meant I could keep coming back to the City for another rights issue at a very shallow discount. This, then fuelled our ability to acquire more and more.

However, I was also aided by another fact. We were a Birmingham company based in Sutton Coldfield. Our acquired funeral directors were nationwide. However, Kenyon and GSG were predominately southern and even London based.

They seemed initially frightened to come out of London. Therefore, I was acquiring all over England and Wales while they were only acquiring in London or the Home Counties. This gave me a huge advantage.

I was able to buy away from the south at a modest price while buying in London or the home counties at a higher multiple due to their competition.

However, as they were only buying in London and the Home Counties their overall multiple was much higher than mine and so I could outbid them when I wanted to while still having a much lower cost of acquisition per funeral across the UK overall. This, along with our vastly superior economies of scale operation, meant not only were we expanding faster but also were doing so in a more economically efficient fashion.

Most journalists are not investigative and can be a trifle lazy. So, over the next few months, the fact that I starred in several Sunday colour supplement magazines, helped me get this point across.

The large four page spread in the Sunday Times with a huge photograph of me in a graveyard wearing a white double-breasted overcoat and brown fedora under the banner 'Mr Death' set the tone and all other Sunday supplements wanted to have their turn to have me appear in their publications. This led to me having to turn down many silly requests, like being photographed with a scull in my hands like Hamlet.

Then I was named as one of 'Maggie's Dozen of the Decade, also in the Sunday Times. This was followed by 'Howard's Way' a BBC 2 television documentary. That led to over 35 other TV programmes between then and 1990. This was more than any other UK company – a lot of whom were bigger and much more profitable. However, they lacked this Robin Walker concept of a rock star kid called 'Mr Death.'

This welter of publicity was all well-orchestrated by Simon Preston Associates, a corporate PR agency introduced to me by CCM prior to flotation. The company was managed by the charming and urbane Simon Preston. He was convinced that he won our account because he understood what I wanted. Actually, he got it because I thought he looked like a funeral director and would shield me from too much exposure.

How little did I know myself. From very early days I had become addicted to that very exposure, and he had to remind me not to do TV interviews with facial and voice impersonations of Paul McCartney instead of me being just plain me.

Shortly after the favourable press reception to its first results as a public company, Hodgson launched its tenth bid since going public for a Doncaster firm called J. Steadman. Still the acquisition trail blazed.

Now I had gathered a team of loyal guys around me as I had some twelve years before. This time however, it was to concentrate on acquisitions.

Nevertheless, I still had my hands firmly grasping the tiller of the daily standards of funeral management, which was run by an entirely different team.

So, while my corporate team were working very hard to ensure we kept the shareholders happy with increased profits due to acquisitions, I still needed to ensure that bereaved families were being well cared at the time of their need. This was both my calling and essential to keep the business successful.

This Life In Death

Given my own commitments to both the growth of Hodgson and the continuing high standards of service, I knew that I needed extra executive help with funeral operations as well as keeping investors happy.

This was particularly important as, unlike the much bigger success I was to have with Memoria over a decade later, where growth was organic, and therefore every new employee only knew our way of doing things, this growth was by acquisition, and we were inheriting staff already engaged in funeral directing and with much lower standards than our own.

I selected a man called Stevie Gauld. He was a Scot who had been a funeral director and worked his way up the Wylie & Lockhead business in Glasgow. Before its sale to the House of Fraser, he had left and joined the Great Southern Group.

We met at an NAFD conference by chance. We chatted. I like his sensitivity, loyalty and concern for the bereaved. I called him a few days later and asked him if he wanted to join Hodgson Holdings plc. He jumped at the chance. I had made an excellent signing. Stevie was then and still is today, a man I have total admiration for.

I was driven by a tireless desire to win and knew that drive, determination and energy were my key USPs, and I didn't care how long it took me every day to oversee that everything was perfect.

The dedicated plc team included Graham Hodson, who had become my number two, was a good legal document guy for us and seemed only too happy to get as far away from conducting funerals as he possibly could; Steven Heathcote, who had been at West House with me, had joined the Board just before flotation as company secretary and remained thereafter as a non-executive director and Simon Ramshaw of Edge & Ellison, the solicitors acting for SUMIT when they took a holding in Hodgson in 1985. He built an acquisition team for us at Edge, and we kept it busy for the next three years.

This Life In Death

I then added a new Finance Director, Ron Middleton, who by sheer coincidence, as Birmingham 'well-to-do' society is but a village community, had also been at West House along with Steven and me.

The final member of my top plc team was brought in specifically to search out funeral directors and seduce them into selling to Hodgson Holdings plc. He was, and still is, at now 82, Dennis Amiss MBE.

Dennis was a former England cricket star of much skill, who became famous as part of that 1970s opening England batting partnership of Boycott and Amiss.

When he finished his wonderfully successful career in 1987 there were plenty of firms chasing his signature. He and I had become friends via the Jordans, and he asked me to advise him on who to choose.

However, it occurred to me that he would be an excellent acquisitions manager for us. I knew most funeral directors loved cricket, and some would give a lot to have a famous England international sit in their office and talk to them about his many amazing innings.

Dennis said yes and I went off for a weekend ski to Courchevel in the French Alps very pleased. However, my brick of a mobile went while having lunch on the slopes on Saturday and it was Graham to tell me that Dennis had called to say that his wife, Jill, had said no so he couldn't join.

I got Graham to invite both Dennis and Jill to lunch with him and me on Monday. We had a very long lunch when I was at my most persuasive while batting back loads of searching questions about death and funerals.

Eventually, Jill got up to go to the ladies. As she did so she looked at me and said, "Dennis will be happy to join you at Hodgson Holdings."

I had passed the audition. My toughest for some time. Once she was out of hearing range, Dennis lent forward and said, "I was going to join anyway guys."

This Life In Death

"Fuck off Den", was my reply.

However, before any of this took place and therefore Dennis had commenced his blitzkrieg attack on the funeral directing acquisition market, Hodgson Holdings were doing pretty well without him as we steamed through 1987. We bought WH Wigley, our first London acquisition, for £415,000 in February and within days E. Seymour in St Albans for £325,000.

The acquisitions since flotation some nine months earlier had now cost £2.4m, which was a lot of money in those days.

However, this is why I had floated, so I was determined to exploit public company status by issuing 1.76 million shares at 170p to raise another £2.85m net of expenses.

Such was the image of the company now and its 'enfant terrible' CEO that the market took the issuing of more paper in its stride with the Investors Chronicle commenting: 'Fair value even though the shares are much more highly rated than those of other undertakers.'

The existing shares jumped up 16p to 200p on the news. However, the real excitement was yet to begin.

At various stages of a business career, whether buying or selling, you may be faced with 'a very big deal' and you must get it right. Do so and you will have underpinned and correctly exploited all the hard work connected with the day-to-day running of the business.

However, get it wrong and you could destroy all those years of toil. In my case going all the way back to 1975.

Occasionally, along comes a deal like that. They are bigger and more important than others: the acquisition of Ingalls was such a deal for me.

On 2nd April 1987 under the headline, 'Major deal on the cards at Hodgson Holdings' the Birmingham Post announced that I had asked the Stock Exchange to suspend dealings in Hodgson pending an announcement.

In bear markets, suspensions usually imply there is a disaster around the corner. However, in bull markets they foretell glad tidings.

The Post went on to predict, 'Watchers of the way Mr Hodgson has pursued his ambition to establish a national chain took the move as a signal that the House of Fraser has accepted his offer for their considerable funeral operations.'

Ingalls was originally an engineering company based in Wolverhampton, that had diversified into funerals. In 1985, the Birmingham Co-op had made an offer for them, and Ingalls had, rather ironically, not wishing to become part of the Co-op, considered making an offer for Hodgson & Sons Ltd instead. However, I had made it very clear that I was not about to exit, and as I was the majority shareholder by some way, my decision was final.

Moreover, once the Birmingham Co-op made a formal offer it became impossible for Ingalls, as a PLC, to bid for Hodgson.

Then, following the Birmingham Co-op's 80p offer a share for Ingalls, the House of Fraser, which already had got extensive Scottish funeral interests of its own, entered the battle and offered 110p a share. The Co-op did not improve their offer and so Ingalls became part of House of Fraser instead.

However, over the next two years the House of Fraser became completely distracted by a battle for control between Tiny Rowland and the Al Fayed brothers.

The Al Fayed brothers were ultimately successful. They were most interested in the flagship Harrods, the world-famous London department store; less so in the other House of Fraser retail outlets; and not at all in Ingalls.

Moreover, as Muslim Egyptians, they thought that owning a large funeral business might prove to be unlucky. So, it became known they were prepared to sell Ingalls which was now a private company again as part of the House of Fraser.

Naturally, I was interested but I knew it was too big for me. It was conducting 22,000 funerals a year, when you included the House of Fraser Scottish funerals. Collectively this amounted to £16m annual turnover, and the asking price was £30m.

Hodgson Holdings had by now grown to 9,500 funerals per annum. This might mean that we had come a long way from the 400 per annum that I bought twelve years before, but it was a colossal jump to a new total of 31,500. It seemed a bridge too far. I believed that the market, if not the Exchange itself, would prevent me from bidding.

However, I talked to my now friend and Fleet Street's foremost financial journalist John Jay, who had supported me so much at the time of flotation and since. He told me that I must find a way. It was an opportunity that I must take. It was a quantum leap that might never occur again.

I knew he was right, and I knew I had to find a way. Then it came to me that, while the whole deal might be a bridge too far, half might just be possible and half the cake would still take us to 20,500 funerals per annum.

I turned to Michael Kenyon of Kenyons PLC and offered to go 50/50 with him. He turned me down. Something he was later to forget apparently when giving an interview to BBC's Money Programme about me.

I then telephoned Bruce McDougall, Managing Director of the CWS (Co-operative Wholesale Society) Funeral Division and said, as in the words of that famous Bob Dylan song, "Do you want to make a deal?"

McDougall replied curtly that he didn't need Hodgson Holdings to help him buy Ingalls.

I replied that if that was true for him, it was also true for me as I intended to "buy the bloody thing and you run the risk of getting nothing."

I went on to say, "You may have every Co-op in the UK behind you, but I have the London Stock Exchange behind me. Remember, you telephoned me at the time of the Hodgson flotation and said that you had heard that the capitalisation was £7.2million but that had to be a joke. Well, the market capitalisation, 10 months later is over £14million and who's laughing now? I was willing to share the deal with you, so we didn't push the price any higher but if you want me to go and see the GSG instead...."

"Okay, you made your point. Let's have lunch."

They say bullshit baffles brains, and this had been pure bullshit and it had worked. Nevertheless, one point was correct. I had made up my mind to buy the 'bloody thing.'

xxxxxxxx

I was invited to lunch at the CWS Head office and was shown into their board room at the very top of a large building in Manchester. I had taken Graham with me, and we gazed out over Manchester to Strangeways Prison far below, my mind wondered what my father would have thought about his son doing a deal with his biggest enemy after Adolf Hitler and Yank service men – the dreaded Co-op.

The CWS top brass turned up without Bruce. This was apparently too big a deal to be dealt with by a mere divisional head. So, Graham and I were to have lunch with the best the CWS could offer and I soon realised, by their choice of wine and even water, that I wasn't over impressed with their top brass.

This Life In Death

Nevertheless, if they were to be my partners, I had to trust them and treat them with respect and without suspicion. We struck a deal to split the numbers in half. Therefore, we would offer the asking price subject to due diligence. This would cost us £15million each.

Almost straight away we ran into a serious problem. The CWS announced in the press that they had struck a deal with Lambeth Council in London to do free funerals on the rates. I was furious.

I rallied support amongst funeral directors countrywide to oppose such a waste of public funds and to protect our industry from such an idea of discouraging competition. I considered this to be very important. Others thought that I was being alarmist and that the take-up would be small.

I had just been voted 'USM Entrepreneur of the Year' and was due to go to a large gala dinner in London to collect my gong. I sent Graham to collect it on my behalf instead with the message in his acceptance speech that I was working. This was because the dinner coincided with a meeting about 'funerals on the rates' which I had called back in Birmingham on the same night.

We repaid the CWS's hospitality by inviting them to lunch in Sutton Coldfield. Even before the first course was served, I launched into a tirade of anger over their action. Graham looked nervous that I was taking this aggressive attitude.

He was, of course, right, but I was not able, even in this moment of my great fight to win this deal, to lose my father's defence of honourable funeral directors, despite their apparent hatred of me and my success.

I was completely messed up by his presence in my head of what the right thing to do was. I knew that I must pull this deal off. However, surely not at the expense of my integrity.

So, I was suddenly and amazingly prepared to lose this deal that I was so utterly committed to, because I was even more dedicated to defending my fellow funeral directors' professionalism and livelihoods.

The CWS team melted under my tirade and promised to cancel the Lambeth project. I was amazed but pleased. Graham let out a huge sigh of relief as I could have easily blown the whole deal by following my father's lead of putting integrity over profit and success.

We indicated our interest to the House of Fraser. Initially, Hodgson and the CWS were given time by them to get our act together, and having signed heads of agreement, were just about to make our offer when we were told that Al Fayed had sold his funeral division for £30million to another party.

I was devastated. It was a Friday and I had to attend a dinner party that evening. I sat there quite numb. A corporate finance adviser friend sitting next to me said, "Forget it. It's gone. It's lost."

I turned to face him. "Oh no, it's not. I refuse to lose it" I replied.

CCM had given up, the CWS had given up too, but I found an ally in Tim Seymour of County NatWest, the CWS's corporate advisers. I called him over the weekend, and this resulted in him telephoning Brian Walsh, the House of Fraser CEO, to tell him that I had said that he was not a gentleman, as he had 'welshed' on our deal.

Walsh had only been acting on Al Fayed's orders, and the other bidder had offered the asking price before us, so my criticism was hardly fair.

However, as an Australian with a very senior job in London, Walsh, nevertheless, was acutely keen to avoid the 'Aussie convict' tag and so hated the thought of not being a gentleman. Our gamble paid off and we were invited to meet him in their HQ in Howick Place, Westminster on Monday morning.

We all trouped and bid £31million on the understanding that our bid was accepted there and then. Walsh left the room to phone Al Fayed,

This Life In Death

Chris Callaway and Don de Groot of CCM and I looked nervously at each other.

He returned and told us that Fayed had ordered the other bidders, who were by now doing their due diligence, off his premises and that we had a deal if it was signed in next three weeks to meet House of Fraser tax requirements. I was elated. I was going to buy 'the bloody thing.'

Or was I? The next body-blow came from the Takeover Panel. They warned that I would not be allowed to exceed £15.5 million without getting the approval of my other shareholders, which could not be done within the three week deadline.

The agreed price was £31million and so our share was £15.5million and this was still just acceptable without shareholder approval. However, in a second ruling, the Panel insisted that Hodgson Holdings and the CWS could not split the House of Fraser funerals down the middle, but that Hodgson must buy the English Ingalls business so that it could prepare a proper long form accounting report for our stockholders.

The CWS professed that it was happy to buy Wylie & Lockhead, the House of Fraser funeral business in Scotland. However, this gave me a huge problem because it resulted in our share of the deal going up to £17.5million as the Ingalls business in England was larger. Now we would be forced to seek shareholder approval, and this could not be done within the three-week deadline.

Everybody involved from our stockbrokers, bankers, accountants and lawyers thought and thought again. No one could come up with a solution. So, all the King's horses and all the King's men couldn't put Humpty together again.

I retreated with Marianne and the boys to the South of France for Easter. I went sailing in my First 456 on my own and thought and thought again and again because I was not going to lose 'the bloody thing.'

This Life In Death

Then the miracle happened. I thought I might have a solution. What if I asked the House of Fraser to leave the creditors in Ingalls, I would pay them off after the acquisition and the amount would be subtracted in total from the acquisition price?

I came about and headed 'Fat Girl' (my boat) for Port Grimaud. I got on the phone straight away to Price Waterhouse and asked them how this would affect the acquisition price.

"But it's Easter Howard" was the answer.

"I couldn't give a fuck" was my reply.

An hour later the phone rang, and the answer was that the price would be reduced to £15.3m. Oh yes! I was not going to lose 'the bloody thing.'

Another huge hurdle had been jumped and I had done it not because I was cleverer than my advisers – indeed I was not. I had done it because I had wanted to win more than any of them.

At the start of the negotiations over the contract contents to be signed by all parties, we had had to give a lot of concessions to the House of Fraser in case the other potential purchaser was invited back in to replace us.

However, as the deadline approached, I was able to claw most back as I realised that they were now stuck with the CWS and us if they wanted to meet their own deadline.

It was not my style to unagree matters which had been agreed, and it never has been, but when dealing with Mr Fayed, one had to play by his rules and if they were good enough for him to crucify my shareholders, they were good enough for me to protect them too – much to his annoyance.

Simon Ramshaw and Graham Hodson were very steadfast in helping me in this as we dug in during sessions which went on into the early hours of every morning day after day.

This Life In Death

Just before the completion date, a massive tactical meeting between CWS, Hodgson Holdings plc and both our growing armies of advisers took place at the Co-op International Bank in the City.

Tim Seymour shook our side by opening with a statement that the CWS was not happy with its long form report and wanted to negotiate the price down, postpone the deal, and if they did not get what they wanted, to call the whole thing off.

I was sure that they suspected we were having problems with the Panel and would instantly agree to their proposal.

We were so many in number in this huge room that we were even talking into microphones which were placed all over the ginormous board room table.

I grabbed the one nearest to me and without a moment's consultation with my own army of advisers announced that we were happy with our long form report and asked to be released from the heads of agreement with them in order to buy both Ingalls and Wylie and Lockhead.

My team looked horror-struck, but I believed that this could be my only reaction. I was prepared to call their bluff because I thought that if I could buy Ingalls now, my market capitalisation would rise and therefore I could return to buy Wylie and Lockhead in the autumn without having a problem with the Panel.

I also suspected that the House of Fraser would agree to this, because an Ingalls deal by the deadline with a promise to buy the other part within a few months was better than no deal at all before the tax deadline.

I finished my speech and the room buzzed with both sides whispering to each other – as my side was just as shocked by my statement as the CWS were.

This Life In Death

The CWS asked for an adjournment. Within ten minutes they were back. They had changed their minds about their long form report. Now they were happy with it and the deal was on again.

A furious Tim Seymour asked Chris Callaway if I did all my own corporate finance advice or did CCM occasionally help me?

I was not going to lose 'the bloody thing' and I promised myself again that nothing and no one was going to stand in my way now.

On the completion day, a Saturday, we all gathered at the House of Fraser solicitors, McKenna's offices in the Aldwych. The day was to become the subject of a BBC Radio 4 programme.

We were still nowhere near getting matters over the line and there were scores of protagonists arguing minutiae in a dozen rooms as I wandered from one to another.

Everyone was making or conceding or refusing to concede points. Ties were loosened and jackets removed. What about the women? There were hardly any there. A very different picture then from today.

Hour after hour went by as both temperatures and tempers rose. The House of Fraser was holding firm that it wanted a £28.8 million package in total and that this had to be agreed by midnight.

Chris Callaway and Don de Groot, the latter had replaced Michael Hackney, who had been posted to Milan by ANZ, popped into the morning session, satisfied themselves that the lawyers, Graham Hodson, and I were doing a good job and so took themselves off for lunch at the Savoy. Tim Seymour told me, with a smirk, that he hoped I was not paying them fees for this.

Discussions had been going on for over twelve hours and we only had two hours to the deadline, when something cropped up re the Ingalls articles of association. The lawyers told me I was unable to ignore the point as CEO of a quoted company. Oh, surely not now. I could almost taste the success of winning. Please God no!

This Life In Death

Thank God, the House of Fraser's solicitor, Simon Renton of Mckenna's came to my rescue by agreeing to have the Ingalls articles changed.

Brows were mopped and the arguing re-started as the atmosphere remained edgy. I was still refusing to lose 'the bloody thing.'

Shortly before midnight, Brian Walch, CEO of the House of Fraser, came in to sign the agreement – but agreement still had not been reached. Then in true Hollywood style it was reached with two minutes to go!

I led my team into a room where a huge cast was waiting and announced the five most glorious words ever announced on behalf of Hodgson Holdings plc to date, "Gentlemen we have a deal."

I had not lost 'the bloody thing.'

It was a deal which brought Hodgson Holdings to a value of £30million and gave it the responsibility for 23,000 funerals a year. This represented 4% of all funerals per annum in England and Wales.

We had overtaken Kenyon and the Great Southern Group at a stroke and were now the unrivalled major force in our profession. I had refused to lose 'the bloody thing' and indeed I had won this fantastic prize only a little over a decade from the ghastly first day in charge of Hodgson & Sons Ltd.

McKenna's threw a dinner in celebration. It had come within two minutes of being thrown out of the window, but it was a decent gesture, diminished only by the Co-op party's insistence that they were going back to Manchester instead of enjoying the hospitality on offer. They explained that it was so late - but then their departure was unexpectedly delayed as they couldn't arrange any transport, notwithstanding the huge number of CWS limousines garaged in London.

This Life In Death

At the age of thirty-seven, I was now the force that mattered in my profession. I was on an unimaginable high, and I was in no hurry to come down.

An army of thigh stroking 20-something year old PR girls wanted to make it to my hotel room whether I stayed in London and like a coke head with cocaine; or an alcoholic with booze; I just could not say no. I felt little for most of them, only liked a few and loved just one – but my appetite was gigantic for the unknown and the more publicity I got, the longer the queue became.

I arrived back at Eden Wood at 9:00 on the Sunday morning. Marianne was furious as she suspected I had been satisfying the PR queue rather than working. I collapsed into bed and drifted off to sleep while the boys were telling her to 'leave Daddy alone.' However, I was up and ready for Sunday lunch at Edgbaston Priory Tennis Club later that morning.

I would never miss a Sunday lunch with Marianne and the boys. I worked hard – but when it was the weekend, they took preference, not golf or going boozing with the boys.

As the press affection for their new 'enfant terrible' had grown, it had fuelled a jealous reaction from my competitors.

Michael Kenyon had appeared in the Sunday Times saying he failed to understand why Hodgson was rated so much more highly than Kenyon.

Colin Field had appeared on BBC's 'Money Programme' and had inferred that Hodgson paper was overrated.

I had always taken John Jay's advice on the matter, "If they want to waste their column inches talking about you – let them. The one thing the three of you seem to like is talking about is Hodgson Holdings. This is very good for you." So, I had never commented about either of them. Indeed, I liked Michael Kenyon as I did old man Field and his 'adopted son' Eric Spencer at Great Southern.

This Life In Death

But then Colin Field did something to upset me. I can't remember what now nearly 40 years ago – but I was angry. So, at the press conference to announce the Ingalls success, I opened with the line, "I walked over the Fields to work this morning." The press roared with laughter but Don de Groot of Capel Cure Myers was not amused and rightly tore a strip off me afterwards, saying, "Stay likeable Howard, nobody likes a smart arse."

The Birmingham Post, which had supported me from the time of the flotation was able to pat itself on the back for its prediction a month earlier:

'Just as we indicated when Hodgson Holdings' shares were suspended at the beginning of April, Mr Howard Hodgson, Handsworth's funeral director extraordinary, has clinched a deal to buy the former Ingall Industries business from the House of Fraser – thereby increasing the size of his fast-growing business by 140%.

To raise the money - and another £1.5million for good measure – he is issuing new shares at 240p through the placing and open offer to existing shareholders at 240p, compared with the 275p suspension price, on the basis of five new shares for every eight held.

The institutions have been persuaded to go easy with their fees by the guarantee of more than 50% of the new shares. This is possible since Mr Hodgson and SUMIT, holder of 4% of the equity, have agreed not to take up their entitlements. The effect will be to dilute Mr Hodgson's controlling stake to about 30%.'

The national press wrote much the same kind of article as Mr Neville Boyd Mansell of the Post had and the general feeling in the press and the City was that I had pulled off a brilliant deal.

Chapter XI

The Really Big Deal

1987 – 1989

However, while things were going so well at work, there was a crisis looming at home.

Michael Hackney had become, along with his wife Consuela and daughter Clara, good friends to us in 1986. He and I had ceased to work together after the flotation as he had been sent to represent Grindley Brandts in Milan and so had left my corporate finance needs to be looked after by Chris Callaway and Don de Groot.

Nevertheless, the Hackneys came to stay at our house in Port Grimaud, France in the summer of 1986. We all went skiing together in early 1987. Then, as Consuela had become pregnant, Michael came on his own to join us on a sailing trip on my yacht 'Fat Girl' from St Tropez to San Remo in Italy and back after I had completed the Ingalls deal later that year.

I could increasingly tell that Michael was becoming infatuated and seriously drawn to Marianne. However, no thought entered my head of Marianne being attracted to Michael. This was not because he was an unattractive man. Indeed, he was a very handsome fellow, but because, Marianne had always been completely dedicated to me and had constantly craved both my love and attention.

I had, in my perfect arrogance, not considered what it must have felt like for her to have someone adore her rather than having to worry about which PR girl I might be in bed with.

At the end of this sailing holiday, they had the briefest of flings. I discovered it and was both hurt and furious. I left for England. The boys wanted to come with me and so the three of us drove home.

This Life In Death

It felt like the Susan Best episode of seventeen years earlier all over again. And of course, it was because I had yet again pushed a loving and decent woman too far by my ongoing infidelities.

So, I looked in the mirror and saw a man who clearly made one rule for himself and another for his wife. How could this be fair or just. If I was to live by the sword then I must be prepared to die by the sword I told myself.

Marianne called me from France and we decided to put the episode behind us. She flew back to England, and we were happily reunited.

However, before I give you the impression that I had suddenly become a wonderfully enlightened and reformed man, I should add that her one act of indiscretion allowed me, in my own mind's eye, to consider that from now on I could bed as many women as I wanted without any shred of conscience.

Indeed, before she had even arrived back at Eden Wood, I had a one-night stand with a mature lady who owned a small hotel just off the Hagley Road in Birmingham in an orgy of lust to escape from the pressure of work.

This was no basis for the marriage to work and had been made worse by the fact that I had put Jamieson in our bed, between us, since birth. This was a place he would stay until he was twelve years of age.

I had done so not to avoid Marianne, but because I needed this child there like a child needs a teddy bear. I had been that badly damaged by the loss of Charles and my own inability to come to terms with it.

My mother warned that this was a recipe for disaster, but I refused to listen, preferring to be loving, kind and generous to Marianne while doting on Howie and J at home but living the life of a male gigolo when not.

Therefore, I can say, without any doubt, that it was not Marianne's understandable affair, nor the death of Charles nor the pressure of work that caused our marriage to fail eventually, but my own wilful indiscipline when it came to women.

So, how could a man who had worked so hard to resurrect his family's good name; was a very loving family man; cared greatly about all his staff; and was a standard bearer of fair play, compassion and business ethics, behave so badly when it came maintaining a monogamous marriage?

In my head, I believe I was simply, like all addicts, in denial. I did not see the contradiction of this behaviour to the other values that I had inherited from my father and had fiercely upheld all my life.

Casual sex was a sport and not an act of love in my mind. Like a Victorian grandee, I expected to lead a very respectable family life and be admired as a good person, while leading a second and secret life of sexual indulgence.

As a result, in my mind, women were like ski runs. I might have a favourite, but I could never resist a new one that I had not skied before, even if it was not a particularly pretty slope to ski down.

Perhaps, it also had something to do with my genes. George, with his 'six branch office mistresses', Ossie, known as the 'Stallion of Handsworth' and my father reputed to 'have shagged half of Birmingham', had all been sexaholics before me.

I'm not certain even now how such schizophrenic behaviour could survive alongside each other without creating some form of self-doubt. But this kind of hypocrisy seemed to have worked well for the Victorian empire builders that I admired so much, and I suspect that is why it did for me too – not only then but as a recurring theme over the next thirty years of my explosive life.

Either way, such selfish and hypocritical behaviour makes it extremely unlikely that any marriage could survive such a strain put upon it forever.

Therefore, the blame rests 100% with me, because, although I was now a successful man in his late thirties, I still behaved, whenever the mood took me, like a teenager who could not control his carnal desires.

I had grown up in the '60s, still thought that 'free love' and sexual conquest was a totally essential recreation and secretly still wanted to be the 'sex, booze and rock 'n roll' Beatle, that I had abandoned in order to rebuild the Hodgson name and fortune.

Despite this, the marriage was to last another five years in mostly very happy circumstances and produced the wonderful Davinia Clementine Marianne Hodgson in 1990 – my only and most treasured daughter. More about her in volume II.

Moreover, my ability to confront my own behaviour meant that I knew who was to blame ultimately. So, I held no resentment towards Michael or Marianne whatsoever when the split eventually and inevitably happened due to yet another affair I was to have.

We all have remained the very best of friends ever since. Moreover, Michael was to play a major part in the building of my greatest business, Memoria, along with Jamieson, during the first two decades of the next Millennium.

xxxxxxx

Naturally, as I'm sure you have already realised, I did not allow such domestic distractions to stop the Hodgson Holdings express train from zooming on like a tornado.

The CWS side of the Ingalls deal soon ran into trouble with the Monopolies & Mergers Commission as its purchase of the House of Fraser Funeral Division gave it 21,000 of Scotland's 50,000 funerals each year, which led the Guardian newspaper to headline 'DEATH:

This Life In Death

IT'S NOT ALL AT THE CO-OP', in a slight mickey take over the CWS's TV ad slogan of the time, 'it's all at the Co-op.'

The article went on to say 'the CWS is already the country's largest undertaker but a recent move to expand its Scottish business is to come under the scrutiny of the MMC.'

However, I had no such problems in England and pressed on with three more acquisitions which had all been under negotiation at the time of the Ingalls purchase.

The first was Ashton Ebbutt, the same firm that had taken me in when my father had fired me seventeen years earlier. That felt very good and even better the owners were related to the Kenyon family by marriage. Moreover, Hodgson and Ashton Ebbutt were now mine and that meant that I only had to acquire James Summers to own all my previous employers.

At £2.2million it was, after Ingalls, easily my largest acquisition so far and gave me 12 further offices in London.

The second was a small funeral director, John G. Ashton, in Manchester for £106,000 and the third was a secret favourite of mine, Coyne's of Liverpool, who conducted 1,000 funerals per annum, mainly Roman Catholic around the rough 'Scotty' Rd area of Liverpool. This business cost £1million (about £4million in 2024 money).

The media went into an orgasm of praise as these announcements were now making the financial headlines almost weekly; it was all about the great taboo of death; I looked like a rock star; and the company had not been floated on the London Stock Exchange for a year yet!

I was compared many times over with the most admired Lord Hanson, but Marketing Magazine thought the likeable Gerald Ratner was a better comparison, as he had expanded a family business by acquisition too.

This Life In Death

The New Statesman was more annoying with:

'A Roman Polanski lookalike with long hair, cufflinks and buttoned-up, buttoned-down air, he talks smoothly of creating new market opportunities for his trade and planning a more comprehensive service for clients with financial advice for the bereaved.' This was over 30 years before funeral plans were to appear on every other ITV 3 advert.

Now national newspaper cartoons started to appear about either the firm or me regularly, comedians on TV cracked jokes about me and even taxi drivers were asking me for an autograph.

So, as the bull market rolled on, Hodgson Holdings was on its crest and this personal and corporate publicity that I was receiving in abundance had the huge benefit of keeping the Hodgson share price on the boil. As the Director Magazine reported just after the acquisition of Ingalls in the early summer of 1987:

'Just how he has fired the City's imagination can be judged by the competitive p/e ratios of the three publicly quoted funeral companies. Kenyon Securities languishes in the high teens; Great Southern Group, the Sussex based firm run by the Field family, sits in the low twenties; Hodgson is double that.'

My seventeenth acquisition of this period was a small firm in Bedford, R. Circet, conducting 165 funerals-a-year, which I bought in August for £145,000. In the same month I bought Tovey & Morris of Newport, Gwent for £160,000, which added a further 125 funerals per annum. Within a week came the nineteenth, Howard's of Stockport which only conducted 50 funerals-a-year.

Large firms were becoming harder to find at this pace but, as we now had a national network, these were all in areas where they could be rationalised into an existing 'cluster' to ensure we could sweat the assets and thus improve their finances as well as their standards of service.

This Life In Death

Suddenly, this perfect business world of 1987, just like my private world of 1982 had, came crashing down.

On Thursday the 18th October, I had dinner in the Howard Hotel overlooking the Thames in London with my favourite PR girl. She was just 23-years-of-age, and I really did have genuine feelings for her. I had forsaken all others but Marianne for her and tried very hard to respond to her love and devotion with as much of my own that a married man with two young boys could.

I left her that evening in a room upstairs having enjoyed a perfect evening by wiping away her tears with a smile and a promise to see her next week, I left to catch the last train back to Birmingham International and on to Eden Wood.

I woke the next morning to a nightmare. Overnight there had been a hurricane. A lot of the UK, especially the South of England, had become paralysed by the disruption caused with buildings collapsing and uprooted trees damaging properties and blocking roads.

My young love had sat up in the Howard Hotel since 4am watching five feet waves roll down the Thames in fear of her life as the building shook in the wind, and she wondered when the windows would be blown in. Luckily, her workplace was just around the corner, and it was but a two-minute walk to work.

I had little time to concern myself with her report of that as we had several hundred funerals to conduct on Friday 19th October 1987.

I had hundreds of staff struggling to get to work. If they did, the corteges had to get to home addresses and on to services and committals on time so that they could repeat the process again and again throughout the day.

I am today, some 37 years later, proud to report that all but two of these funerals were carried out. The two that weren't was due to them both involving horse drawn hearses in South London and no horse would venture out of its horse box due to the wind. We offered both families motor hearses instead to continue that day. However, both preferred to postpone until the following Monday with the horse drawn hearses as planned.

Hodgson Holdings, as the major financial force in the industry, had also impressed amazingly well on the day as a company dedicated to the highest standards of service and facility.

Its small minded and jealous much less pressed local London competitors had failed to live up to these results with cancellations being reported everywhere. I was immensely proud of my staff that evening.

The mass destruction of the hurricane meant that the London Stock Exchange remained closed on the 19th October 1987. Elsewhere around the world the bull market bandwagon was being derailed.

The City and most of the stock markets around the world had been wallowing in an orgy of self-love. A communist command economy does not work as Russia, Eastern Europe, Venezuela, Cuba and other countries have proved a hundred times over. However, this does not make a capitalist economy perfect.

In June of 1987 in the UK the Thatcher Tory government had swept to another landslide victory and were in for another five years; Reaganomics in the US was proclaimed as a great success across the world and Gorbachev was starting to respond to the Soviet Union people's unrest that socialist command economies left working people behind in a state of poverty.

However, bull markets will always become bear when investors realise that they have talked themselves up too high. It had happened before and has several times since.

In early October 1987 the world markets were on their way up after the usual summer hiccup when it all stopped.

Suddenly on 19th October 1987 the world stock markets fed off the bad news from initially New York and then became a self-fulfilling prophesy as they all crashed in a massive spiral down as each became a pit of screaming and yelling hysteria.

The market steadied after a 25% fall. However, some super stars fell by over 70%. Was the party over? Would companies like Hodgson Holdings, dependent on acquisitions for their growth and so dependent on a strong and rising stock market to sustain their share price to make such acquisitions, be able to survive?

The Hodgson takeover of Ingalls had been financed by a £17million rights issue at 240p. Subsequently, the shares had risen to 304p within a year of being floated at 80p. However, the crash saw them fall to 200p.

However, I had built this business on acquisitions, it had always delivered good standards of service and the profit growth brought about by acquisition followed by rationalisation had been spectacular.

So, both the City and Lloyds Bank rallied to support this stock market darling and keep the takeover train rolling. On the 22nd December 1987, just two months after the Crash, the Financial Times announced:

'Hodgson Holdings, USM-quoted funeral director, has acquired four more funeral directors for a total of £800,000 cash, including £212,000 for properties. The purchases will add 800 funerals-a-year, making Hodgson's total more than 28,000.'

The effect on the share price was the same as in earlier and headier days – it moved up to 208p. This was more muted than before, but we were still sailing when most ships had gone aground.

Nevertheless, the damage to the Hodgson share price caused by the Crash was influencing my ambitions. I wanted to buy the part of the House of Fraser funeral business that the MMC was by now ordering the CWS to sell.

This Life In Death

However, it would be impossible to ask my shareholders for more cash while the Hodgson share price was below the 240p that I had asked them to stump up for the Ingalls purchase.

So, for big acquisitions at least, the train had been halted. Nevertheless, I comforted my wildly ambitious self that, in hindsight, I had been extremely lucky that Al Fayed had insisted on such a tight timetable in that spring, or the Crash could have wrecked the 'super' Ingalls deal, as at 200p a share it would have been much less attractive even if it could have been 'got away' at all in such hectic conditions.

There was now a different economic climate and some people in the City and in politics foresaw the end of the universe in the Crash. However, out in the real world and away from the City champagne bars, life went on much as before, and I determined to push ahead with our acquisition programme of other independent funeral directors and find alternative forms of funding if rights issues on the back of a galloping share price were no longer open to me.

Therefore, when the MMC told the CWS that they had to dispose of some 7,000 funerals recently acquired from the House of Fraser in Scotland, as part of the Ingalls deal, I happily gobbled them up for £10 million, despite not being certain how I would reduce that debt going forward, as there was no appetite for any form of institutional placing.

Nevertheless, this was still a huge acquisition and caused us to pull even further ahead of our rivals.

Then, late 1987 saw me, still undaunted, in negotiation with a large London firm Dottridge & Sons. A deal was struck, and we shared a bottle of champagne in the Hodgson Holdings board room with their directors, as the owners did not work in the business.

However, Michael Kenyon of Kenyon Securities was still smarting from me buying Ashton Ebbutt, a relatively large London business, from under his nose that summer. This resulted in Kenyon's upping their offer to a wholly unrealistic level for the Dottridge business and taking it from us.

I didn't realise this at the time and thought that this was because they preferred the pleasant Michael Kenyon to me.

Nevertheless, I was furious, in particular with the Dottridge directors for going back on their word and announced to the Hodgson Board that we would not drink champagne in that room again until Dottridge was ours. FD Ron Middleton looked perplexed and said, "But that would mean buying Kenyon Securities."

"Precisely", I replied.

"Oh Jesus Christ", he muttered under his breath.

When we later discovered that Michael Kenyon had upped the price from our £9.5 million to an extra-ordinarily high £11.5 million I was jubilant as I knew this mistake would make Kenyon very vulnerable in the next 12 months when, because of this barmy price having been handed over to the vendor, it would seriously dilute their earnings per share.

However, initially, we did not know this and had to sweep this disappointment to one side. So, we continued into 1988 acquiring other funeral directors, while working on new ancillary services such as pre-arranged funeral plans which were to be launched in 1989 under the name 'Dignity in Destiny' (taken from Charles' headstone) to such headlines as 'Pay First – And Die Later' (Financial Times); 'The Bottom Line .... And How To Go In Style' (Today); and 'Mr Death Undertakes A Revolution' (The Sun).

The press had decided that my 'press ID' was now 'Mr Death' after a headline across a 6-page spread in the much read and highly acclaimed Sunday Times Colour Supplement Magazine had christened me with this title.

The Financial Times also greeted the pre-arranged development as 'long awaited' and indeed it had been a long time in gestation.

This Life In Death

Pre-arranged funeral plans where the price is fixed at the time of purchase are commonplace today. Indeed, turn on ITV 3 or 4 in the afternoon and you will see every advert break extolling the benefits of direct cremation funeral plans by various providers.

However, although an established product in Australia and the USA, they were unheard of in the UK in the late '80s. Their launch here had an immediate impact – not on the public, who largely ignored the concept for many years, but on the funeral directing industry where immediate panic set in.

My major competitors might have become obsessed and frightened of Hodgson Holdings' success but the rest of the UK funeral directing community still saw us as a marvellous form of exit. They could comfort themselves with the thought that Mr Death would always be happy to buy them out when the time came.

The launch of Dignity in Destiny changed all of this. The story that I had launched pre-arranged funeral plans to steal their market and therefore have no need to buy them spread like wildfire.

This was potentially very damaging because how could I buy someone who refused to even meet me. I solved this problem by engaging the hugely entertaining and immensely popular England International cricketer Dennis Amiss and he re-opened all current doors and a lot of new ones too.

But with no pre-emptive placing of shares through my brokers to rely on due to the Crash how was I going to fund the Dignity in Destiny launch as well as continue to make funeral company acquisitions?

The press launch of Dignity in Destiny contained an announcement that B&C Ventures, part of the financial conglomerate British & Commonwealth Holdings, was taking a stake of 20% in the separate company, Dignity in Destiny Ltd (I had gifted 5% to Help the Aged and Hodgson Holdings owned the remaining 75%).

B&C Ventures was also providing Hodgson with £14.5 million capital by subscribing for 15 million 8.5p convertible preference shares at a

This Life In Death

100p. So, I had fixed my funding gap, and I was very pleased with myself as a result. It seemed to the outside world that Mr Death had done it again.

British & Commonwealth had originally been a shipping company built up by the Cayzer family. However, since the end of World War II it had become a conglomerate with many interests. By the 1980s the Cayzer family had been bought out for about £500 million, and the shipping arm had been ceased.

John Gunn, who had made his name building a money-broking business called Exco had become CEO after his company had become part of B&C and at the height of the bull market, he was one of the Thatcherite financial tigers who was revered and, with the B&C share price at an all-time high, his reputation was well deserved.

However, the Crash of October 1987 had made life a lot tougher for conglomerates like B&C. Unfortunately, the company was to compound these difficulties by making some poor investments – most notably Atlantic Computers, for which they paid £400 million only to discover that the leases of this computer-leasing company were flawed.

So, by late 1988 B&C were finding life tough on all fronts, and they needed a solid deal to restore confidence. I was Mr Death and funerals were an extremely safe and secure investment.

However, in reality, I needed the very likeable John Gunn even more than he needed me. For the truth is that without him I was in a tricky place.

The Crash had frightened institutions certainly but nothing like as much as private punters. Everyone expected a second crash sometime in 1988. Therefore, the Market drifted on low volume trading with little appetite to invest even in the magical Hodgson Holdings.

This Life In Death

Nevertheless, I was still forced to acquire other funeral directors, because I was locked into a race with Kenyon and Great Southern to acquire the best of the available independents.

And I also had to continue to acquire them to keep our earnings per share rising or I might see sellers in the Market and a fall in the share price as a result. This would cause a downward spiral as intense as the one that had seen me spiral up to become a household name over the last two years.

By the autumn of 1988 Hodgson's borrowings were approaching £15 million when the UK Chancellor of the Exchequer, Nigel Lawson, responded to an overheated economy by raising interest rates sharply during the summer and autumn of that year.

This was bound to hit our profits and therefore our earnings per share and, as a result, our share price. Therefore, it was highly likely that the magical Mr Death could spiral down just as he had exploded up from nowhere.

So, we needed an equity injection of cash to ease these strains on our profits, earnings and balance sheet.

Without one it seemed likely that the party was over and the 'enfant terrible' of funeral directing was heading for a fall that would make so many in the funeral industry jump with glee.

I had been aware of the problem for months. However, being aware and finding a solution were two different things.

Nevertheless, with my usual fevered simple but determined brain working into the night, eventually I thought I had found a solution. I started negotiating with the USA's largest funeral company, Service Corporation International, known as SCI.

I knew that they wanted to buy Hodgson Holdings as a start of a drive into Europe. I hated that idea but wanted to keep the dialogue going.

This Life In Death

They wanted me to drop the idea of Dignity in Destiny in favour of their 'Guardian Plan.' This was just an insurance plan, and I did not believe it was suitable to compete against the Great Southern plan 'Chosen Heritage' with its price guarantees, as a result.

Instead, I offered them 50% of Dignity in Destiny and 20% of Hodgson Holdings for £15million. I presented this deal to them at their HQ in Houston, Texas and my offer was accepted. Hooray, Mr Death had saved himself, or had he?

Everything was set up for the launch of Dignity in Destiny while curing the horrid Hodgson Holdings debt mountain when disaster struck.

I was on my way to yet another 'Top 40 Under 40' reunion when I received a call from Graham Hodson, who told me that he had taken a call from the SCI FD who didn't sound happy. Graham suggested I gave him a call on my car phone (remember those?).

I did and was told that the SCI stock price had fallen by $2 on the previous day and they needed every dime to buy in their own stock to stop the slide. Therefore, despite six months of negotiation and an agreement at the end of that, the deal was off.

I still don't know how I held it together during the reunion. Not even sitting next to the beautiful and flirtatious Debbie Moore was a consolation. Some years later, she and I did spend a lot of fun time together, in between my marriages, but on this night my mind was far away. This was no time to be thinking about sexual pleasure.

I needed to forget about the press flash bulbs, the banter, the slender Debbie, any thoughts of sex, and concentrate on the fact that I now needed to find £15 million in the next two months or face the consequences. It was a bear market; I had borrowed all that I could; and my advisors were starting to look nervous.

Then, on the drive back to Birmingham later that night, I had an inspiration. What about B&C? As it happened Dennis Amiss had played golf with John Gunn earlier that summer at a pro-am tournament which had infuriated me as I did not believe that our

This Life In Death

Acquisitions Director would come across many funeral directors for sale there.

Later that summer, I had also met the B&C CEO John Gunn at Lords Cricket Ground, having been invited into his box with the famous Martin Sorrell of WPP and we had had a friendly natter about cricket. The subject of funding never came up.

Russell, my brother, whom you will recall worked for CCM as a broker, had been headhunted by UBS Phillips & Drew, around this time, on the promise of a great salary if he could persuade me to bring my huge corporate finance annual fees to them instead of Capel Cure Myers.

UBS started to make a market in Hodgson stock and put the price up 30p in a week. I was impressed and switched.

However, UBS were against any deal with Gunn when I explained my idea of offering him preference shares. They said that B&C were 3rd division and that I was scraping the barrel.

I replied that beggars could not be choosers and that I intended to talk to him unless they could suggest something better. They had floated the idea of a preference share issue with the Prudential and other institutions but there was no interest even at an 8 or 9% coupon. This is how nervous the City still was a year after the Crash.

I decided to act with or without their blessing. I called Gunn and we met. I explained what I wanted, and John put his accountants to work to thrash out a deal.

The B&C team and the Hodgson team struggled to reach an agreement as the B&C terms were too severe, would have made the money very expensive indeed, infuriated our institutional investors and so would have only made matters worse.

However, John Gunn secretly had eyes on Hodgson Holdings becoming part of B&C in due course. This investment would be their foot in the door. He cleverly never told me that at the time, but insisted his team made a deal acceptable to me. They did and the matter was settled, and immediate disaster averted.

Nevertheless, some institutional shareholders were critical even though they had been offered very similar terms and refused them. Their main complaint was that the 8.5% coupon was too high.

I was furious and upbraided them at the shareholders briefing saying:

"Interest rates are much higher now; we have £15 million of borrowings; a pre-emptive placing is impossible unless deeply discounted, which would send the share price plummeting; and the risk associated with this level of borrowing could seriously affect the share price of Hodgson unless something is done.

"Moreover, it's only a three-year contract, not an eleven-year window like quoted preference shares. Furthermore, coming from you (it was as usual the Prudential who were vocally complaining), it's a bloody cheek as you turned this offer down saying that the coupon was not good enough. So not good enough for you; but too good for Mr Gunn!"

The brilliantly calm and ever tactful Chris March of UBS stepped in at this point before I went any further and suggested that we break for lunch.

In the document to shareholders offering them a chance to subscribe for 7,500,000 of the 15,000,000 convertible preference shares on offer the board's strategy was clearly laid out both for now and the future.

However, most importantly, it made it very clear why this preference issue was essential. The need for the cash was not for the launch of Dignity in Destiny, although some was needed for this purpose. But the truth was that cash was urgently needed to redress the balance sheet following a huge acquisition programme which had seen sixty-four businesses bought in the 12 months to 31st March 1988 at a cost of £26 million and after the Crash it had proved impossible to bring down the debt by our trusted route of a rights issue while the cost of that debt had been rising due to rises in interest rates.

It went on:

'The Group has achieved a rapid but carefully planned expansion, leading to the establishment of Hodgson Holdings as the largest and geographically best-represented publicly quoted national chain of funeral directors conducting in excess of 40,000 funerals on an annualised basis from more than 240 branches.'

I feel quite exhausted now just thinking about what had happened over the thirteen years since I was told on that first morning as owner of Hodgson & Sons Ltd that the Midland Bank intended to close us down and I had set about conducting 400 funerals per annum in the hope of surviving.

Not too bad an effort for a little boy who had been stupid enough to ask if his family funeral directing business had done Julius Caesar's funeral.

Indeed, looking back, I now see that I had managed to show the same resilience in the face of calamity in 1988 as I had in 1975 and had won through in those difficult times which was much less fun but equally, if not more, important than galloping to Footsie stardom in the bull market of 1986 and '87.

The launch of Dignity in Destiny took place at the Savoy Hotel in London. It was a large and rather splendid affair. It was also the subject of yet another BBC TV documentary programme made solely about Hodgson Holdings and called 'Dignity in Destiny' much to the fury of my competitors.

It was starring me along with Marianne as a most stunning co-star, as the cameras captured her strutting into the Savoy reception very elegantly attired and followed by an army of directors, advisors and press photographers.

This Life In Death

Before this however, a select group of journalists had been briefed by me in PR Simon Preston's office in the Aldwych, which was only two hundred yards away.

The press, with one exception, didn't place as much importance on the Dignity in Destiny launch as it did on my other announcement made on the same day that I was going to place a financial value on the many local brand names that I had bought.

The Financial Times was non-committal, confining itself to reporting that 'a funeral director has become the first UK company to value the names of its subsidiaries in its accounts.' It further added that WPP Group, the huge advertising and marketing services company and others were considering following my example.

It added that:

'Hodgson Holdings' decision to put a value of £42 million on the names on 80 groups of funeral companies could open a new chapter in the continuing debate over brand names. Last year, Rank Hovis McDougall, the bakeries and food group, stirred up controversy in the accounting profession by becoming the first company to put a value on existing brands in its balance sheet. Hodgson argues that when buying a funeral business, goodwill and the value of the trade name are one of the same. The group says this is because undertakers rely on the loyalty of clients to that local name, generation after generation.'

The world-famous financial newspaper also noted that Price Waterhouse, Hodgson's accountant, approved of my decision to change our accounting policy.

However, the Tempus column in the (London) Times did not like it as much. This was the first hint of criticism that the 'enfant terrible' had received since shooting into financial stardom nearly three years earlier.

'Mr Hodgson is unhappy about the effect of writing off goodwill against reserves, which all but wiped-out shareholders' funds in the

328

previous financial year. Under his new scheme funds are shown at £47.6 million.

'Any predator looking at his group would be likely to base its worth on the number of funerals conducted, he claims. With Hodgson now paying the equivalent of £1,500 a funeral for its latest acquisitions, this would value his group at about £75 million allowing for the work he has done in rationalising his network.

'Hodgson's market capitalisation is about half this: Mr Hodgson claims the company is something of a victim of its own success. The large number of acquisitions he has made is acting as a brake on further expansion.'

The journalist might not have liked the idea that much from his tone rather than his words, but he had more or less reported the facts correctly.

Moreover, I was right. If the company was to be subject to a takeover, then the value placed on it would have been at least £75million and not its market capitalisation, which was much lower at close to £40million.

However, the real criticism was yet to come and was not born out of anything wrong with what Price Waterhouse and I had decided was a justified change to the treatment of goodwill. It was rather that I had inadvertently made an enemy in the small and highly competitive circle of financial journalists that followed companies like Hodgson Holdings and who were always hoping for an exclusive titbit of news.

At the press briefing that morning, the journalists were given a pack containing two press releases to take away to help them write their pieces for the following day's morning additions.

One journalist, a Jason Nisse of the Independent, had led with the launch of Dignity in Destiny. He was the one exception referred to above. Everyone else had led with the new revolutionary accounting principle. His editor called him in and gave him a severe rollocking about how he had spent the day with me wining and dining and had missed the main piece of news.

Apparently, the press release about the accounting method change had been missed out of his pack.

Mr Nisse was furious and decided that I had ordered this to be done. This was simply not true. In reality, Simon's people had not put a copy in his pack by mistake.

Nisse was angry with me; I was angry with Simon; he was angry with the personal PR on our account, a certain 23-year-old lady called Pip Rosen, who Simon claimed should have checked all the packs. Simon knew, as others might not, that I would forgive her.

I phoned Jason personally, in an attempt to repair the damage, as he had always been a big supporter, but he refused to take my call.

Instead, a day later the financial pages of the Independent led with an article which, from start to finish, was full of venom directed at Mr Death. It claimed that I was so arrogant, due the acclaim that I had received in recent years, that I believed that I could now even drive a coach and horses through established accounting principles which were hundreds of years old and had been born in the home of the world's most stable quoted enterprise market – London.

This feud was to rumble on as we shall see. It was only ended when I decided to adopt the same non-objective and ruthless attitude to him as he had displayed towards me. Therefore, the matter was eventually settled in a scene more reminiscent of a typical JR performance from the famous TV 'Dallas' series of the time, which my children were addicted to, rather than truth or constructive discourse as I decided to fight fire with fire and hit him where he was vulnerable. You don't 'fuck' with the Peaky Blinders comes to mind, and that was who I really was if pushed too far. But this is for the future.

This Life In Death

Two interesting possibilities that, in the end, never happened came out of this episode of my desperate need to raise funds, after the Crash in 1987 and during 1988.

If I my deal with SCI had gone ahead, it is most unlikely my next and biggest deal ever would have happened because my association with SCI would have prevented it.

Moreover, the SCI deal did not go ahead because it needed to buy back its own stock due to its falling share price. SCI went on to have a very difficult future in the 1990s. If I had got into bed with them, I would have been sucked into their crisis and would have probably been sold off, as we were not a US venture, to the highest bidder in a fire sale. Wow, that was a lucky escape.

On the other hand, if I had not pulled off my biggest deal ever in 1989, I would have been facing the prospect of B&C, or the liquidators of B&C, as that company collapsed in 1990, holding 20% of Hodgson equity. That was also a very fortunate escape too.

As a postscript to the launch of Dignity in Destiny and my controversial capitalisation of the brands, Hodgson moved up to a full London Stock Exchange listing. We believed that we would benefit from the fact that certain large institutions were prevented from investing in anything but a fully listed company. In the event the effect of the share price was limited as many institutions decided to wait and see how my controversial capitalisation of the brand names would pan out.

Nevertheless, it was yet another huge step forward from a tiny little funeral director in Birmingham conducting just 400 funerals-a-year but 14 years previously. I wished so very much that my father had lived to see this.

And to put two fingers up yet again in the direction of the NAFD, the NSM, the Birmingham Funeral Directors' Guild and now Jason Nisse, we announced just two days after the spectacular Savoy Hotel launch, and on the same day as Jason's poisonous article, the acquisition of a further eleven companies for £2.6m in cash: three in Scotland, three in the north of England, two in the Midlands, two in the southwest, and one in the mid-northwest.

I knew that I was the most ethical man in the industry, that I had a very genuine compassion for the bereaved and believed in honest and decent British Empire behaviour as learnt on my father's knee and so well portrayed by the eccentric Professor Henry Higgins in 'My Fair Lady.'

I knew that I wasn't just a fair-weather sailor with a pretty face. This was because I also knew that I came from Birmingham, I was tough and if you messed with me, you did it at your peril.

In total we had added a further 2,200 funerals to the group's annual total and, despite the Independent challenge to my accounting ideals, 'Bearbull', in the Investor's Chronicle, added Hodgson Holdings plc to his defensive portfolio on the same day.

In 1988 I was also presented to HM Queen Elizabeth II My initial reaction to being invited to St James's Palace to be presented to her as a leading businessman, was one, as a loyal monarchist, of great pride.

However, I wasn't nervous. Why should I be? Dennis had already been to Buckingham Palace to receive an MBE and that was vastly more important than this I told myself.

However, things were to change somewhat two days before I was due to go. I received a phone call from a trusted Regional Director Harvey Hewitt to say that there had been a serious incident at one of the recently acquired Ashton Ebbutt funeral homes in London.

Apparently, a removal ambulance returning from collecting two deceased people from a hospital had arrived back to see a loaded hearse and two limousines was blocking the drive while the chauffeurs were grabbing a quick cup of tea before leaving.

This Life In Death

As a result, he had abandoned the ambulance with the engine on and the driver's door open in the middle of the road to go in search of the funeral director and his chauffeurs. This was, of course, inviting trouble in South London.

He returned less than two minutes later but the ambulance had vanished and with the two bodies inside!

Harvey was immediately called, and he called me. I asked him to call the police and then inform both families what had happened.

I was asked if we shouldn't wait to see if the police recovered the ambulance. I said no as honesty was always the best policy. The families were duly contacted – one by Harvey, the other by David Bonham. They were told exactly what happened, that we accepted total responsibility and that that we would not be charging for either funeral.

The police sent up helicopters in an intense and desperate search, but the ambulance was not found after 24 hours.

Marianne and I arrived at the Stafford Hotel, which was just behind the Ritz, to get changed to go to St James's Palace, which was only walking distance away. I was extremely worried that I would come out from being presented to her Majesty the Queen to headlines about two bodies having been inside a stolen ambulance on News at Ten.

I proceeded to St James's, I attended the reception with Marianne and was then ushered into another room to be presented. My mind was somewhere else, but I managed to pull myself together, compose myself and concentrate on talking to HM when she eventually got to me.

Then the champagne flowed, and I was tapped on the shoulder. There was a call for me. My heart stopped. I walked to the phone. It was Graham. He thought that I might like to know that the ambulance had been found in a cul-de-sac about 500 yards away from where it had been stolen. Both bodies were still as last seen. The thief had obviously looked over his shoulder, seen what he had stolen and panicked.

As a postscript both funerals took place on time, despite the ambulance theft and neither family received an account as promised.

Perhaps, as a result, both went on to use us again in the future, while a near PR disaster had been averted by the skin of our teeth.

However, even if the worst had happened, no one could have accused us of a cover-up and I'm prouder of that honesty than anything else.

xxxxxxx

On the domestic front life had returned to normal at Eden Wood. The boys were growing up and were happy in both their splendid home and at West House school – where my father, Russell and I had been educated before them.

Howard was proving to have a career there not dissimilar to mine of nearly thirty years earlier. He excelled at cricket, hockey and football but did not always give of his best in the classroom. Nevertheless, he was more academic than me and nothing like as disruptive. When lecturing him about his behaviour and lack of effort, I rather tended to ignore my own history at the school until it came to the winning of the 'Pound Cup.'

Marianne and I got on well, despite J sleeping between us, and my constant trips to London, as keeping the share price going up was by now taking as much time as it took to run the business.

Then Marianne discovered my affair with the Hodgson PR account holder and so war broke out which meant she called Michael and spent her weekends with him while the boys and I entertained the young lady either in hotels in the Cotswold countryside or by the sea in Dorset.

The boys naturally adored their mother but found it very hard not to like this Bohemian girl, who rolled her own cigarettes, drank scotch and had a husky voice. She was closer in age to Howard than me and could talk about all kind of things to them that I knew nothing about – such as the 'soap' Neighbours.

After a couple of months, Marianne and I decided it might be best to make a more permanent separation, and this accidently caused a stir in the City, as she and Michael had no money but needed a place to live.

They decided they would like an apartment in Evelyn Gardens, just off the Fulham Rd, in London. I sold some shares in Hodgson Holdings to raise the funds to buy it for them.

Upon the news hitting the streets that Mr Death was selling shares, albeit a very small percentage, in his own company, there were other sellers and the share price fell.

I instantly issued a statement that explained that I needed to buy an apartment in London to stop running up hotel bills there and didn't think that Hodgson Holdings should buy this for me and therefore needed to sell a few shares to complete the transaction – as all my wealth was invested in Hodgson Holdings. This was taken positively by the investors and the share price immediately recovered.

Given the mass media attention of the time and the fact my children and I were seen constantly in London, Dorset or Birmingham restaurants at weekends with a twenty-three-year-old beautiful but rather Bohemian girl instead of their mother went unnoticed was most unlikely. However, to all our surprise, no headlines came along to interfere with this arrangement.

However, in the autumn of 1988, Marianne collapsed in a malaise of unhappiness and decided she needed us all to be back together.

This Life In Death

Now, the young PR girl was extremely unhappy and talked of killing herself if I left her. She called me at home. But Marianne answered with, "Aren't you dead yet?" The latter was still that fiery French girl that had sworn at me some 15 years earlier.

I was exceptionally fond of the young PR girl but knew that I had to put Marianne and my children first and so I agreed but typically kept my affair going secretly, or at least at a very low-profile, for another two years until the birth of Davinia, when I decided that I really needed to grow up. I was determined to try to be monogamous but how long would that conviction last?

The surprise that the summer of 1988 separation had gone unnoticed was because Hodgson Holdings plc had become the most talked about company in the UK due to the number of column inches written about it and the amount of TV and radio programmes dedicated to it.

The flotation of a funeral directing company in 1986 with a chief executive who looked most unlike the preconceived idea of what a funeral director looked like alerted the press and by 1987, prompted by the Ingalls deal publicity and the huge Sunday Times colour supplement article by Michael Watts with its controversial photograph by Barry Lewis, the press attention grew and spread from the financial to the feature pages, followed by the colour magazines, and the television and radio appearances started to become more frequent.

Indeed, in 1987 I was asked to appear on television in one form or another about every three weeks. This was at the height of the bull market and certainly it seemed that entrepreneurs had replaced soccer players as the bedfellows of rock stars.

Richard Branson and Virgin had the longevity of Macca and the Beatles, whereas Hodgson Holdings and I were the Bay City Rollers of these four years – a very bright shooting star to dazzle everyone before fading away to be forgotten.

This Life In Death

Simon Preston vetted all approaches to me and gave the green light to most. He advised against just three – a programme by the BBC criticising Chancellor Nigel Lawson, one about being a sex symbol and one about a delightful old chap, Teddy Corbett-Winder, who wanted to do a DIY funeral. I accepted Simon's judgement on the first two but overruled him on the third – which turned out to be a great advertisement for both Hodgson Holdings and the whole industry as it gave me an opportunity to explain what went into the arrangement, administration and conducting of a funeral.

When I got home from appearing on this live show, I asked the kids to show me the recording. They had been watching a recording of the US TV series Dallas while the programme was on, so not only had they not seen it, but they hadn't even recorded it. Such were the frequency of my television appearances at the time they had got blasé about them. I had to borrow a tape of this one from Ron Middleton as a result.

However, if we thought that almost being a permanent guest on various TV chat shows in 1987 was all very exciting, it paled into a quiet life compared to 1988. The combination of being presented to HM Queen Elizabeth for business achievement; included in Who's Who, named by the Sunday Times as 'one of the dozen businessmen of the decade' and then placed in Money Magazine's 200 wealthiest people in the UK above two Beatles and my neighbour in France Joan Collins kept the press fascinated.

Adding the national treasure Dennis Amiss to my team and making 100 acquisitions in that year merely poured petrol on the media fire.

The press's headlines were always a source of irritation to me but looking back I should not have been so precious about them because it was part of the attraction to the press and thus their fascination with me.

Here is a small selection from 1988 – Body Shopping (Daily Telegraph); Pay Now Die Later (Sunday Mirror); Hodgson Is Dying To Grow (Today); Nothing Funereal About Hodgson (Financial

This Life In Death

Times); Rising From The Grave (Evening Standard); Bodies Count (Investor's Chronicle); Ashes to Ashes For Amiss (Daily Mail); It's All At the Co-op for Hodgson (Investor's Chronicle); Syntactical Cricket (Guardian); Pennies From Heaven (Business); Firm Buries its Rivals (Today); Life After Death (Daily Express); Funeral Firm In Talks With Unknown Body (Guardian); Undertaker Is Over-taker (Sunday Times) and Howard Hodgson's Parlour Game (Sunday Telegraph).

In fairness, there were over 400 articles about either Hodgson Holdings or Mr Death in 1988 so quite a lot had appeared below sensible headlines and, moreover, the fun of seizing on such an opportunity to write the above headlines was part of the attraction to the nature of the business and its new 'enfant terrible' leader.

Furthermore, the press had been very kind to me and consistently backed me and my future image and plans for our ancient profession against increasingly irritated and obviously jealous competitors.

My self-belief made me fairly rattle proof in the face of competitor disapproval. Mainly, because I was a 'real' funeral director, and they weren't. I knew that I both knew what I was doing more than they did and was prepared to work harder than them to achieve what I wanted to.

So, thanks to John Jay's advice, I was pleasant about the competitors' criticisms in public while working with extreme drive and determination to beat the shit out of them in private.

Colin Field's (Great Southern Group) 'green with envy' performance on BBC2's Money Programme in 1987 was a huge mistake by comparison. The programme was easy for me because I had won the Ingalls deal and was basking in the glory of my best deal to date, which is why the cameras were there in the first place.

Michael Kenyon had lost but did his image no harm by behaving like a perfect gentleman. However, Field, in a poor media performance which did not become someone so intelligent, insisted that the House of Fraser had made a great deal as sellers of the business. The inference being that I, as the acquiror of the business, had done a bad deal.

Not only did I smash his credibility into the ground in the next year by rising earnings per share from 6.6p to 11.6p – a perfect deal, which confirmed my coronation as 'King of England Funeral Director' – but the next day everyone was saying, "Who was that little jealous guy on 'your' show last night?"

Television led to radio, radio led to the papers and the papers led back to television in an orgy of light-hearted amazement at how a dour and crusty Victorian nineteenth century business such as funeral directing could have suddenly become so sexy.

Then came the French, German, and Italian magazines and even one from Japan. However, none of us expected to be on the front page of the Cape Times in South Africa with an article under the headline 'Hodgson Breathes Life Back into Undertaking' but we were.

It was about this time that the UK daily 'Today' newspaper started to produce 'Hodgson Holdings' cartoons to accompany news stories about the firm. Many people in the funeral profession were outraged, but actually, I found them inoffensive and even funny.

The next year, 1989, continued much in the same vein. BBC's 'Dignity In Destiny', was followed by another show featuring Mr Death called the 'Enterprise Culture' and the huge acquisition programme kept the press permanently interested.

Dignity In Destiny was shown in June. The Radio Times, understandably promoting their programme about Hodgson, dedicated a whole page to a good interview with me even if it appeared under the usual silly headline, 'Grave New World.'

When the programme appeared on the screens it was reviewed the next day by virtually all the national press. Everyone thought that the programme was great. Most were also extremely complimentary about Hodgson Holdings. The TV critic of the Independent even queried how I had had managed to persuade the BBC to make a corporate video about Hodgson and then air the same to the nation on a prime-time slot.

But then there was Peter Tory of the Daily Express. He seemed to like the programme, perhaps even the company but he obviously disliked me. I was described as vain, slick, arrogant and far too clever for his liking.

I was astonished, but somehow not offended. I thought it unfair and wrong, but I wasn't that bothered. If he had attacked the company or even the funeral profession I would have been seriously upset – but me? Well, I thought he was wrong, whereas, as he had never met me, he couldn't be sure that he was right.

Simon Preston et al, me included, loved to quote him and then roar with laughter. Was this a defensive device invented by us all to protect me and a delicate ego? I don't think so, but then it was half a lifetime ago.

So, Peter Tory had joined the Jason Nisse 'not a fan of Howard' club that wanted funeral directors to look and behave as Victorian obsequious gentlemen. They then left other journalists to try and explain what I was attempting to do.

I think the Investors Chronicle captured what was happening rather well:

'If Great Southern Group claims that it is constantly wooed by businesses wanting to come under its wing; Hodgson is more forthright – 'I don't know why funeral directors like to appear like blushing virgins. Of course we approach people'.

Hodgson wears swanky double-breasted suits, long hair and dark sunglasses. He professes to abhor the unctuous manner of the traditional undertaker and his conversation is far from lugubrious .... A recent profile in the Sunday Times – which labelled him Mr Death – has confirmed him as the anti-hero of the funeral profession'.

This Life In Death

Perhaps, this anti-hero image would have been diminished if I had ever bothered to point out that actually I was the only genuine funeral director on offer.

Nevertheless, it went on to report that I had stated, in a thinly disguised reference to Kenyon and Great Southern, that funeral directors who bought other funeral directors with the claim that they would change nothing were either lying or incompetent.

Moreover, the figures supplied by the Investors Chronicle supported the fact that Hodgson was financially in a different league to the other two.

They measured growth between 1984 – 1988 in all three companies.

They quoted that the compound % growth in turnover was year on year:

Hodgson Holdings 85.6%

Kenyon 27.6%

Great Southern 16.5%

The compound % growth in pre-tax profits year on year:

Hodgson Holdings 102.4%

Kenyon 41.2%

Great Southern 23%

The compound % growth in earnings per share year on year:

Hodgson Holdings 62.4%

Great Southern 20.2%

Kenyon 10.5%.

Game set and match to Hodgson. I might be Mr Death, the anti-hero of the funeral profession; but I was the only properly qualified and historically serving funeral director as a quoted CEO in the public arena; and I could deliver, as a result, both standards of service and returns on investment which left the other two drowning in the wake of my forging wash.

Writing this now, I'm impressed how I had listened to John Jay's advice and had not blasted my competitors small-minded and jealous criticisms when I had shaped the future of the industry despite their opposition. This was against my every instinct.

However, I seem to remember now also that their much-voiced criticism put a pressure in my own head, at the time, to make me almost apologise for who I was. Perhaps, this was because of my father and the British Empire order of pre-1960s. Perhaps, it was because that, secretly, I loved the acclaim and felt that that was a betrayal of this honourable profession.

However, looking back now and with the knowledge of what has happened since in the tragic world of personal and very painful bereavement, I know my conviction was 100% right, and that I shook up a sleepy industry and sent it to a better place from the consumer's point of view.

Therefore, I now realise now that I was much more important than my own self-doubt allowed me to believe at the time. I think that was because, somewhere, deep down, there was still enough of that little boy self-doubt that had shown itself so much in the first decade of my life, to cause me to believe in the criticism of others.

Nevertheless, I had sent my family business and my chosen profession on a journey where the bereaved client came first and small, cosy and incompetent funeral directors, who dealt in a twilight world of little competition and no choice were eliminated, as the taboo funeral world had been chucked under a spotlight by one who craved success but knew that this must be based on client satisfaction – both morally and for financial longevity.

xxxxxxx

This Life In Death

If the Ingalls deal in 1987 had been a very 'big' deal – which it indeed had been by making me 'Mr Death' and Hodgson Holdings the undisputed champion of the British funeral market, the Kenyon Securities deal was 'really big' and a fitting end to volume I of these memoirs.

Hodgson had continued to expand in the south of England, but to make any significant future progress, it had to either buy or merge with either Great Southern or Kenyon Securities.

This was important because to keep the Hodgson share price fuelled on growth by acquisition percentage expansion year on year was becoming more difficult to maintain a PE of circa 30 x earnings.

Turning 7,500 funerals per annum into 15,000 had taken a lot of acquisitions, turning 15,000 into 32,000 had taken the Ingalls deal. Now there were fewer funeral directors for sale, many less of a decent size, we were having to up the price to all for Amiss to attract new ones and we had had the Crash; and yet I had to maintain the growth or see the PE fall on lowered expectation. Therefore, the share price would fall and with it the value of Hodgson Holdings.

Over the last two years I had had discussions on the possibilities of a tie-up with both other quoted firms. However, increasingly while both resisted my advances, Kenyon looked more vulnerable and would be forced to deal with me for two reasons.

The first was the Dottridge acquisition, as already mentioned earlier, where Michael Kenyon had paid a ridiculous price out of desperation following my acquisition of the Kenyon family connected Ashton Ebbutt business south of the river in London.

I knew that this would cause Kenyon a serious earnings dilution. Therefore, this would bring about the second reason – the annoyance of the huge monopolistic French company, PFG.

It was a major holder of Kenyon stock and would be furious with the earnings per share dilution caused by the folly of the Dottridge acquisition.

This Life In Death

Initially, PFG were not quite so quick witted as me, and they took the opportunity to increase their % of Kenyon from 10 to 28% in the placing that Kenyon had to get away to complete the acquisition.

PFG did not understand what was happening as well as me and therefore, I knew that I just had to wait for my phone to ring with a call from them and a request to save their bacon.

PFG now had enough Kenyon stock to control the future direction of the company. They were a French monopoly, having buried or cremated 235,000 French folk in 1987 as well as manufacturing 230,000 coffins.

The company also was the largest funeral director in Belgium, enjoyed 9% of the Swiss market, and for some illogical reason, 10% of the Singapore market.

PFG was itself controlled by the Lyonnaise des Eaux group, which was a major French utility company involved in water supply, heating and waste management.

PFG also faced the potential approaching nightmare of the French government's desire to de-monopolise funeral directing in France.

Such concerns were astutely picked up on by the USM magazine when making some interesting predictions following the increase in PFG's stake in Kenyon at that time.

Having analysed the reasons for PFG's interest in Kenyon in the first place, it predicted:

'It seems to us that the process of concentrating UK market shares into fewer hands is likely to continue for some time, probably at the current rate of acquisitions for two to three years. But conditions are going to get tougher, margins are probably going to reduce and access to finance is going to be less easy. Earnings per share growth in 1988/89 could also begin to slow. Kenyon, via its tie-up with Pompes (PFG), would seem to have got the ideal solution although, because of the Take-over Code, Pompes cannot own more than 30%

of Kenyon without triggering a bid. It is therefore going to be difficult for Kenyon to expand further via share placings without being vulnerable to a bid being triggered from Pompes. And Pompes would be very sensitive to any Francophobe slogans which the competition would be quick to produce. For these reasons investors should be alert to the possibility of a different sort of restructuring in the industry.

We would guess that in three years' time there will probably be only one quoted player left in the funerals business, possibly two. We see Kenyon being used as a take-over vehicle by Pompes and taking out either Hodgson or Great Southern or both'.

I read this at the time and thought how very perceptive. However, the USM magazine clearly did not know my personality too well. I had not come this far and shown greater skill and courage than Kenyon in every competitive situation to be taken out by them with or without PFG.

In fact, later in the article the writer seemed to acknowledge this:

'We believe a Pompes inspired bid for Hodgson or even a Pompes inspired Hodgson bid for Kenyon is a distinct possibility. The logic for the French of 30% of a merged Hodgson/Kenyon business carrying out almost 50,000 funerals a year and probably run by the inspirational Howard Hodgson could be overwhelming'.

And so, it was. A very perceptive article – despite the fact the combined new total would be 60,000 funerals a year rather 50,000 as quoted.

Throughout 1988, when talking to SCI, I had kept in touch with Hervé Racine,the PFG finance director. This was because I knew I needed help from some source or another. In the end that had come from John Gunn and B&C.

Hervé was a man I really liked. He was from Marseilles, not the usual stuffy, bureaucratic Parisian, straight out of the elite INSEAD Business School with little to no entrepreneurial skill.

This Life In Death

Kenyon's foolish deal over Dottridge caused a deeply discounted rights issue and after it the share price continued down.

I knew that that the price paid was too much and I also knew that Kenyon had zero skill in rationalising the new firm so earnings would not be enhanced to repair the damage of their folly.

Now Hervé wanted to be my friend as much as I had wanted the year before to be his. Our conversations continued into 1989. We had hatched a plan together in 1988 which the Kenyon board had scuppered, but now they were not considered as important by PFG having failed so badly with Dottridge. PFG wanted me and I wanted Kenyon.

We kept talking, and finally in July 1989, while in Port Grimaud, in the bosom of my entire family: Marianne, Howard, Jamieson, my mother, my stepfather, Baker, my beloved parents-in-law Samuel and Raymonde, my much-adored brother-in-law Alex and his very beautiful wife Beatrice; after a super lunch, I boarded a plane from Nice to Paris.

The deal was struck without Michael Kenyon, or his board, being consulted except for one, named Tony Warburton, who had thrown in his lot with PFG.

The Independent seemed to sum up all this situation accurately:

'The Merger between funeral director Hodgson Holdings and Kenyon Securities seems to give all the parties what they want. Howard Hodgson becomes chief executive of Britain's largest funeral director chain; the French Group Pombes Funebres Generales swaps a 28% stake of Kenyon for 25% of the enlarged group, PFG Hodgson Kenyon International; and Michael Kenyon gets a nest egg and a non-executive directorship.'

It also pointed out, correctly, that it was clear that Hodgson and PFG had hatched the deal and had presented the Kenyon Board with a fait accompli and also pointed out, again correctly, that Michael

This Life In Death

Kenyon was probably unhappy having his company tied in with Hodgson.

'Mr Kenyon has never made a secret of his dislike of Hodgson's way of doing business. Both groups, in common with Great Southern Group, have been expanding aggressively in recent years, buying up independent outlets. Mr Kenyon has often said that the directors who sell to him would not have considered joining Hodgson. Now these directors have been sold to the company they rejected lock, stock and barrel.'

This article was probably written by Jason Nisse. I can't remember – but he was the Independent financial journalist who should have covered the story. However, it was, as one might expect from such a bitter guy, complete nonsense.

The only funeral director who ever turned Hodgson Holdings down in favour of Kenyon Securities was Dottridge and that was purely over Kenyon madly offering £2 million more than us.

Nevertheless, I determined to keep Michael on as I needed him as an ally against French bureaucracy – and understandably he hated them much more than he hated me - and because I wanted him to help me integrate the two companies.

We met for dinner in the neutral Stratford-Upon-Avon, and I charmed him to stay on as my equal number two with Graham Hodson in the new ridiculously named PHKI as an executive director.

Now we move to the press conference to announce the merger. This huge and hurriedly put together event was a nightmare for the French to organise and more than a little difficult on the day.

Michael Kenyon, who at this point had not been wooed by me, most understandably since he had not known about the merger until 72 hours earlier, was being awkward and causing many delays, while I had not been to bed for 48 hours.

This Life In Death

Then the press conference had to be further delayed due to Michael's refusal to agree the press release and without an agreed release the information couldn't be posted on the Exchange screen. Until it was on that we couldn't start the conference.

The Savoy Hotel, where the huge conference hall had been booked, and was full of journalists, who were being kept waiting. The hotel had promised me a razor, as I hadn't shaved for three days, but it didn't materialise. It was a very hot day; the air conditioning was poor and there was a rail strike on.

Next Michael decided he didn't like the slide show as he claimed it showed Kenyon in a bad light. Sandy Fraser of UBS said that the slides were both accurate and essential as PHKI needed to demonstrate how Hodgson's vastly better financial performance was going to apply to Kenyon in the future and thus lift earnings per share in the new group.

Meanwhile, Simon Preston left a paper with the companies' code names, which are always used to keep matters secret in advance of an announcement, lying around which was seized on by Michael Walters of the Daily Mail. The names were Famine, Pestilence and Plague. This led to the Mail's headline the next day 'Plague and Pestilence Put 19p On Hodgson'.

The press and analyst audience of around 200 were getting more and more edgy with the delay as the sticky heat was not pleasant, and they were worried about getting home due to the rail strike.

We were now more than a bit late. Still the damn announcement, which Michael had now signed off, did not appear on the screen. Hervé was calm but his Parisian colleagues were looking as shaky as their parents might have done as the Germans approached Paris in 1940.

I said to Sandy Fraser, "I'm going for it now. I'm not waiting anymore."

This Life In Death

"No, you can't, Howard, there's a guy over there with a mobile phone (not too common back then) and it's still not on the screen at the Exchange" he replied.

"OK, go and take the phone off him and if he won't give it up, take him behind a pillar and beat him up and then take it – because I'm starting now." And I did.

Michael Kenyon did his bit very well, despite his truculence beforehand. I did the slide show. Philippe de Margery and Claude Pierre Brossolette, of France's very confident and largest funeral director and Kenyon's largest shareholder opened and closed proceedings respectfully.

While Philippe de Margery was speaking, I shaped my hands into the sign of prayer as I concentrated on his words. I knew the hordes of photographers present would not be able to resist such a shot. I also knew, as a result, that it would be me who was the photographic accompanist to the next day's headlines. I had learned my media trade well.

So, to questions. The French were supposed to take the lead here to ease the Michael vs Howard position. They were not well prepared and wholly unprepared for the rudeness and aggression of a mass gathering of an impatient, hot and tired British press.

Michael Walters of the Daily Mail came in with his usual, "What worries me is" after a few awkward questions which de Margery and Brossolette had fumbled as the press started to smell blood and 'Froggie' blood at that.

I had had enough, be it my place or not, I decided to take over proceedings and swung Brossolette's microphone over to me and interrupted, " What worries me is every time we meet you always start every sentence with 'what worries me is' and you know if what worries you is the Hodgson valuation in this deal then perhaps if you hadn't spent most of the last three years describing me as either a

Third Division footballer or an ageing rock star then maybe the valuation would be higher."

The audience laughed and the tension lifted a little. Then I took control as I demanded "Next question – ah, you OK, stand up and, please, tell me your name."

I had instantly taken over and had shown that I was not going to be intimidated by this audience. I knew a lot more about the subject than them and by getting them on their feet I was making it into a one-to-one contest with me holding all the knowledge and a pocket full of the one liners that I had used against the Prudential or anyone else who wanted to challenge me in the last three years.

The questions became friendly, as did the press articles the next morning. The French were grateful and congratulated themselves on the leader they had appointed 'en Angleterre' but they had been terribly shocked by the British press's behaviour and so decided to leave everything to me in that regard in future – for which I was extremely grateful having just witnessed their performance. Moreover, this was a very big signal that I was still running the show.

The next day the press comment was surprisingly favourable considering that we launched the conference 45 minutes late on a hot day with a rail strike going on and with ill-prepared French directors and one very disgruntled English one.

The Guardian reflected much of the media and, although they all seemed slightly incapable of being wholly serious about anything to do with funerals, they delivered a better result than perhaps we deserved:

'The architects of the deal presented a varied picture at yesterday's slightly less than smooth-running formal ceremonies. Claude Pierre Brossolette, who will be chairman of the new company, is a former head of France's Treasury department and served as President Giscard d'Estaing's chief of administration staff. Flanking him was Hodgson Holdings' chairman, Howard Hodgson, whose youth and

This Life In Death

near shoulder length blond locks have seen him compared to a fourth division footballer…. Kenyon Securities chairman, Michael Kenyon, was unsurprisingly, puzzling as to whether his description, as a "middle aged, retiring man, very much the popular image of an undertaker", was flattering or not.'

Nevertheless, the deal had got away and had been by and large well received by everyone from institutional investors to the press. Everyone that is except for the usual critics.

I was now in charge of 60,000 funerals per annum – a long way from 400 I had initially bought. I was still master of my own ship and now commander of the funeral profession. I was well known and had made my mark on English life by totally changing a taboo industry. I was still only 39 and had had to survive many slings and arrows to get here. Some of which had been of my own making.

It had taken me fourteen years of manic fanatism and dedication to combine a belief in standards of service and facility for bereaved families of any race or religion with my financial plan to make both our family name and fortune bigger and better than ever before.

Fourteen years from those seemingly impossible early days in 1975. I knew that I owed so much to my father's knowledge and teaching, my mother's inherited fortitude, my wife and children's devoted love and the wonderfully loyal and dedicated staff who had worked so hard to get me there. Together we had created so much and against all odds.

It also still seems almost impossible that a stupid little boy who was proud of the comment 'fair' on any school report and who was happy to daydream at the back of the class could have ended up here. But I had and with much, much more yet to come.

And so, to new and very important chapters in 'This Life in Death'. How will these turn out along with everything else in my hectic existence?

This Life In Death

You will have to wait for that because this is a good place to end volume I and take a 'breather' at half time before completing the tale.

Volume II continues the story for another 35 years with as many highs, lows and shocks as before both in my business career, home life and own struggles to deal with the schizophrenic me.

There will be births, marriages, deaths and more love affairs; desperate struggles, business failures away from the funeral industry, a triumphal return to it with the creation of Memoria, and the reasons behind the writing my biography of King Charles III.

I look forward to telling you more about 'This Life in Death' in Volume II.

Book Index

This Life In Death

This Life In Death

This Life In Death

This Life In Death

This Life In Death

This Life In Death

This Life In Death

This Life In Death

This Life In Death

This Life In Death

This Life In Death

This Life In Death

This Life In Death

This Life In Death

This Life In Death

This Life In Death

This Life In Death

This Life In Death

Reference Index

Index

Milton Keynes UK
Ingram Content Group UK Ltd.
UKHW011708071224
452098UK00007B/84